This book is our gift to you. We hope you enjoy reading it as much as we enjoyed creating it. There is so much to see and do in the Greater Prescott region. We tried to include a little bit of everything.

- With love from everyone at ROX Media Group

Photo: Christopher Marchetti

- Custom Furniture
- Custom Upholstery
- Designer Fabrics

NEED HELP STYLING YOUR HOME?
CALL US FOR AN IN HOME CONSULTATION

& Beautiful Home Decor

Stop in and be inspired by our Showroom.

115 W. Willis Street Prescott, Arizona 86301

928-458-7275

WWW.BELLAHOMEFURNISHINGS.COM

Bella
HOME FURNISHINGS

ARTFULLY UNITING **EXTRAORDINARY HOMES** WITH **EXTRAORDINARY LIVES** ®

LIVE PRESCOTT

For those ready for what's next

Only one real estate brand gives you that feeling. The feeling that you're in the presence of the world's best. The Sotheby's International Realty network achieved $112 billion in global sales volume in 2018, and reaches nearly every corner of the globe, with more than 990 offices in 72 countries. For those who seek exceptional service and results in Prescott, there is only Russ Lyon Sotheby's International Realty.

— Only —

Russ Lyon | Sotheby's INTERNATIONAL REALTY

2971 Willow Creek Rd. Prescott, AZ 86301 | 928.227.2435 | russlyon.com

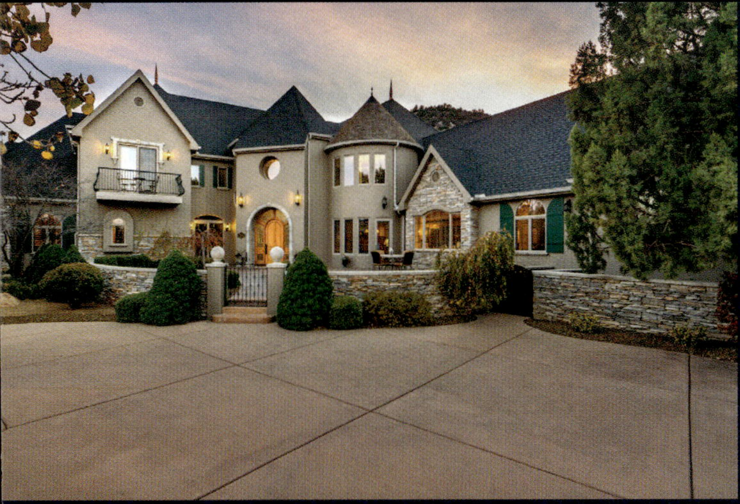
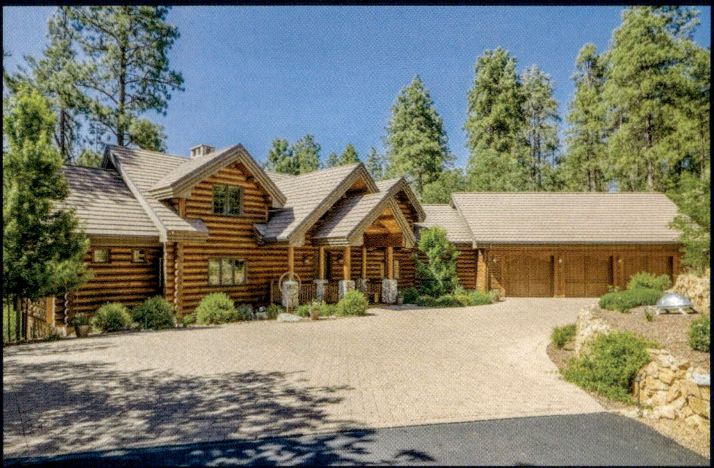
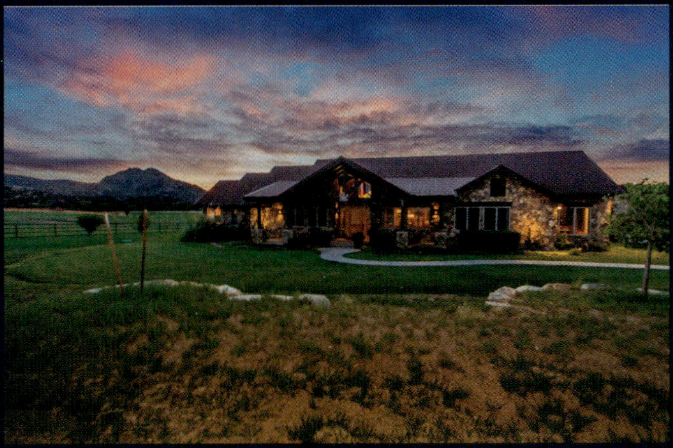
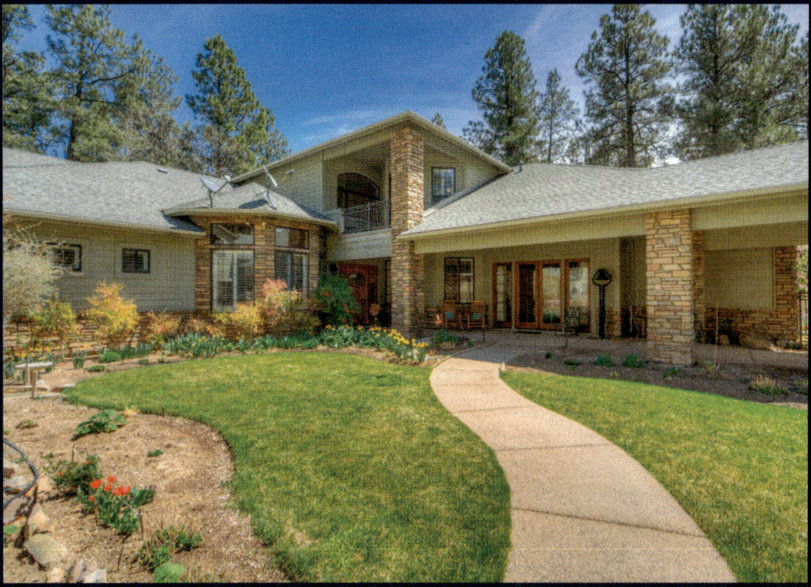
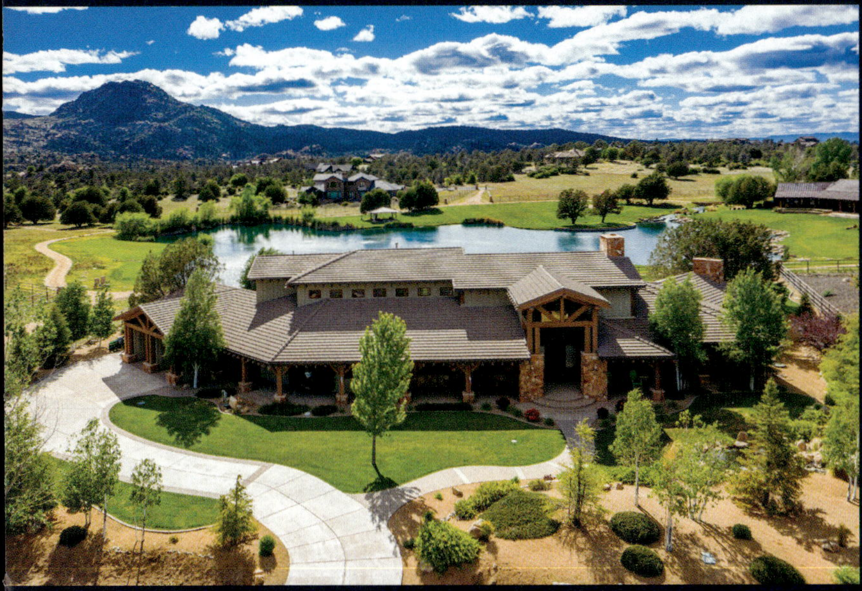
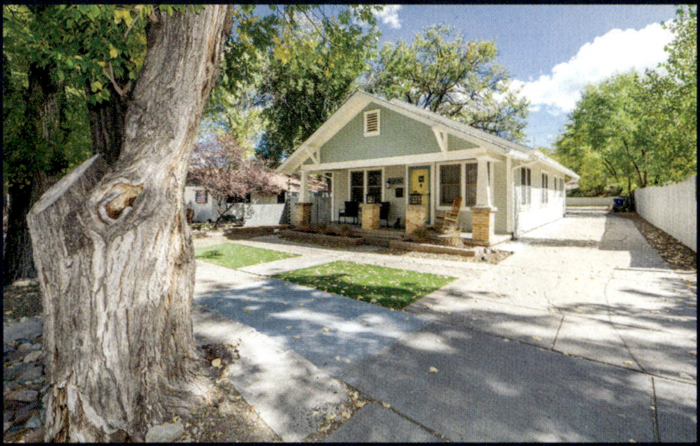
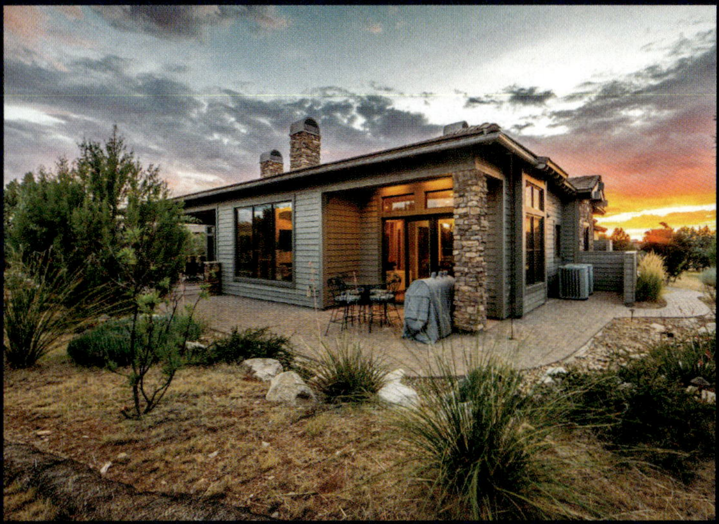
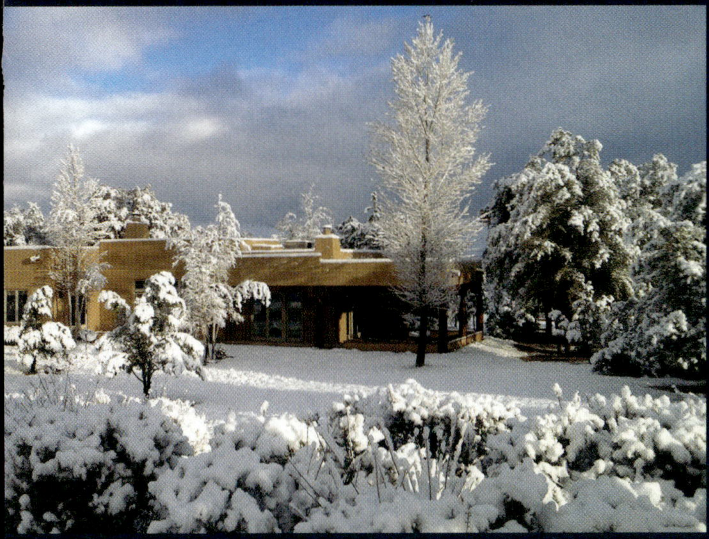

AMERICA'S OLDEST, ARIZONA'S BEST

EST. 1888

PRESCOTT FRONTIER DAYS

PRESENTS

WORLD'S OLDEST RODEO

AUTHENTIC EST. 1888 WESTERN TRADITION

PRESENTED BY

Coors Banquet — PRORODEO PRCA

COWPUNCHERS RANCH BRONC RIDING

PRESCOTT'S MOST ANTICIPATED

― **NAMED BEST OF THE WEST** ―
BEST HISTORIC RODEO
- TRUE WEST MAGAZINE

2015 | 2016 | 2017 | 2018 | 2019

© MILLER PHOTO

EVENT OF THE YEAR!

FOR TICKETS VISIT:
WORLDSOLDESTRODEO.COM
OR CALL: 928-445-4320

FINDLAY TOYOTA CENTER | Prescott Valley, Arizona
NORTHERN ARIZONA'S PREMIER MULTI-PURPOSE FACILITY

The Findlay Toyota Center (FTC), located in Prescott Valley, AZ is a 6,200 seat multi-purpose facility which opened its doors in November 2006. The FTC leads the field among venues in north and central Arizona and is home to the Northern Arizona Suns, the NBA G-League affiliate of the Phoenix Suns. With 165,000 square feet of extended floor space, the Findlay Toyota Center is ideal to host concerts, sporting events including basketball and hockey, family shows, conferences, banquets, and cultural programs. The arena features a single concourse and has 22 suites and 2 party suites, as well as a large club lounge for dinners and parties. The technical expertise and dedication of the FTC staff ensure that audiences will be dazzled and entertained with shows they will never forget.

The Findlay Toyota Center is owned by the Town of Prescott Valley and managed by Spectra Venue Management. The arena has hosted headlining acts such as Heart, Dierks Bentley, Stevie Nicks, Miranda Lambert, Jeff Dunham, Godsmack, Eric Church, Chicago, Willie Nelson, ZZ Top, WWE, Blue Man Group, PBR, Harlem Globetrotters and Cirque du Soleil.

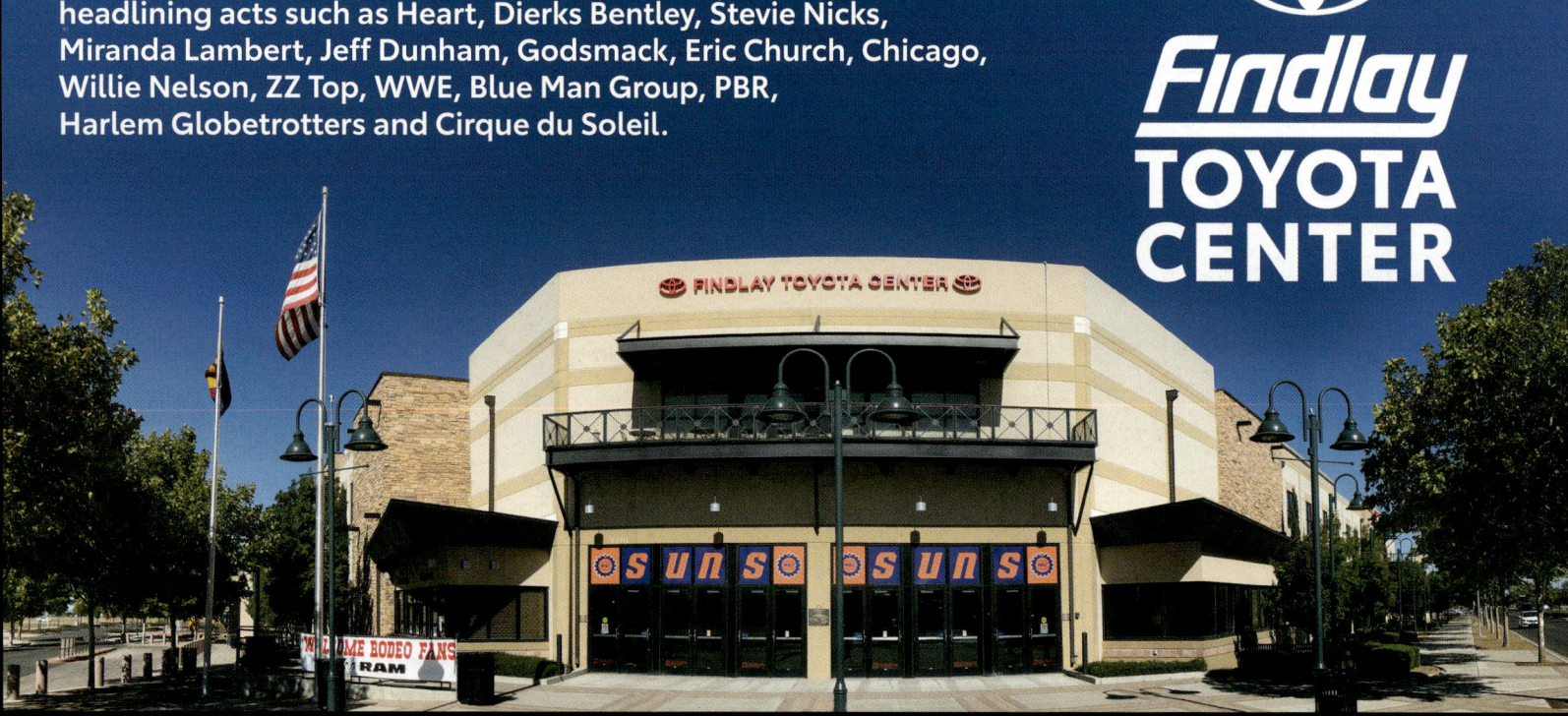

Findlay TOYOTA CENTER

Visit FindlayToyotaCenter.com for upcoming events and venue information!
ADDRESS: 3201 N. Main St. | Prescott Valley, AZ 86314   PHONE: 928-772-1819

Pre-Loved... ready to be *Re-Loved!!*

Scarlett's Women's Boutique

Spoil yourself

with our latest curated collection of new and pre-loved clothing and fashion accessories

Scarlett's CURATED COLLECTION
Pre-Loved ready to be Re-Loved

928.227.2581

107 N. Cortez St. • Prescott

scarlettsinprescott.com

CHRONICLE ARTS

YOUR LIFE YOUR STORY YOUR FILM

CREATING YOUR LEGACY

SHARING YOUR VALUES, WISDOM, AND HOPES FOR YOUR FAMILY IS AN IMPORTANT PART OF THE LEGACY YOU LEAVE.

Everyone has a story worth telling and no one can tell your story better than you!

There are many important things you can give your family, but a film about you is a one of a kind gift.

Chronicle-Arts films honor the tradition of storytelling with the technology of digital filmmaking to beautifully archive history so it can be passed down and preserved.

Create a beautiful time capsule today.

Share your dreams for the future.

Be remembered.

WWW.CHRONICLE-ARTS.COM

1-888-474-3456

COBHAM AEROSPACE COMMUNICATIONS

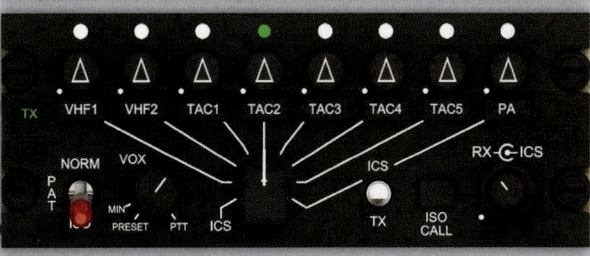

COBHAM

Specializing in the design, development, sales and support of avionics and connectivity systems globally for airborne platforms at the leading edge of technological development. In the fields of defense, security, and commercial aerospace, the innovative, high performance solutions we provide enable our customers' assets to perform to their maximum potential.

PART OF UK-BASED COBHAM PLC	1 OF 105 LOCATIONS ACROSS 24 COUNTRIES
IN BUSINESS SINCE 1970	160+ EMPLOYEES

928-708-1550 | 6400 Wilkinson Drive | Prescott, AZ

The expertise to heal.
The passion to serve.

Not-for-profit healthcare brings out the best in people. We see it at Yavapai Regional Medical Center where our team delivers exceptional healthcare that's wrapped in a 75-year mission of caring for people of our community.

YAVAPAI REGIONAL MEDICAL CENTER
Proudly Caring for Western Yavapai County

YRMC.org   YRMCHealthConnect.org

ARIZONA All Service Plumbing LLC

RESIDENTIAL - COMMERCIAL

Don't waste time to find the line, Call a *Professional* first.

When buying your new home, have your sewer line checked with our camera before you finalize your inspection.

Family Owned and Operated
42 Years Experience   ΙΧΘΥΣ

Accredited Green Plumber

- Tankless Water Heater
- Water Heater Repair and Replacement
- Sewer and Drain Cleaning up to 250 ft
- Garbage Disposals & Water Softeners
- Mobile Home repairs and Re-Pipes
- Water and Gas Line Repair and Installation
- Toilet and Faucet Repair and Replacement
- Sewer and Gas Line Locater

Licensed Bonded Insured
ROC308192 CR-77

928-775-6550
928-925-6809

azallserviceplumbing.com

Affordable - Honest AND Reliable.

REALTY ONE GROUP
MOUNTAIN DESERT

Jill Hunsucker, Realtor®

Jill Hunsucker
YOUR PRESCOTT REALTOR®

I absolutely love living life in Prescott, Arizona! I strongly feel that when it comes to buying or selling in the growing Prescott area, hiring a Realtor® who values honesty and integrity with a vast knowledge of the community and real estate market is what matters most. As a real estate agent, it's truly a joy and an honor to showcase this gorgeous historical city on a daily basis!

928-848-9710

100 E. Sheldon Street, Ste 200
Prescott, AZ 86301
email: jill@jillhunsucker.com
www.jillhunsucker.com

In addition to my 16 dedicated and rewarding years of real estate experience in Arizona, my husband Kevin Hunsucker and I are owners of Elk Ridge Development LLC, a company that specializes in building stunning custom homes and home sites tailored to our clients' specific wants and desires. We are committed to working closely with our clients to help them find that perfect home or build their dream home on a property they love.

Elk Ridge Development LLC is a family owned general contracting company specializing not only in custom home building, but also in custom home sites including excavation and grading, custom garages, and light commercial buildings.

With over 30 dedicated years in the business, we help remove the fear of the unknown by walking our clients through the building process, educating them every step of the way. We take great joy in making our clients dreams become a reality and are committed from start to finish!

ELK RIDGE DEVELOPMENT LLC
Prescott, Arizona

Kevin Hunsucker
928-848-9707
www.elkridgedevelopment.com
elkridgedevelopment@gmail.com

Each office is independently owned and operated.

FLY-U SHUTTLE
SPACE AVAILABLE

Fly-U Shuttle is a locally owned and operated *premier shuttle service,* that was founded to address the growing needs in Prescott and the rest of Northern Arizona for an *executive transport and tour service.* Recognizing the demand for a premier shuttle service from the local community, you can now *ride in style* in our executive vans.

THE FLY-U SHUTTLE DIFFERENCE

RIDE IN EXECUTIVE STYLE COMFORT, IN RECLINING LEATHER CAPTAIN'S CHAIRS

UNDER NEW OWNERSHIP • MIMA BONNETT, NEW OWNER

CHARTERS • WEDDINGS • SPECIAL EVENTS • GROUPS

- One way and Round trips to Sky Harbor Airport
- Seasonal Tours to Grand Canyon and Sedona
- Inquire about our Charters to Mexico.
- Home Pick up and Pick up locations around the Quad City area.

HOME PICK UP
Call or Visit our Website for areas
INCLUDES ALL OF THE LOCAL HOTELS

REGULAR PICK UP SPOTS
MAIN PICK UP LOCATION: Home Base at Gateway Mall. Multiple Pick Up Spots from Prescott to Cordes Junction

928-445-8880
3250 GATEWAY BLVD., SUITE 252
INSIDE GATEWAY MALL, ACROSS FROM JCPenney

FOR HOME PICK UP AREA & REGULAR PICK UP SPOTS, PLEASE VISIT OUR WEBSITE.
YOU CAN ALSO BOOK YOUR RESERVATION ONLINE AT:
Fly-UShuttle.com

Your nest is empty, but the work isn't done.

Grow your retirement account with confidence. I can help you with solutions from respected companies such as AXA, Lincoln Financial Group, Protective, and Prudential. Call me today.

Robin Binkley
928-772-0322

7749 E. Florentine Rd. Prescott Valley, AZ 86314
robinbinkley@allstate.com

Allstate
You're in good hands.
10408609

Securities offered by Personal Financial Representatives through Allstate Financial Services, LLC (LSA Securities in LA and PA). Registered Broker-Dealer. Member FINRA, SIPC. Main Office: 2920 South 84th Street, Lincoln, NE 68506. (877) 525-5727. Check the background of this firm on FINRA's BrokerCheck website http://brokercheck.finra.org. © 2018 Allstate Insurance Co.

Protect the life you've built.

Don't take any chances when it comes to your dreams for retirement. Make sure they're protected with life insurance from Allstate. Call me today.

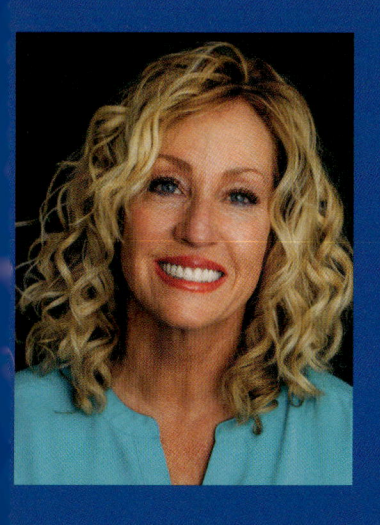

Robin Binkley
Binkley & Associates
928-772-0322
robinbinkley@allstate.com
allstate.com/robinbinkley

Have any other coverage needs? Call anytime!   10680832

Allstate
You're in good hands.

Life insurance offered through Allstate Life Insurance Company and Allstate Assurance Co., 3075 Sanders Road, Northbrook, IL 60062, and American Heritage Life Insurance Co., 1776 American Heritage Life Drive, Jacksonville, FL 32224. In New York, life insurance offered through Allstate Life Insurance Co. of New York, Hauppauge, NY. © 2019 Allstate Insurance Co.

Table of Contents

Publisher's Letter	20
Jim and Linda Lee Planetarium	30
Music & Performing Arts	70
Western Heritage Center	116
Highlands Center for Natural History	120
Prescott	130
Elks Theatre and Performing Arts Center	144
Prescott Valley	156
Chino Valley	168
Prescott Frontier Days	180
Day Trips	188
YRMC and the Community	204
Featured Photographers	240

Special Sections

Prescott: History and Heritage	Parks & Recreation	Prescott Valley: Talking Glass	Dining Directory
33	78	99	210

Every Home, Every Season

At Watters Garden Center We Believe Gardening Should be *Natural, Safe & Organic*

We Design, Deliver & Plant everything we grow

WattersGardenCenter.com
1815 Iron Springs Rd., Prescott, AZ | 928.445.4159

WATTERS
GARDEN CENTER

Letter
from the Publisher

All of us at ROX Media Group would like to express a sincere thank you to everyone in the community who contributed. The beautiful photography, as well as the articles and information, were provided by these generous partners featured throughout the publication. We couldn't have done it without you. We truly hope you enjoyed visiting the greater Prescott region featured throughout our pages.

Elaine Earle

Elaine Earle
Publisher, Prescott LIVING Magazine

Photo: Blushing Cactus Photography

roxmedia.net | info@roxco.com

Northern Arizona's *First* Tribal Casino

Bucky's and Yavapai Casinos offer a wide variety of entertainment with slot machines, Blackjack & Poker. Bucky's Café and Yavapai Cantina offer great food, drink specials and live broadcast sporting events.

Voted Best Casino and Top 50 Best Casinos in America!

EAST HWY 69 & HEATHER HEIGHTS
1.800.756.8744 • BUCKYSCASINO.COM

Must be 21 years of age or older. Problem Gambling Call: 1-800-NEXT-STEP ©2019 An Enterprise of the Yavapai-Prescott Indian Tribe

From the Publishers of

Prescott LIVING MAGAZINE

Greater Prescott
Annual Showcase 2020
PRESCOTTSHOWCASE.com

PUBLISHER
Elaine Earle, CPA

EDITOR-IN-CHIEF
Bea Lueck

CONTRIBUTING WRITER
Ray Newton

DIRECTOR OF SALES & MARKETING
Laurie Fisher

REGIONAL ACCOUNT MANAGER
Georgie Myers

ADVERTISING EXECUTIVES
Scott Metteauer
Jamie Wagner-Brashier

CREATIVE DIRECTOR/GRAPHIC DESIGNER
Tim Clarke

GRAPHIC DESIGNERS
Rebecca Bowen
Shannon Price

CUSTOMER SERVICE/AD TRAFFIC MANAGER
Julie Kahn

PUBLIC RELATIONS & MARKETING MANAGER
Julie Turetzky

COMMENTS & IDEAS
editor@roxco.com

CALENDAR INQUIRIES
calendar@roxco.com • prescottlivingmag.com/calendar

SUBSCRIPTIONS
info@roxco.com • prescottlivingmag.com/copies

ADVERTISING INQUIRIES
info@roxco.com • prescottlivingmag.com/advertise

130 N. Granite St., Prescott AZ 86301 • 928.350.8006

Corporate Office:
442 W. Kortsen Rd, Ste 101
Casa Grande, AZ 85122
520.426.2074

ROX MEDIA GROUP

Prescott LIVING is published by ROX Media Group dba RAXX Direct Marketing. Editorial content is provided by affiliates of ROX Media Group, community members and local organizations.

© 2020. All rights reserved. No part of this publication, including but not limited to editorial content, illustrations, graphics and photographic images, may be republished, reproduced or reprinted without the prior express written consent of the publisher. The publishers of Prescott LIVING assume no responsibility for errors or omissions of any advertisement beyond the actual cost of the advertisement. In no event shall the publishers be liable for any consequential damages in excess of the cost of the advertisement. Prescott LIVING shall not be liable for inaccuracies, errors, omissions, or damages from the use of information contained herein. Submitted articles do not reflect the opinions of the owners or management of Prescott LIVING. Information contained within submitted articles had not been verified for accuracy and readers are responsible for forming their own opinions.

ADVERTISER INDEX

A Valley of Vitality Wellness Studio	237
Allstate Insurance & Financial Svcs- Robin Binkley Agency	16
Ameriprise Financial	29
Arizona All Service Plumbing LLC	13
Bella Home Furnishings	2
BiGA	217
Bucky's & Yavapai Casinos	21
Capital Canyon Club	148
Chronicle ARTS	10
City of Prescott - Heritage Trail	68
Cobham Aerospace Communications - Prescott	11
Elks Theater & Performing Arts	235
Findlay Subaru of Prescott	67
Findlay Toyota Center	8
Findlay Toyota Prescott	243
Findlay GMC Prescott	242
Fly-U Shuttle	15
Grand Highland Hotel	23
Gurley St. Grill	214
John's Chophouse	217
JT's Septic	223
Maid To Order	229
Murphy's Restaurant	214
Pepe's Painting	225
Premiere Tax & Accounting Services PLLC	233
Prescott Flooring Brokers	233
Prescott Outpatient Surgical Center	237
Prescott Western Heritage Foundation Inc	35
Prescott Window Coverings	229
Purple Clover Boutique	235
Raskin's Jewelers	Back Cover
Realty ONE Group Mountain Desert - Jill Hunsucker	14
ROX Travel	209
Russ Lyon Sotheby's Int'l Realty - Debbie Dunbar	231
Russ Lyon Sotheby's Int'l Realty - Tod Christensen	4
Scarlett's Curated Collection	9
Scottsdale Plastic Surgery	231
Sumner Commercial Real Estate	239
Talking Rock Ranch	172
The Office Restaurant & Bar	215
Thumb Butte Medical Center & Urgent Care	34
Two Mamas' Gourmet Pizzeria	219
Watters Garden Center	19
Western Heritage Center	35
World's Oldest Rodeo	6
Yavapai Regional Medical Center	12

THE GRAND HIGHLAND HOTEL

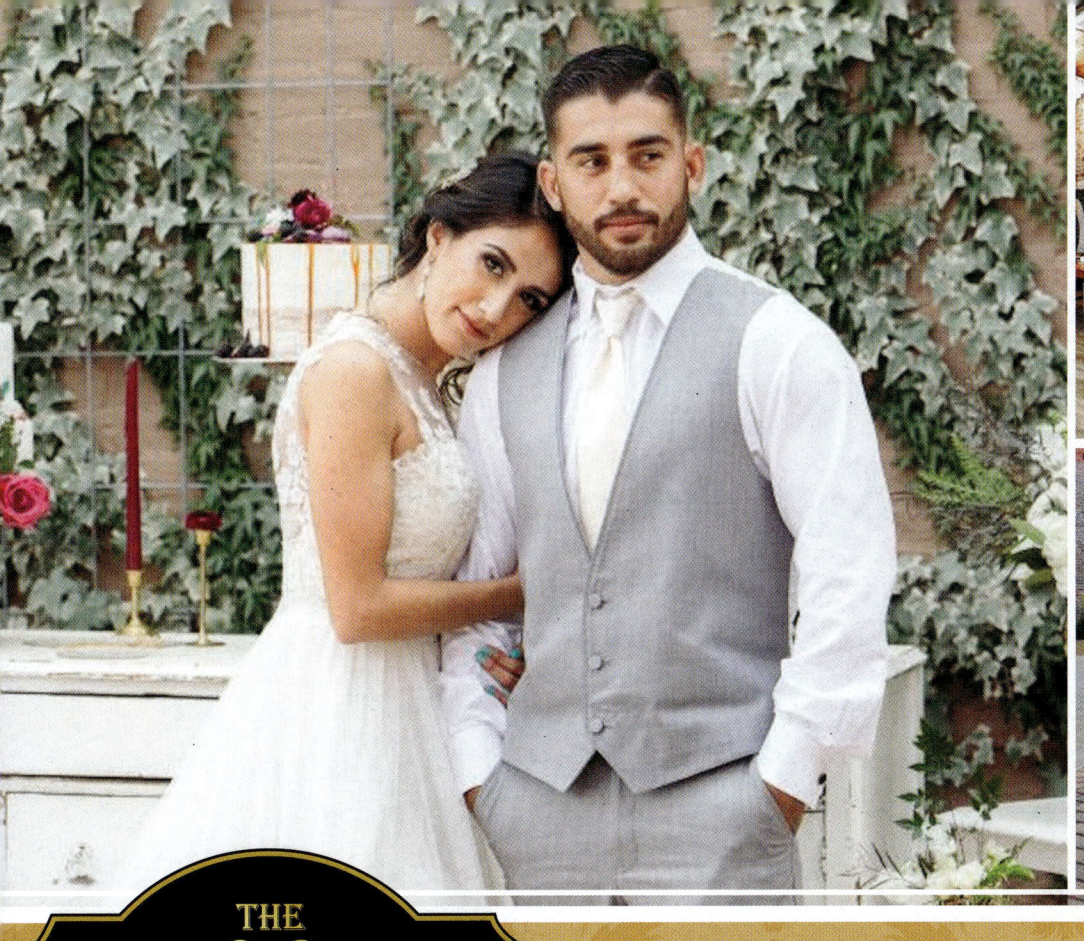

"Visit the Holiday Venues to Begin Planning Your Day, Your Way"

- Weddings & Receptions
- Corporate Events & Meetings
- Retreats & Reunions
- Private Parties
- Concert & Performances
- Have something in mind, let us know!

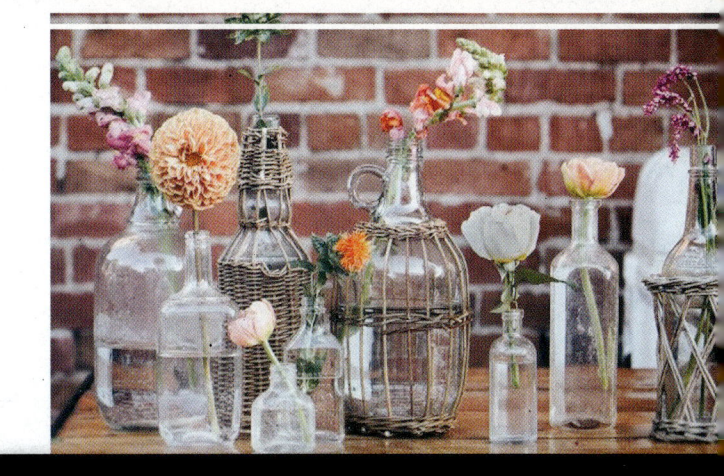

The Grand Highland Hotel offers three unique spaces:

The Holiday Courtyard
A unique outdoor venue that accommodates up to 300 guests right on Downtown Whiskey Row

New in 2019
Holiday Ballroom
A beautiful historic indoor venue that accommodates up to 150 guests

Holiday Hub
An ideal indoor venue space that accommodates up to 50 guests
All amenities included & outside vendors & alcohol permitted

Contact us at
events@grandhighlandhotel.com &
928.224.2746

154 South Montezuma Street,
Prescott AZ

WWW.GRANDHIGHLANDHOTEL.COM

Curiosity is the tip of the intelligence iceberg.

- WB Dedman

Photo: Rod Hendrick - Doll Face Rock at Watson Lake

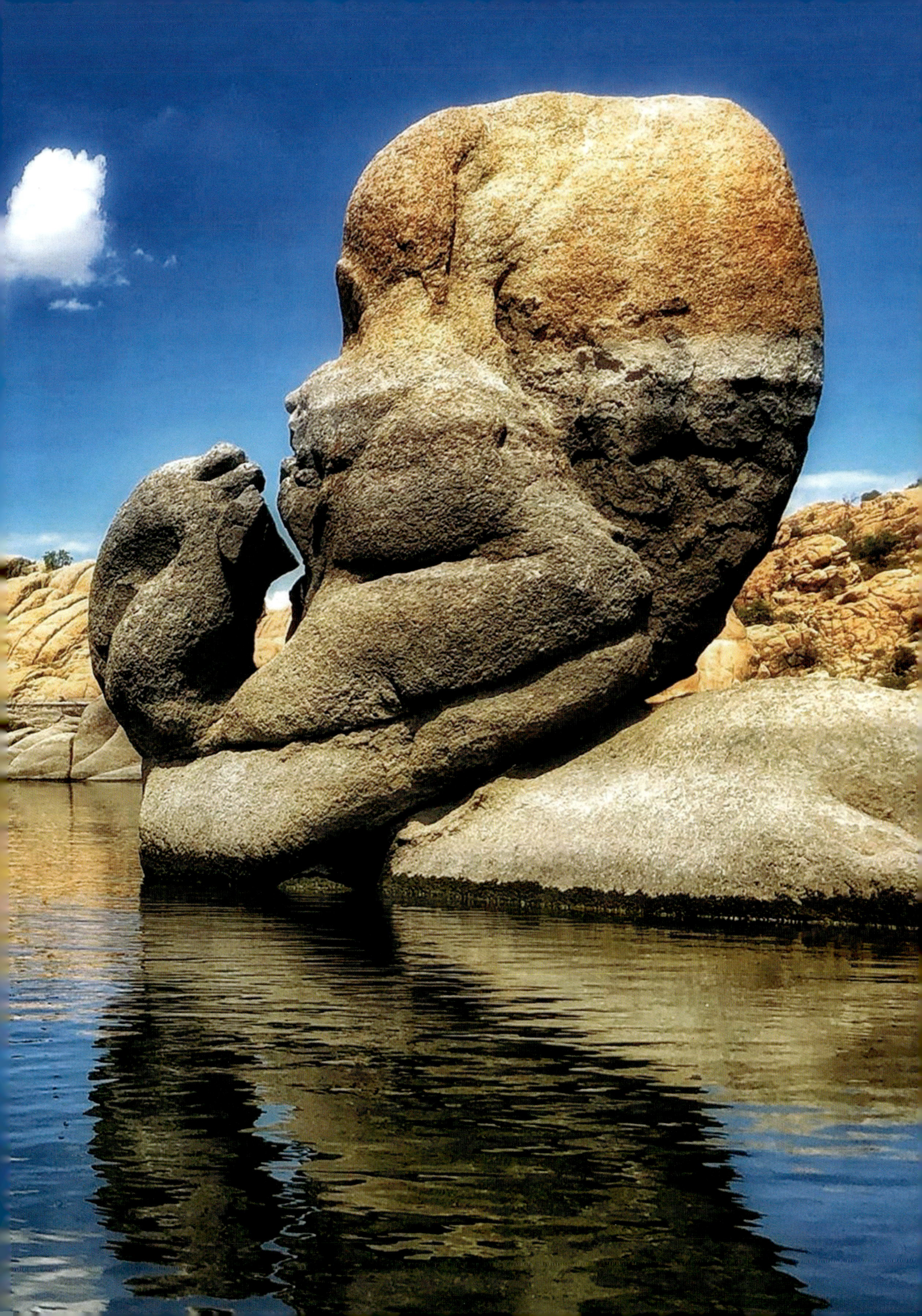

Location

Prescott

AWARDS & RANKINGS

One of the Coolest Downtowns in North America
Expedia Viewfinder

No. 5 Top Visitor Attraction in Arizona
USA Today (6/17)

Top Visitor Destination in Arizona for Nature Lovers
Expedia Viewfinder

Five Must-See Towns in Arizona
USA Today (10/17)

"Best Place to Live Like an Old West Cowboy"; "Best Old West Town to Live In"; "Best Historic Rodeo"; "Best Pioneer History Collection"
True West Magazine. (10/17)

13 Adorable Small Towns in Arizona you need to visit.
Narcity.com (9/18)

Top 20 Best Places to Retire
55Places.com (9/18)

America's Top 25 Best Small Towns for Christmas (2017, 2018)
Country Living Magazine

CLIMATE

Average	Average High (F)	Average Low (F)	Average Precip. (in)	Snow (in)
January	54	24	1.9	4.9
February	54	24	1.9	4.9
March	59	28	1.7	5.1
April	67	34	1.0	1.3
May	75	41	0.5	0.2
June	86	49	0.4	0.0
July	89	57	2.9	0.0
August	86	56	3.3	0.0
September	82	49	1.7	0.0
October	72	37	1.2	0.2
November	60	27	1.3	2.1
December	52	22	1.6	4.7

DISTANCES

Distance in Miles / Distance in Kilometers (matrix showing distances between Albuquerque, Durango, Flagstaff, Grand Canyon, Las Vegas, Moab, Prescott, Petrified Forest, Phoenix, Tucson)

PRESCOTT CHAMBER OF COMMERCE & VISITOR INFORMATION CENTER

117 W Goodwin Street, Prescott, Arizona
928.445.2000 or 800.266.7534

Visit The Prescott Chamber's Visitor Information Center for local, area and statewide visitor information. The Center is conveniently located in historic downtown Prescott, across from Yavapai County Courthouse Plaza in a historic brownstone building dating back to 1898 when it was once the City Jail & Firehouse.

MONDAY THRU FRIDAY:
9:00 AM TO 5:00 PM

SATURDAY & SUNDAY:
10:00 AM TO 2:00 PM

For information about the City of Prescott Tourism Office go to the About Tab at
Visit-Prescott.com

Prescott Valley

AWARDS & RANKINGS

Arizona's Safest Cities (No. 11)
Safewise (2019)

International Water Deal of the Year
Global Water Intelligence (2007)

Distinguished Budget Presentation Award
GFOA (2018)

Certificate of Achievement for Excellence in Financial Reporting
GFOA (2018)

Popular Annual Financial Reporting
GFOA (2018)

Safest City in Northern Arizona
National Council for Home Safety & Security (2018)

Best High School in Arizona - Bradshaw Mountain High School (No. 96)
US News (2017)

Chamber of Commerce Community Improvement Award - Boys & Girls Club
Chamber of Commerce (2019)

Tree City
Arbor Day Foundation (15 Years)

CLIMATE

Average	Average High (F)	Average Low (F)	Average Precip. (in)	Snow (in)
January	52	24	1.4	2.5
February	55	27	1.7	3.5
March	60	31	1.6	2.9
April	67	37	0.7	0.9
May	76	45	0.5	0.0
June	86	53	0.4	0.0
July	89	60	2.3	0.0
August	86	59	2.9	0.0
September	81	51	1.7	0.0
October	72	40	1.1	0.0
November	61	30	1.1	1.1
December	52	23	1.3	1.3

www.bestplaces.net

DISTANCES

Distance in Miles / Distance in Kilometers (matrix showing distances between Albuquerque, Durango, Flagstaff, Grand Canyon, Las Vegas, Moab, Prescott Valley, Petrified Forest, Phoenix, Tucson)

PRESCOTT VALLEY CHAMBER OF COMMERCE

7120 Pav Way #102, Prescott Valley, AZ
928.772.8857

Visit the Prescott Valley Chamber of Commerce for local business information and events.

The Chamber is conveniently located off of Highway 69 and open Monday thru Friday.

MONDAY THRU THURSDAY:
8:00 AM TO 4:30 PM

FRIDAY:
8:00 AM TO 4:00 PM

For information about the Prescott Valley Chamber of Commerce, visit:
www.pvchamber.org

Greater Prescott LIVING at Its Best!

*It's human nature to stretch, to go, to see, to understan(d)
Exploration is not a choice, really; it's an imperati(ve)
– Michael Colli(ns)
Astronaut, crew member of the Apollo 11 moon missi(on)*

Photo: Jess Berry

What matters most to you in life?

It's a big question. But it's just one of many questions I'll ask to better understand you, your goals and your dreams using our *Confident Retirement*® approach. All to help you live confidently – today and in the future.

Parshalla Wood, MBA
Financial Advisor

928.777.0500
3613 Crossings Drive Suite B
Prescott, AZ 86305
parshalla.wood@ampf.com

CA Insurance #0J01038

Ameriprise Financial | **Be Brilliant.**

The *Confident Retirement* approach is not a guarantee of future financial results. Investment advisory products and services are made available through Ameriprise Financial Services, Inc., a registered investment adviser.
© 2019 Ameriprise Financial, Inc. All rights reserved. (11/19)

The Jim and Linda Lee Planetarium

Located on the Prescott campus of Embry-Riddle Aeronautical University, Northern Arizona's only planetarium can project 360-degree, 4K imagery of the night and day sky and its heavenly bodies, the human body, favorite films or almost anything else onto its 47-foot diameter dome, using state-of-the-art software to provide crisp, vivid visuals. With a seating capacity of 116, it has been an invaluable resource to ERAU students majoring in astronomy, biology, business, engineering, gaming and simulation science – it goes on down the list

Numerous educational groups from around Prescott and the surrounding region have been brought in to the planetarium and eight laboratories which make up the STEM Education Center, engaging youth who might not have much contact with science, technology, engineering and math courses and careers by bringing them to the same rooms where current students and staff conduct research..

Shows for the general public are offered most Friday nights and Saturday afternoons, taking audiences from the edges of the universe to a close-up look at relative celestial neighbors. The planetarium can also show shared NASA content and coverage of major astronomical events, such as solar eclipses. There are even laser shows synchronized to the music of Led Zeppelin, Queen and other legendary bands.

Tickets to most shows are $6, and discounts may be available to ERAU students, faculty and staff for some events. For information about and to purchase tickets for upcoming shows, visit www.prescott.erau.edu/about/planetarium, call 928-777-3422 or email prplntrm@erau.edu.

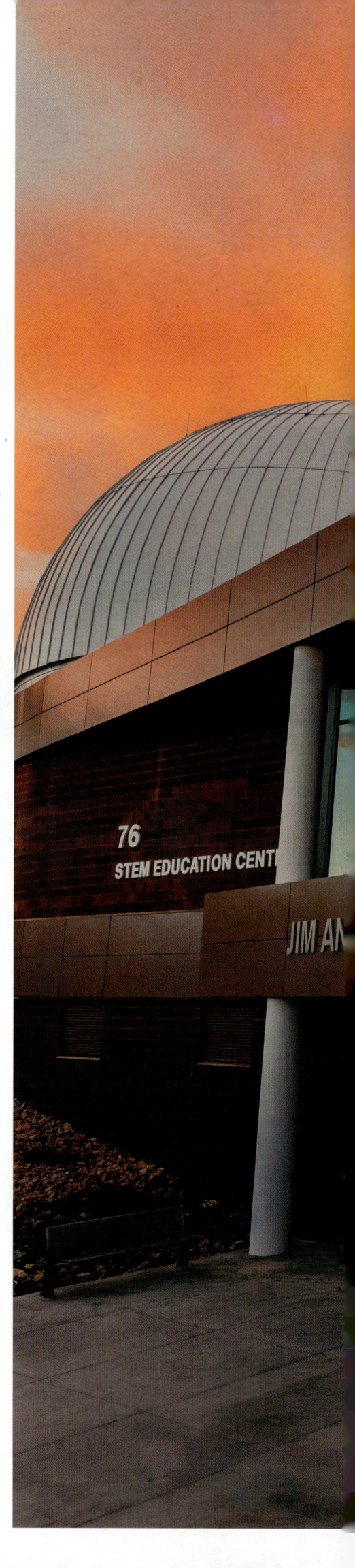

30 ANNUAL SHOWCASE EDITION 2020

LEE PLANETARIUM

The Jim and Linda Lee Planetarium

Winter Bliss

Laura Zenari - "Pronghorn in the Snow"

Nancy Maurer

Jess Berry - "Flora Snow"

SUGGESTED DONATION:
$5.00

Prescott

HISTORY AND HERITAGE OF...

Sharlot Hall Museum

Phippen Museum

Smoki Museum

EVERYBODY'S HOMETOWN

THUMB BUTTE MEDICAL CENTER & URGENT CARE

Multi-Specialty Clinic

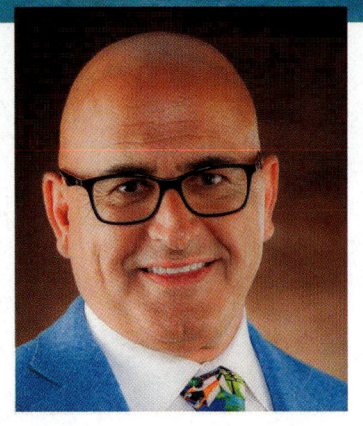

Hojat Askari, M.D.
Founder, Medical Director
Board Certifed Internal Medicine

"We treat patients like family."

Walk-ins Welcome | New Patients Welcome
All Ages | Medicare and Most Major Insurance Accepted
NOW ACCEPTING WORKMAN'S COMP

- State-of-the-art 20,000sf Multi-Specialty Clinic
- Thumb Butte Radiology, *coming soon*:
    - Large bore, highest defnition MRI in the nation - no noise!
    - CT Scan with greatest resolution
    - Ultrasound & X-Rays
- Metro Lab & Lab Corp located inside the Clinic for your convenience
- House calls available for homebound patients or 85-years old & above

TWO LOCATIONS TO SERVE YOU

3224 Willow Creek Road
Prescott, AZ 86301
Monday - Friday, 7 a.m. - 5 p.m.
928.445.7085

6496 E. Hwy 69
Prescott Valley, AZ 86314
Monday - Friday, 8 a.m. - 5 p.m.
928.775.9007

www.ThumbButteMedicalCenter.com

WESTERN HERITAGE CENTER

A unique and creative showcase of museums & other organizations that preserve & promote our heritage

Visit Our Mercantile Featuring Local Artists, Authors, and Craftsmen

Located on Historic Whiskey Row · 156 C S. Montezuma · Prescott, AZ
Please visit www.visitWHC.org for seasonal hours of operation

Prescott Western Heritage Foundation Inc. is a Charitable 501(c)(3) Non-profit Corporation

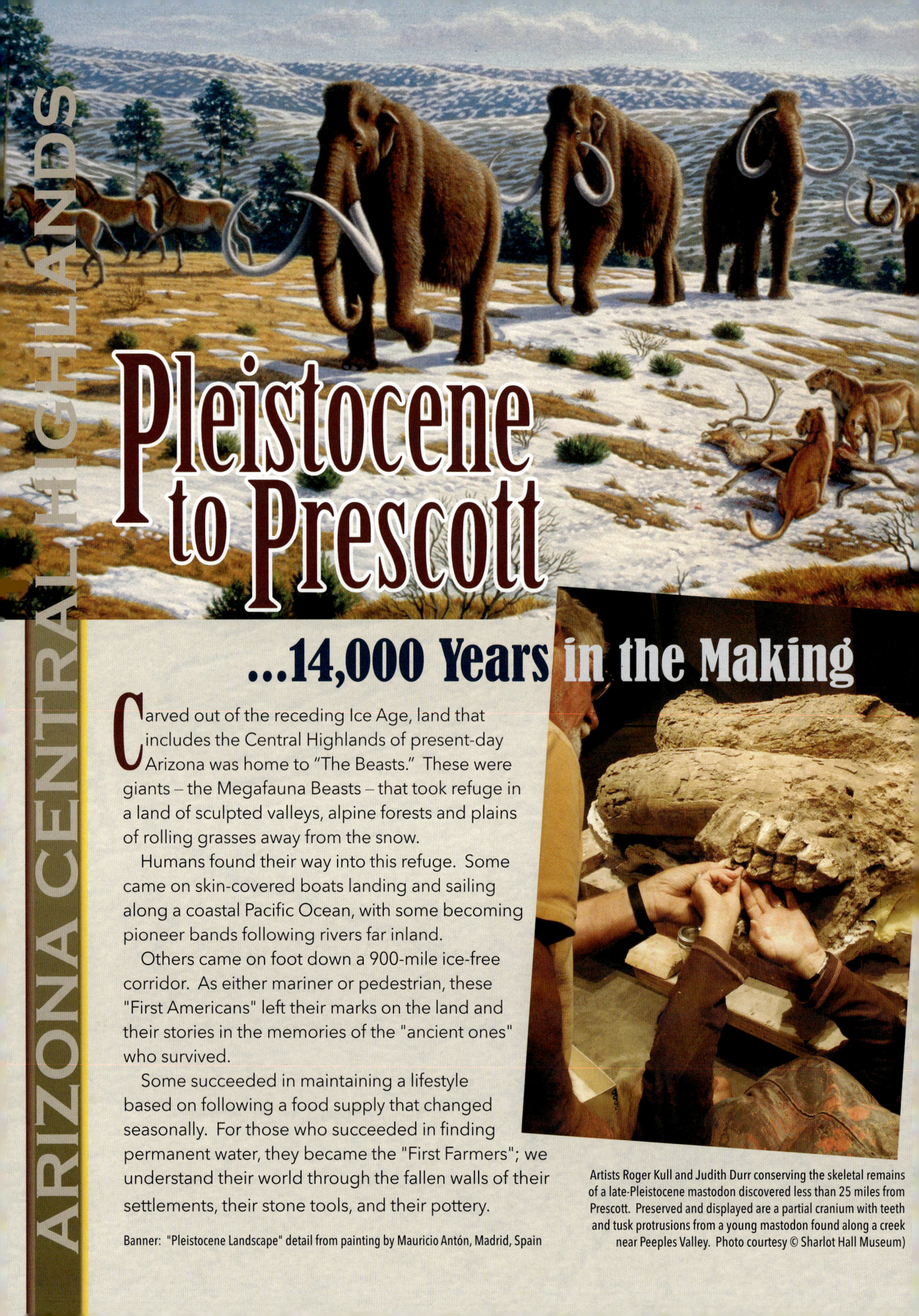

ARIZONA CENTRAL HIGHLANDS

Pleistocene to Prescott

...14,000 Years in the Making

Carved out of the receding Ice Age, land that includes the Central Highlands of present-day Arizona was home to "The Beasts." These were giants – the Megafauna Beasts – that took refuge in a land of sculpted valleys, alpine forests and plains of rolling grasses away from the snow.

Humans found their way into this refuge. Some came on skin-covered boats landing and sailing along a coastal Pacific Ocean, with some becoming pioneer bands following rivers far inland.

Others came on foot down a 900-mile ice-free corridor. As either mariner or pedestrian, these "First Americans" left their marks on the land and their stories in the memories of the "ancient ones" who survived.

Some succeeded in maintaining a lifestyle based on following a food supply that changed seasonally. For those who succeeded in finding permanent water, they became the "First Farmers"; we understand their world through the fallen walls of their settlements, their stone tools, and their pottery.

Banner: "Pleistocene Landscape" detail from painting by Mauricio Antón, Madrid, Spain

Artists Roger Kull and Judith Durr conserving the skeletal remains of a late-Pleistocene mastodon discovered less than 25 miles from Prescott. Preserved and displayed are a partial cranium with teeth and tusk protrusions from a young mastodon found along a creek near Peeples Valley. Photo courtesy © Sharlot Hall Museum)

For more than 10,000 years, native bands and villages developed across the Central Highlands. The "ancient ones" survived and developed a flourishing trade that included everything from valuable rock to pottery containers that could hold magical medicines to coveted foods — evolving and competing for limited resources as the tundra changed to forested high country, semi-arid highlands and desert lowlands.

Map graphic identifies possible migration routes, courtesy © Northern Arizona University.

"Clovis Migrators" (left) and "Clovis Cave People" (surprint)
Illustrations courtesy © Wood, Ronsaville, Harlin, Inc.

Archaeological evidence traces these "First Americans" – that is, reading meaning into their stone points, procurement camps and (much later) the stone-stacked walls and ruins we see today. They left their marks on the land and their stories in the memories of the "ancient ones" who survived in forests, as well as arid highland and lowland areas.

Scientists widely agree that – across the Americas – all indigenous people spinning off from the first landings and camps were descendants out of Siberia.

Basketry, pottery and rock art tells us about their creative expression. Some are mysteries, like the rock-art petroglyphs for which we will never find out their meanings. Designs on their tempered clay pottery bowls and jars do tell us about the boundaries of their communities and answer the question: **"How long ago?"**

Indigenous pottery on exhibition at Sharlot Hall Museum.

Pottery and petroglyph rock art became forms of storytelling and creative expression. Such art is found throughout the Central Highlands, with common motif symbols, regardless of clay source and locality. Pottery took many shapes, forms and designs, and became an essential element in the sophisticated mercantile system.

ARIZONA CENTRAL HIGHLANDS

Hilltop sites dot the local landscape...
- an unsolved mystery!

First identified during Amiel Whipple's expedition in the mid-1800s, hilltop sites were not mapped until Ken Austin's work in the 1970s. Whipple had made note of these sites on his surveys recording that these were plentiful and dot the landscape. Their purpose, however, remains as illusive today as when first observed.

For defense? Housing? A lookout post? Ceremonial site? Archaeologists date the construction as far back as 1100CE, and then suddenly stopped about 1350CE.

An exhibit at Sharlot Hall Museum considers possible roles for these sites. Some scholars consider landscape clues for habitation or defense; others identify too many crossover variables to defy singular purpose.

Fortunately, site stewards continue to work to protect these sites from human trafficking and looting, thereby preserving them for ongoing study.

If you see a hilltop site, "take" only pictures, and minimize your imprint on the land and rock formations. Support the site stewards who preserve these fascinating artifacts of the past.

Above left: Petroglyphs site 101. Top: Defensive site wall. Below: "Mills Fort" hilltop site. Photographs courtesy © Sharlot Hall Museum.

Game and grain, heat and rain... impacted the indigenous peoples along trails and trade routes that predated European intervention. Settlements were often miles apart; some formed a communal, village-based structure that probably never had more than 100 inhabitants. Others lived remotely in small, scattered pithouse shelters. Survival was based on availability of resources: food and water. Clan and villages grew from extended families.

Prescott Culture murals depict both scattered and village-based pithouse living scenarios. Illustration photos courtesy © Sharlot Hall Museum.

Spanish Conquistadors explore the Southwest in search of Cibola, the legendary cities of gold. Coronado mural painting, east wall © Coronado Museum.

Replica of Conquistador helmet from Sharlot Hall Museum collections.

When Spanish Conquistadors explored the Southwest in the mid-1500s, few communities of native peoples were welcoming of these new trading partners.

Native communities were ravaged by smallpox and European illnesses. Finding little evidence of material riches, the Spanish moved on, leaving the area alone and virtually forgotten.

For the next 300 years, government oversight of these lands was minimal and, with few settlements, only adventurers and mountain men explored the streams and forests of what is now Arizona, some seeking gold, others seeking beaver pelts.

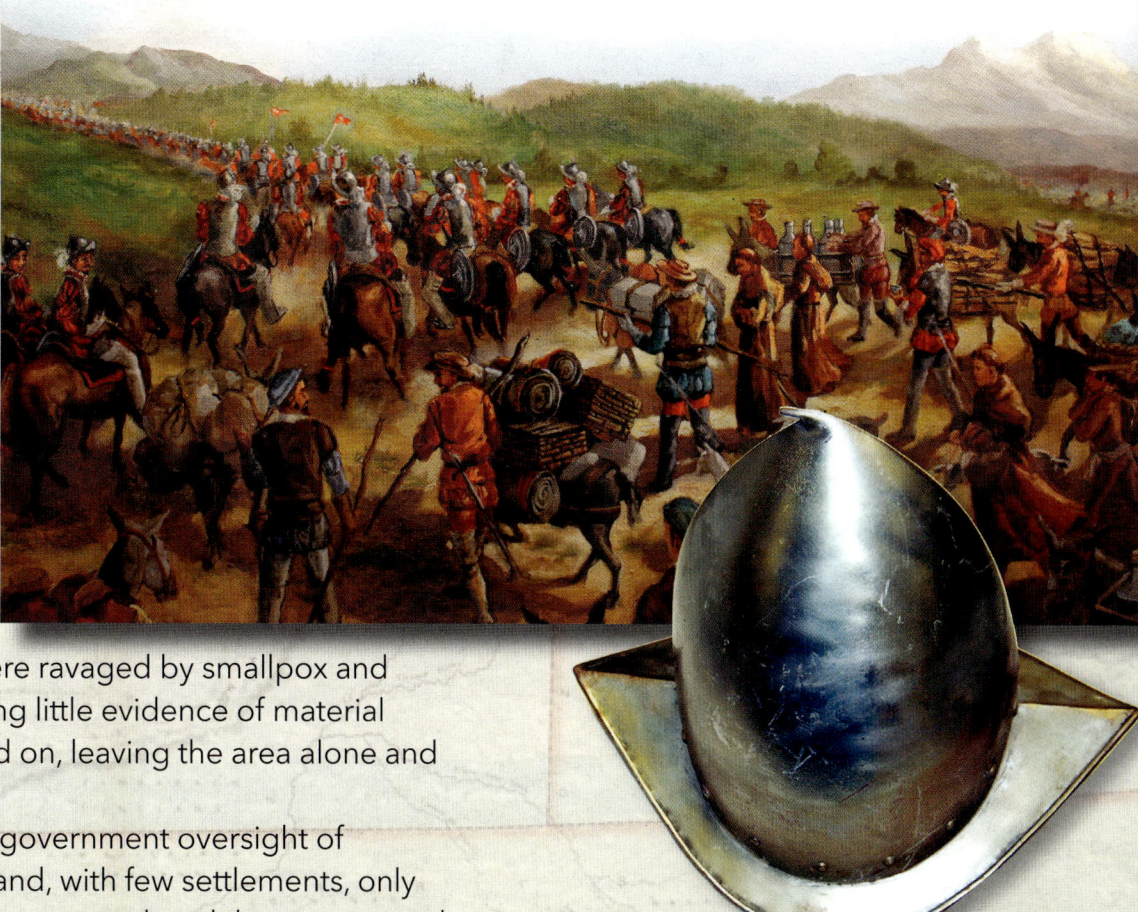

Following the War with Mexico (1848) and the Treaty of Guadalupe Hidalgo, the United States was ceded much of the Southwest, including land that became the territory of New Mexico. Army surveyors were dispatched to explore the new land, find routes west to the Pacific and to map the vast new Territory.

Steamboat *Explorer* illustration by Heinrich Balduin Mollhausen, 1858, watercolor and gouache on paper, courtesy © Amon Carter Museum.

Illustration of Army wagon train, vintage 1850 courtesy © Sharlot Hall Museum.

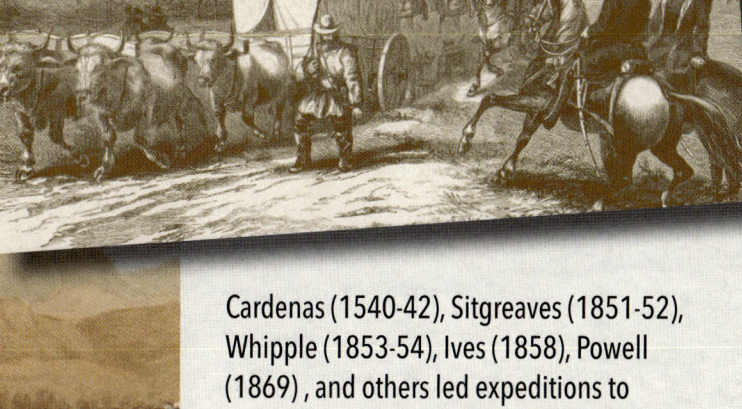

Cardenas (1540-42), Sitgreaves (1851-52), Whipple (1853-54), Ives (1858), Powell (1869), and others led expeditions to map the new territory. While most were overland, Joseph Ives' expedition navigated the Colorado River aboard the *Explorer*.

ARIZONA CENTRAL HIGHLANDS

Some scholars claim Prescott is an historical accident. Place climate, geology and humans together and almost anything can happen.

Those who live here know that, over the millennia, people have been coming to the Prescott area for a good reason: It's one of the world's great places.

The Central Highlands stands as a broad swath of land roughly a mile high and more in elevation, a tall uplift at the very heart of Arizona.

With alternating pine-clad mountains and broad, brushy valleys, this is lush, verdant country compared to the arid Sonoran Desert to the south and the Colorado Plateau to the north.

As storm clouds track north from the Gulf of California, these collide with the great wall of the Mogollon Rim, marking the southern limit of the Colorado Plateau.

Meeting that barrier, clouds turn southward again, shedding rain on the region laced with rivers and streams that feed great forests of ponderosa pine, juniper, oak, manzanita, agave and other plant species green zones that in turn sustain a wealth of diverse animal species.

Elevation, airflow and moisture combine to give the high country a fine, even climate that is neither excessively hot in the summer nor excessively cold in the winter.

At its core is Prescott, a popular destination where residents and visitors meld together to enjoy the culture, history, activities and events.

Northeast view of Thumb Butte, with Bradshaw Mountains in background.

Map 200, U.S. Geologic Society, 1955, courtesy © Sharlot Hall Museum archives

Territorial Seal of Arizona, courtesy © Sharlot Hall Museum

Prescott, the town, was carved out of the wilderness. Amid the chaos of the Civil War, the U.S. Congress enacted legislation, signed by President Abraham Lincoln, that created the Arizona Territory. The War was costly and Union leaders were influenced by the prospect of mineral wealth in the region.

That prospect came to fruition in May 1863 when an exploration party led by Joseph Reddeford Walker discovered gold in the Bradshaw Mountains, south and east of present-day Prescott. A subsequent discovery of gold in the Antelope Mountains set in motion a chain of events:

- establishment of Fort Whipple on the banks of Granite Creek,
- founding of Prescott on May 30, 1864, and
- subsequent designation of Prescott as capital of Arizona Territory, and seat of government for newly created Yavapai County.

Civil War illustration courtesy © Sharlot Hall Museum

Capt. Joseph Walker was 63 years old when he led the expedition that found gold near Prescott. Image courtesy © Sharlot Hall Museum

Depiction of Capt. Joseph Walker and party making first contact with local, indigenous people near Thumb Butte. Painting by George Phippen courtesy Sharlot Hall and Phippen museums.

Settlement of Prescott and the surrounding region came at the expense of native peoples, including the Yavapai who had occupied the region for centuries.

Drawn by the "Go West!" promise of new opportunities and riches, immigrants and settlers competed for the same food, water and space as the native peoples — Yavapai, White Mountain and Tonto Apache to the north and east, Mojave Yavpe to the west and Hohokom to the south.

Above right: On their release from San Carlos Reservation, the Yavapai were returned to historic lands near Prescott.

Above: Viola Jimulla became the chief of the Yavapai-Prescott Indian tribe.

Right: Indian scouts follow renegade tracks during the Indian Wars that ravaged the West, 1864-1889.

Photos courtesy
© Sharlot Hall Museum

Fort Whipple parade grounds, 1870s.

The Indian Wars of the Arizona Territory had a direct impact on the people of the Central Highlands, both settlers and the indigenous population. Gen. George Crook, shown with his Indian scouts, and the U.S. military were engaged against rebellious natives throughout the Territory. Photos courtesy © Sharlot Hall Museum

The inevitable conflict between cultures led to almost 40 years of bloodshed and war. The U.S. military established a series of forts throughout the Arizona Territory to protect miners, ranchers, settlers and pioneer families. Fort Whipple (established in 1863) provided a measure of stability, safety and security to a region embroiled with lawlessness and unbridled ambition.

While many tribal people including the Yavapai were forced onto the San Carlos reservation, skirmishes between renegades and military continued until the late 1880s when Geronimo and his followers surrendered. In the early 1900s, the Yavapai returned from San Carlos to Prescott where — as the Yavapai-Prescott Indian Tribe — they play a vital role in the region's heritage, culture and economy.

Y. B. Rowdy

...was described as an "excellent shot ...old in war (and) loved campaigning and fighting..." according to his commanding officer. As an Indian scout, he was cited "...for bravery in action against Apache Indians" and presented the Medal of Honor on March 7, 1890.

Yavapai scout Y.B. Rowdy served as the eyes 'n' ears of a detachment of the 10th U.S. Cavalry pursuing followers of the "Apache Kid." The patrol closed with and battled the fugitives during the Cherry Creek Campaign in one of the last engagements of the Indian Wars in the Arizona Territory.

ARIZONA CENTRAL HIGHLANDS

Adventurers, miners in search of gold, farmers and ranchers seeking a new beginning on land made available through the federal Homestead Act, merchants, lawyers, and others seeking a new opportunity came to Prescott.

Together they created a community with schools, churches, businesses, other social organizations and, of course, saloons and brothels. Eventually came the railroads and such indicia of 19th century modernization as electricity and public water service.

To be sure, Prescott in its early territorial years was a frontier town and had its share of disasters, crime, rowdyism and occasional gunfights on Whiskey Row. Over time, it matured and developed into a commercial center for the Central Highlands

Two-story brick Courthouse (top) was centerpiece of downtown plaza. Built in 1878, it was later torn down and replaced by 1916.

Whiskey Row became the focal point for the young community of Prescott featuring such establishments as the Diana, Cobweb, Cabinet and Palace saloons, to name a few.

Miners flocked to the area in search of gold, silver and other mineral riches.

Photos and illustrations courtesy © Sharlot Hall Museum

The Yavapai County Courthouse, 1878-1916, on the Prescott Courthouse Plaza.

Electricity and trolley in downtown Prescott along Gurley Street, circa 1904.

Courthouse Plaza and its Gazebo with view of Granite Mountain, about 1905. Photos courtesy © Sharlot Hall Museum

Prescott lost its status as the territorial capital in 1867, when the Territorial Legislature voted to have the capital moved to Tucson.

Regaining it temporarily in 1877, the capital was permanently relocated to Phoenix in 1889 as population and political influence within Arizona shifted.

Despite the political loss, Prescott continued to prosper and develop, and continues to serve today as the county seat of Yavapai County.

ARIZONA CENTRAL HIGHLANDS

A view of downtown Prescott shortly before the Great Fire of 1900.

Anyone who has lived in Arizona knows that, eventually, one topic is bound to surface: drought. When the spring of 1900 rolled into the Central Highlands, an unusually dry spell came with it. Despite a growing number of brick buildings, a multitude of tinderboxes were still in existence in a town still mostly comprised of wood. While the commmunity of Prescott had experienced several major fires previously, the one in July 1900 destroyed much of the downtown. It became known as the Great Fire on Whiskey Row.

Smoke continued to waft from the smoldering remains the morning after the Great Fire. The brick edifice of the Palace saloon was one of the few standing and was ultimately removed. The fire destroyed the Whiskey Row block, parts of Gurley and Goodwin streets, and introduced new legends and folklore associated with its cause, effect and economic impact, and the future of Prescott. Photos courtesy © Sharlot Hall Museum

Railway to Prescott

The Territorial Legislature authorized building a railway in 1864, but it was 13 years before the **Southern Pacific Railway** crossed the Colorado River at Yuma. A line for the transcontinental **Atlantic and Pacific Railway** (A&P) was completed west to Kingman in 1882. What was needed, however, was a rail line to Prescott and the local mines.

The first was the **Prescott & Arizona Central Railway**. It connected with the A&P at Prescott Junction (present-day Seligman) and was completed to Prescott on Jan. 1, 1887. With leased rolling stock and built with lightweight rail from A&P, operations were plagued with construction problems. It ceased to operate in 1893, leaving behind a legal morass.

It was eclipsed that same year by the **Santa Fe, Prescott & Phoenix**, amid railway building inducements provided by the 16th Territorial Legislature. It connected with the A&P at Ash Fork and, by 1895, tracks ran to Prescott over Iron Springs to Congress and on to Phoenix.

Branch lines were built into the Bradshaw Mountains with the **Prescott & Eastern** completed in 1899 and the **Bradshaw Mountain Railway** in 1901-1902.

While railroad operations had expanded in the 1800s, these began to shrink by the mid-1900s. In an attempt to improve service to Phoenix, the **Santa Fe Railway** passenger line bypassed Prescott leaving the town as a spur line with only freight service. This was abandoned in 1983 after a series of winter storms washed out bridges into town.

The Prescott race for an economic base was often centered on freight, both inbound and out. Freight wagons were slow and cumbersome. Ore needed to be shipped, and supplies and trade goods from the East were aided with rail transport.

This developed intense competition for railway connections north to the transcontinental lines near Flagstaff, in tandem with spur lines to the mining camps nearby. This competition became a battleground that almost crippled the Arizona economy.

Over time, rail transport for freight and passengers became no longer economically viable, and service to Prescott was shut down in the 1980s.

Images of the downtown Prescott Depot (top), local rail yard (right), and early locomotives in Prescott (at Point of Rocks, center right) highlight the lure and lore of railroading in Arizona. Photos courtesy © Sharlot Hall Museum

ARIZONA CENTRAL HIGHLANDS

Along with the rest of the county and country, Prescott's population suffered during the Depression years of the 1930s, but also benefited by the post-World War II boom.

The 1980s was a period of significant growth and, by the 1990s, population had increased to more than 25,000 residents.

Today, Prescott is a modern city of more than 45,000, and growing. Mining, ranching and railroading no longer drive the area's economy, having been replaced by government and tourism.

The first courthouse (top) was a two-story wood structure with the courtroom on the ground floor. The sheriff's office and jail were upstairs. This was replaced with....

The 1878 two-story red-brick edifice (second from top). Considered a landmark, it was also drafty, fragile and prone to construction-related issues.

The 1916 granite edifice (above and right) was quarried from nearby stone (inset right) and remains today as the iconic focal point of the Courthouse Plaza.

Photos courtesy © Sharlot Hall Museum

Courthouse Plaza

The central core on which the historic Yavapai County Courthouse now stands was laid out by pioneer surveyor Robert Groom in 1864 as a plaza for public use.

The first county courthouse, however, was in a two-story wooden building with the sheriff's office and jail on the second floor. Court was held downstairs.

In 1878, a brick edifice was constructed on the grounds of the Plaza, which served as both a county courthouse and jail.

Over time, this facility proved to be inadequate (and too fragile) for its intended purposes. By 1916, work began and it was replaced...

utilizing material quarried from the old Simmons Ranch near today's Granite Mountain Middle School. This colonade structure continues to this day to serve the county court system.

The Courthouse Plaza and the businesses that surround it serve as both the center of Prescott's downtown commercial activity and a major attraction for tourism.

Governor's Mansion

In 1864, the historic Governor's Mansion was constructed on a plot two blocks west of the Courthouse Plaza. A "mansion" only in a relative sense, this log structure was built from local Ponderosa pine and served as the residence and offices of the first two Territorial governors – John Goodwin and Richard McCormick.

The cost of construction was $6,000, paid for with private funds.

Following relocation of the Territorial Capital to Tucson in 1867, the Mansion fell into private hands and remained there until 1917, when it was acquired by the State of Arizona for preservation due to its historical significance as the offices and residence of the first Territorial governor of Arizona.

In 1927, a woman named Sharlot Mabridth Hall secured a lifetime lease of the Mansion and opened it as a museum the following year featuring collections and artifacts she had acquired during her time as Territorial Historian (the first woman to hold public office in Arizona).

She worked tirelessly to preserve the local history and heritage of the West Central Highlands of Arizona. Following her death in 1943, the Museum she began was named in her honor.

From its inception, Prescott has been the home of two iconic landmarks—the Courthouse and the Governor's Mansion—both of which are of paramount importance to the local heritage and to the city's reputation as a destination for tourists from throughout the world.

While Prescott's history as a frontier town is a thing of the past, it continues to be recognized as one of the country's top 10 Old West cities. Its cultural past is preserved today in the community's museums:

- The **Sharlot Hall Museum** in downtown Prescott showcases the past for all future generations in its exhibits, collections and archival records, and stands today as a testament to the namesake's remarkable foresight and her pioneer determination.

- The **Smoki Museum** about a mile east of downtown has transformed from an Indian tourist attraction supporting the world's oldest rodeo to a cultural center for native American Indians.

- The **Phippen Museum** about seven miles northeast of Prescott honors the American cowboy and rancher with changing exhibits of Western art.

Sharlot Hall MUSEUM

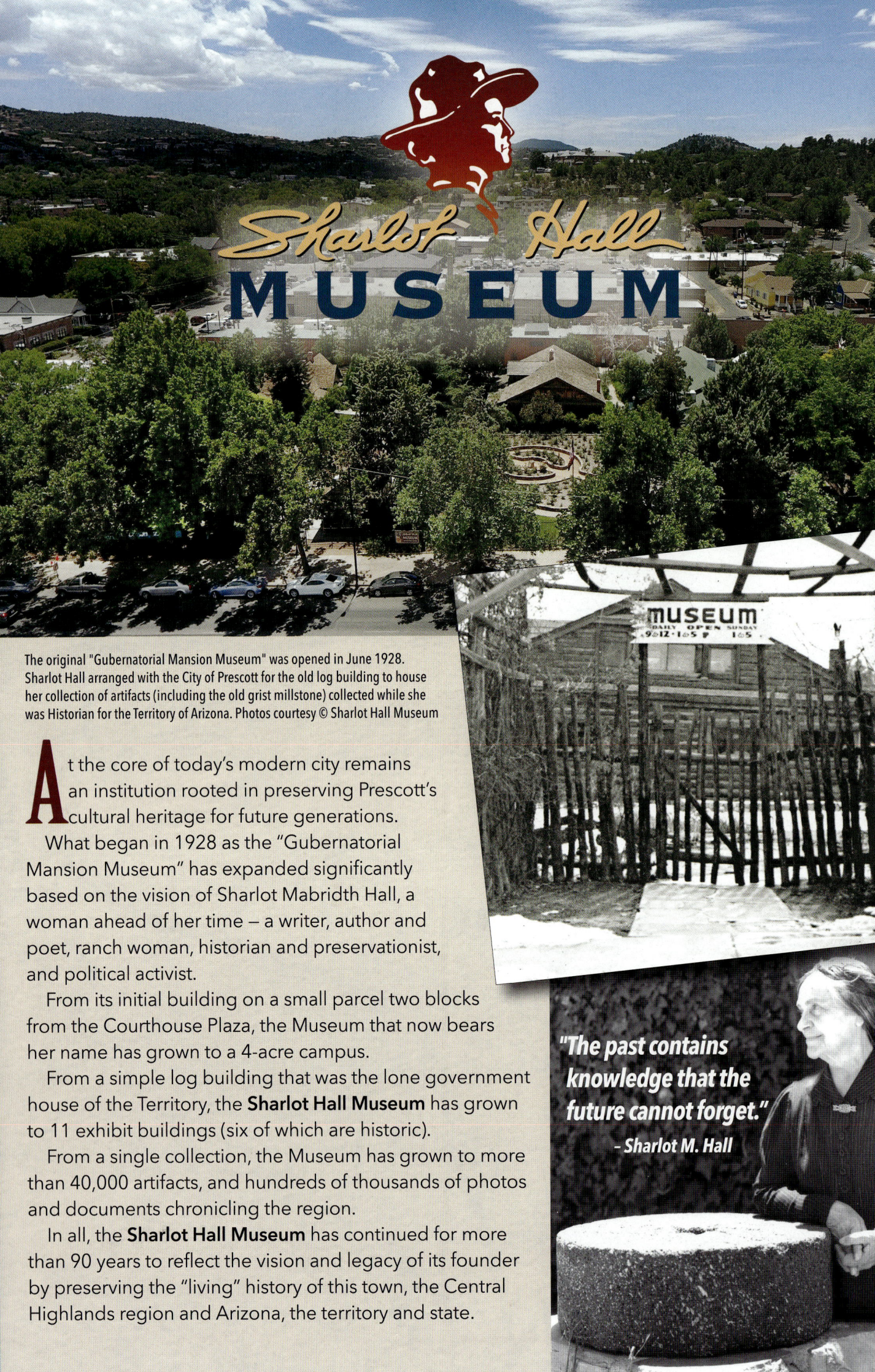

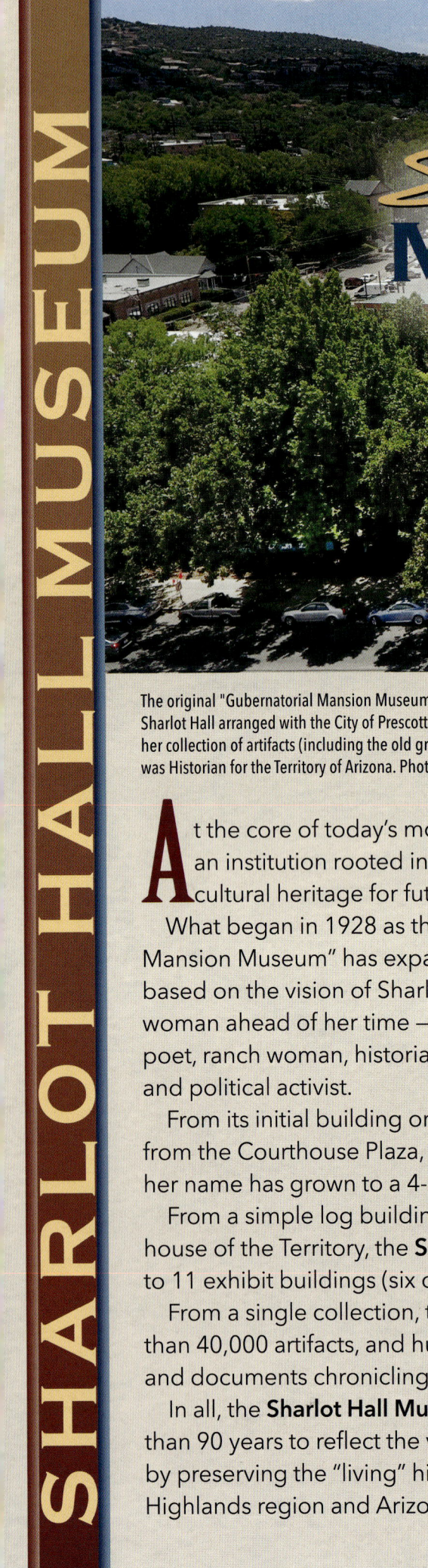

SHARLOT HALL MUSEUM

The original "Gubernatorial Mansion Museum" was opened in June 1928. Sharlot Hall arranged with the City of Prescott for the old log building to house her collection of artifacts (including the old grist millstone) collected while she was Historian for the Territory of Arizona. Photos courtesy © Sharlot Hall Museum

At the core of today's modern city remains an institution rooted in preserving Prescott's cultural heritage for future generations.

What began in 1928 as the "Gubernatorial Mansion Museum" has expanded significantly based on the vision of Sharlot Mabridth Hall, a woman ahead of her time — a writer, author and poet, ranch woman, historian and preservationist, and political activist.

From its initial building on a small parcel two blocks from the Courthouse Plaza, the Museum that now bears her name has grown to a 4-acre campus.

From a simple log building that was the lone government house of the Territory, the **Sharlot Hall Museum** has grown to 11 exhibit buildings (six of which are historic).

From a single collection, the Museum has grown to more than 40,000 artifacts, and hundreds of thousands of photos and documents chronicling the region.

In all, the **Sharlot Hall Museum** has continued for more than 90 years to reflect the vision and legacy of its founder by preserving the "living" history of this town, the Central Highlands region and Arizona, the territory and state.

"The past contains knowledge that the future cannot forget."
– Sharlot M. Hall

Built in 1864, the Governor's Mansion continues as the centerpiece of the Sharlot Hall Museum.

The Territorial Women's Memorial Rose Garden features more than 200 rose bushes and is dedicated to the pioneer women who helped settle the Arizona Territory before statehood (in 1912). In essence, these women prepared the way for many others to make a life in Arizona. More than 500 women are honored, representing nearly all occupations and ethnic backgrounds. Photos courtesy © Sharlot Hall Museum

Sharlot Mabridth Hall

A woman ahead of her time — writer, poet, political activist, historian, and ranch woman — Sharlot rode her way from Kansas to Lynx Creek, Arizona Territory, along the Santa Fe Trail as a young girl of 12 in 1878. On the family homestead, she was homeschooled by her mother and attended a brief term at Prescott School.

It was then she met Henry Fleury, secretary to the first Territorial Governor. He was living in the old log-building and told her stories of the early history. This would impact the rest of her life.

Sharlot began writing, was published in national magazines of the day, became an accomplished author, poet and activist for statehood, women's rights and historic (and cultural) preservation.

She became the Territorial Historian in 1909, the first woman to hold public office in Arizona. She continued collecting artifacts and family histories while traveling the Territory. Her poem *Arizona* had a strong influence on Congress during debates on Arizona's bid for statehood, and she was named as Arizona's elector during the Presidential election of 1925.

Following the death of her parents and wanting to preserve the old log building that had been the Governor's Mansion, she petitioned the town of Prescott to secure the building. In 1927, her efforts were rewarded with a lifetime lease of the building.

She moved her collections into the old log building and welcomed the first visitors to the "Gubernatorial Mansion Museum" on June 11, 1928. She continued to grow the Museum until her death in 1943.

SHARLOT HALL MUSEUM

Living History presentations are held on the Museum campus every month, where docents share the history, heritage and skills of yesteryear with young people and inquiring adults. Sharlot Hall Museum is a place where history comes alive – an Arizona History Adventure.

Photos courtesy © Sharlot Hall Museum

The 1864 log-building Mansion serves as a centerpiece of the 4-acre campus that hosts festivals and special events throughout the year. The Museum is open daily except Thanksgiving, Christmas and New Year's days.

Sharlot Hall MUSEUM
two blocks west of the Courthouse Plaza
415 West Gurley Street • Prescott, AZ 86301
(928) 445-3122 • www.sharlothallmuseum.org

Fort Misery – What's in a Name?

"Why is it called that?" — a typical query that brings out a detailed response from a docent or tour guide relating the history of one of its owners, along with the fact that it has nothing to do with local military history.

Fort Misery — its name is anecdotal in the pantheon of Sharlot Hall Museum. When the building got its name, it was literally a miserable place to live in.

Built in the winter of 1863-64 by Manuel Yrissari, it was hastily constructed from local Ponderosa pine logs with a flat pine pole roof covered with a thick layer of dirt to keep out winter snow and rain. Mud daubing between the logs was a regular maintenance chore, and the dirt roof would no doubt have turned to mud a number of times before it washed away or fell through the poles.

Intended as a temporary shelter and local mercantile, the building was pressed into service as a church and a room for the first term of court in the Territory after the Governor's Party arrived in early 1864.

When Yrissari sold off his stock of goods and left town, the building passed to Mary Decrow Ramos and she turned it into a boarding house. It's possible Judge John Howard was one of her boarders, as he acquired the building when Ramos moved.

The Judge was a man of means, highly respected as a local barrister. The building served as his office and residence, and he improved it to the extent of adding a peaked roof. All of his cooking was done in its stone fireplace, and he was generous in offering his hospitality. He could not begin to compete, however, with Henry Fleury's well-ordered household at the Governor's Mansion.

Fleury himself cooked up meals whose fame spread throughout the territory. Hence visitors of the day compared the little cabin by contrast by dubbing it Fort Misery, according to Sharlot Hall writings in an article for the *Prescott Journal Miner* of March 23, 1934.

Rescued from demolition in 1934 by Sharlot Hall, it was moved to the Museum grounds and saved for posterity.

The oldest surviving log cabin in Arizona resides at the Museum with its unusual moniker: **Fort Misery**. The structure, relocated to the campus in 1934, was built alongside the nearby Granite Creek and served as a mercantile, courtroom, boarding house, residence, law office and church. It was the meeting site for locals in creating the town of Prescott on May 30, 1864. Photos courtesy © Sharlot Hall Museum

What began as a simple log-building, the Museum has grown to a 4-acre, park-like campus that beckons visitors and locals to enjoy its hospitality and respite. Festivals and special events allow plenty of opportunity to live, learn and relax amid the high country flora, fauna, living history and heritage.

As Sharlot M. Hall acknowledged in creating her legacy,

"The Museum is as important as the land itself. It gives this place we call home meaning."

SHARLOT HALL MUSEUM

Since its founding, the Museum has added an array of historic buildings, exhibit galleries, an outdoor amphitheater and education center, plus a research center with its modern library and archives. Cultural and educational programs are presented throughout the year, and the campus hosts such annual events as the **Folk Arts Fair** and **Prescott Indian Art Market** in June, the **Prescott Folk Music Festival** in October, and **Frontier Christmas**.

Photos courtesy © Sharlot Hall Museum

The Museum continues to acquire a wide range of collections and artifacts, from the ancient past to the 20th century, that reflect the historical, social and natural aspects of the Central Arizona Highlands. Among the many treasures are more than 400 Native American baskets. These baskets — only a portion of which are on display in the Hartzell Room of the Sharlot Hall Building — feature examples that are both exquisite as they are utilitarian.

Other Museum exhibits explore the region's natural history and earliest peoples, as well as feature the adventurers, entrepreneurs, miners, ranchers and soldiers who poured through the Territory, ushering in one of the most turbulent and lively periods in Western history. Changing exhibits in the Lawler Museum Center offer a wide array of artistic and cultural experiences allowing the Museum to tell many stories that draw on the rich collections.

Expanding on Sharlot's Work

Many of the Museum's exhibits and dioramas are housed in the **Sharlot Hall Building**, a large stone structure built in 1936 as a Civil Works Administration project. Amid the Depression of the 1930s, it was deemed "the house of a thousand hands" providing work for many.

Exhibits and diorama in the "Stone" building chronicle the founding of a wilderness territorial capital (1863) to statehood (1912), as narrated through displays that reveal the region's rich history of mining, ranching, railroads, military, indigenous peoples and more.

The **Ranch House**, built on-site in the 1930s, is a tribute to the early ranchers of the area. In the single, multipurpose room, cooking, sleeping, bathing and other indoor activities took place. The fireplace was used for cooking and heating. Some families saved for such luxuries as a cast-iron stove and glass windows.

Prescott's first **School House**, built in 1868 near present-day Mile High Middle School, burned in 1948. Local service organization members joined to construct a replica to the west of the Sharlot Hall Building in 1962.

Completed in 1875, the **Frémont House** was built with local, milled lumber. As Governor of the Territory (1878-1882), John Charles Frémont and his wife and daughter lived in the little house. In 1971, the structure was purchased and moved from its location on Union Street to the lot across from the Governor's Mansion.

The **Transportation Building** opened in June 1990 featuring the Museum's collection of rolling stock, including Sharlot's own 1927 Durant Star Touring Car, a Model T farm truck, the Bicentennial Wagon, a stagecoach and numerous buggies, wagons and bicycles.

The **Bashford House** is a Victorian treasure that houses the Museum's gift shop. Built in 1877, it was bought by local merchant William Coles Bashford for his bride. Exhibit panels and artifacts explain who lived here, and the remarkable civic effort to save and move the structure to escape it being bulldozed. It remains one of the few of Prescott's many Victorian houses that is regularly open to the public.

The modern **Lawler Museum Center** (1979) and new **Education Center** (2020) provide theater space for changing exhibits, special presentations, collections and campus events.

FORT WHIPPLE MUSEUM

Fort Whipple Museum

Fort Whipple served as a tactical base for the U.S. Army during the Indian Wars of 1864 to 1889, where it became one of the key centers for military presence in the Arizona Territory.

A few decades later, Whipple became one of the military's largest hospitals for the treatment of respiratory ailments and continues today serving veterans as a VA medical facility.

If your enthusiasm is for historic buildings, you will enjoy touring the vintage 1908 military officer's quarters for its architectural interest.

If you're piqued by the history of military medicine, Museum exhibits feature medical instruments of the late-1800s and the treatment programs of World War I veterans suffering from tuberculosis or respiratory recovery from mustard and chlorine gas warfare.

If your curiosity is vintage Army weaponry, Buffalo Soldiers, military maps, photographs and memoirs written by those stationed at this outpost, you're in for a "Frontier Adventure."

For decades, Fort Whipple and its companies were protecting the Territorial Capital (Prescott), nearby gold fields and early settlers of the frontier.

It also served as the mobilization point for the Rough Riders. By the mid-1920s, Whipple was the fourth largest veteran's hospital in the United States.

Hours: Thursday to Saturday, 10 a.m. to 4 p.m., self-guided. **Admission:** free, donations accepted

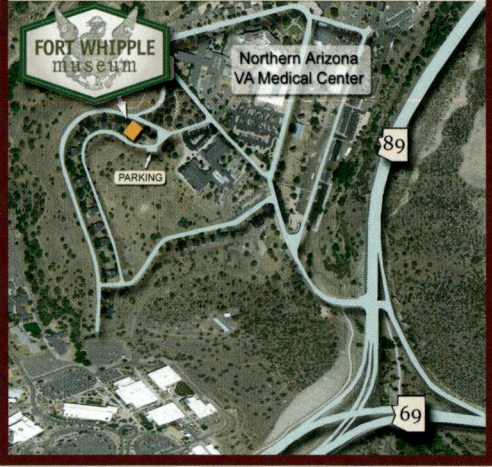

Quarters at Fort Whipple on Officer's Hill were constructed in the early 1900s — this one is home to the Fort Whipple Museum in its historic creme and green colors.

Illustration of Fort Whipple, 1864

Photos and illustration courtesy © Sharlot Hall Museum

Replica of Gen. George Crook's field desk.

The Gatling gun (left) was a hand-driven rapid-fire weapon that saw action in the Spanish-American War by the Rough Riders.

Displays and exhibits at Fort Whipple Museum trace its history and transition from a military and tactical base to a medical and veterans facility.

The "Smoki People" are Born

The Smoki MUSEUM
American Indian Art and Culture

In 1921, the Prescott Rodeo was in serious financial trouble, despite the popular interest in Wild West Shows featuring Wild Bill Hickock and Annie Oakley. Interest in the Rodeo was waning, and something had to be done.

Charles Elrod, Gail Gardner, Ralph Roper and several other notable Prescott men gathered to see what they could do. As they talked, Gardner recounted with awe the Snake Dance he'd seen as a youth on the Hopi mesas. Why not perform a show utilizing imagery from the vanishing Native People to attract an audience?

A performance followed at the Rodeo that June. Nearly 5,000 attended, and word spread. Continuing the imagery show amid growing popularity, the Rodeo was soon back "in the black." The group was having fun pursuing what they saw as a civic duty.

Soon, they needed an identity...a name. The Spanish word for Hopi people is "Moqui," which became 'smokey' and then 'Smoki.'

As a founding member of *The Smoki People*, Gardner said of the effort that he had "never had so much fun, or worked so hard."

Following a communitywide roundup of bull snakes, *The Smoki People* presented their version of the Hopi Snake Dance in June 1922.

Hopi Kachina Dance at the First Village, circa 1910. This was an event that inspired *The Smoki People*. Photos courtesy © Smoki Museum

SMOKI MUSEUM

The Smoki Public Museum

With a grant from the federal Civil Works Administration (CWA) authored by Grace Sparkes, *The Smoki People* received more than $19,000 to construct **The Smoki Public Museum**. It opened on May 29, 1935, which had open shelving displaying a large collection of pre-contact pottery, baskets and "curiosities."

The Smoki People were becoming more well-known. They inducted President Calvin Coolidge as their first honorary member, receiving a "Smoki Stetson" hat. A deerskin was shipped via train to Mr. Coolidge in 1926 with a letter imploring "The Great White Chief" to bring infrastructure to the growing state of Arizona. The deerskin, recently recovered by the museum, has an interesting tale and is on display at the Museum.

The Smoki People organization continued to grow and, in 1941, Barry Goldwater sought membership in the organization. He gave many wonderful gifts to the museum including a full set of the Bureau of Ethnology books. He was the "Voice of Smoki" announcing many of the annual performances. The Goldwater family made another contemporary gift to the Museum

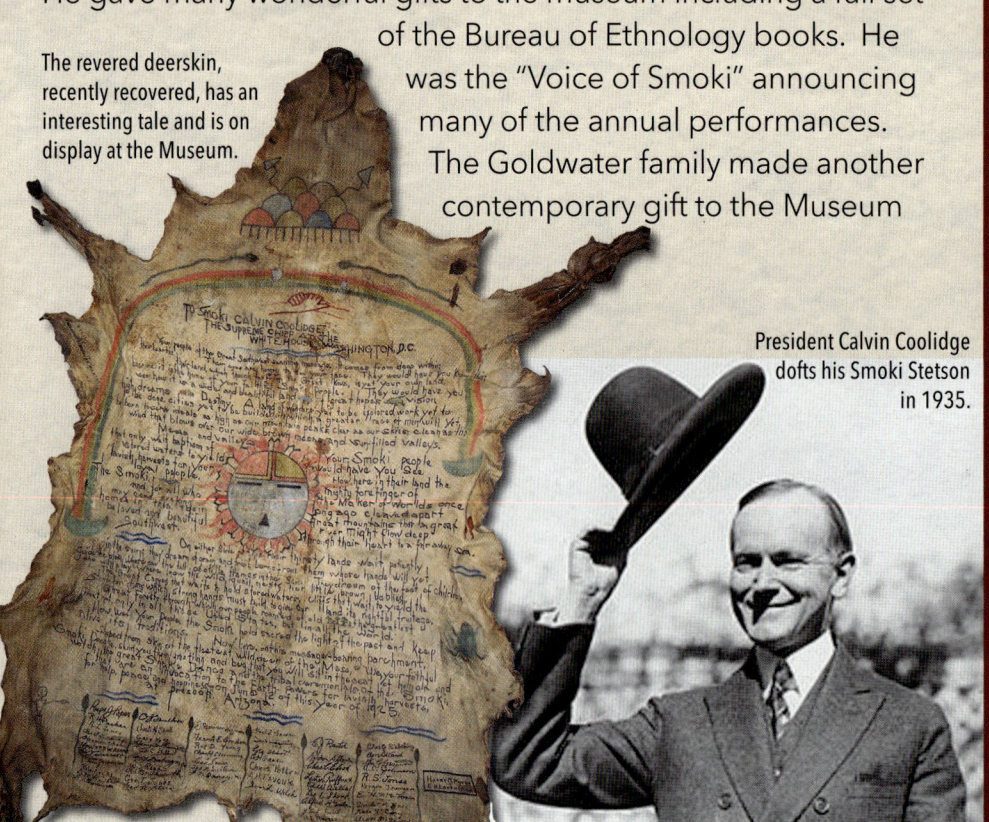

The revered deerskin, recently recovered, has an interesting tale and is on display at the Museum.

President Calvin Coolidge dofts his Smoki Stetson in 1935.

Founding 'Mothers' of *The Smoki People*

Kate T. Cory, artist of Arizona, landed in Prescott in 1912, having lived on the Hopi Mesas for seven years. She became friends with Grace Sparkes and Sharlot Hall at the time Arizona became a state.

With a great appreciation for native culture, the women asked The Smoki People to please continue what they were doing, but in a more respectful way.

Kate Cory witnessed firsthand the impact of white society on native culture; the pre-eminent thought of the time was for it to go away — for indigenous people to be absorbed and blended through the boarding school system.

Kate Cory

Sharlot Hall eloquently provided The Smoki with a "creation myth" and wrote poems about them.

Sharlot Hall

Grace Sparkes, Yavapai County immigration officer, agreed to publicize and promote them. Kate Cory assisted them in accuracy in The Snake Dance performance.

Grace Sparkes

Women became a part of the Smoki by 1926 with their own meetings and dances, and they played a major role in both costuming and fundraising.

With the Joslin-Whipple family gift for The Smoki People land, Cory assisted Christopher Totten, architect of the Pueblo Building in design to make it look and feel like an ancient pueblo structure outside and a pueblo plaza inside. The building was largely completed by 1934.

in 2011 donating many iconic photographs from the exhibit "Arizona's Son: The Photography of Barry Goldwater" to the museum. When he ran for President in 1964, he became an honorary chief – the first in Smoki history. With his "rank" tattooed on his left hand, he held microphones with that hand so everyone could see his tattoo.

The Smoki People's glory days were the 1940s and 1950s when Max Factor provided their makeup and they created Hollywood-level theatrics on the Prescott Rodeo Grounds. "To be Prescott was to be Smoki, and to be Smoki was to be Prescott" was often heard. *The Smoki People* "re-created" not just the Hopi Snake dance, but other dances from North and South American indigenous cultures.

Then came the 1960s. Membership numbers began to drop as families began to drift apart. Native people started reclaiming their tribal voices and rights. Requests to stop dancing prompted a vote of the Bear Council, ruling leaders and past 'chiefs' of *The Smoki People*. The vote was to keep going, to allow younger members still active their opportunity to dance.

In 1989 after more requests to stop, officials of the Hopi were offered an opportunity to witness the dances in person. More than 100 Hopi attended; their reactions went from awe and astonishment, to laughter and then anger. Another formal request to cease and desist was submitted.

It would take a short while and a coordinated protest on the Courthouse Plaza and at the Rodeo Grounds, but the days of *The Smoki People* were over. The final performance was in 1990.

One of Barry Goldwater's famous photographs is known as "The Navajo." While showing his photography around the Southwest in the 1940s, however, he would refer to the man in the photo as a friend named Charlie Potato. One day, someone walked up to Charlie and exclaimed, "Hey! You're Charlie Potato!" Shortly after that, Charlie asked Barry to call him "The Navajo" when giving "his talks."

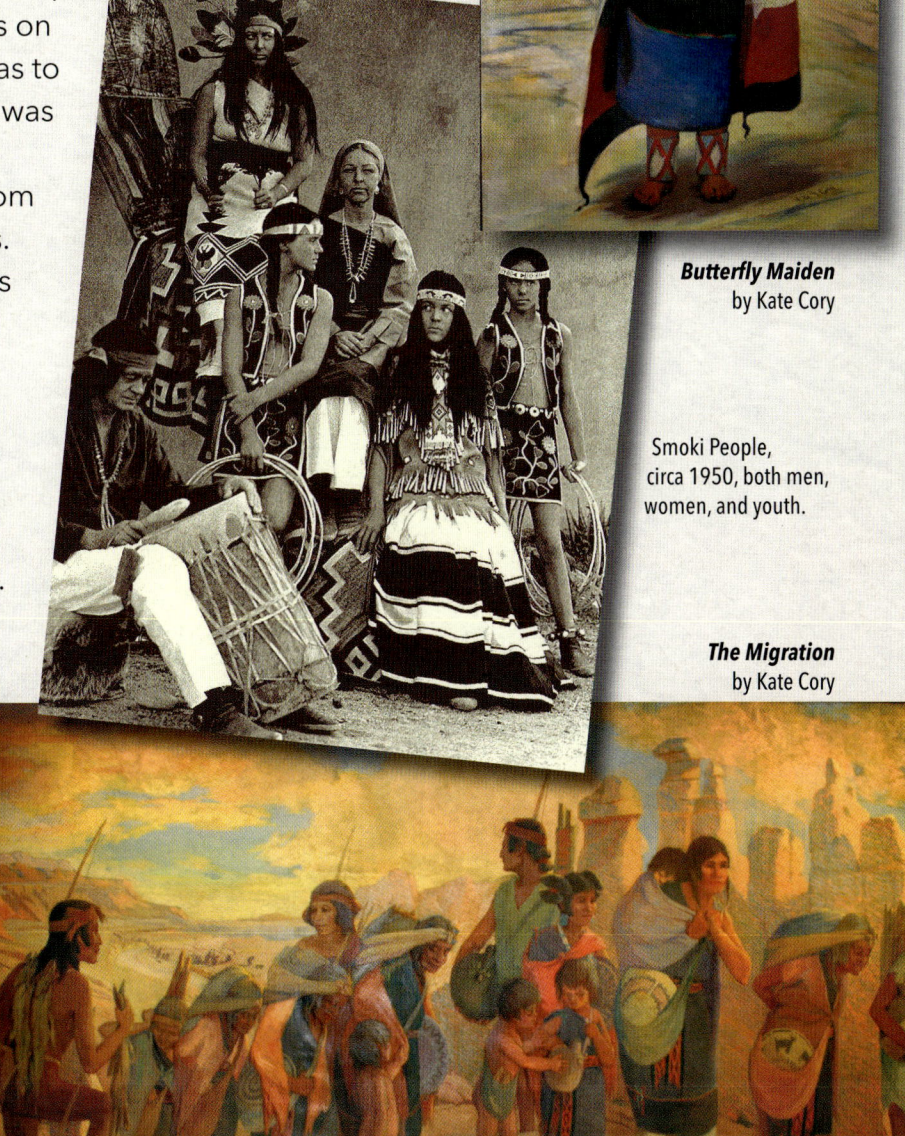

Butterfly Maiden
by Kate Cory

Smoki People, circa 1950, both men, women, and youth.

The Migration
by Kate Cory

Smoki Museum
A New Mission, New Direction

Since its construction in 1935, the **Smoki Museum** was largely staffed, cleaned and run by the women of Smoki and the Renegades—junior members of *The Smoki People*. Major repairs to the buildings were facilitated by the men through the connections they had within the community.

By 1991, those still at the museum expressed a common desire to keep the collections intact and available for public viewing. They joined with other community members and activated the nonprofit corporation formed in 1985.

Education programs were instituted; lectures, events and programming came to the museum. The buildings were placed on the National Register of Historic Places in 1995. The following year, Navajo Rug and Indian Art Auctions came to the museum through traders Jeff Ogg and Bruce Burham.

In 2001, **The Smoki Museum of American Indian Art and Culture** hired its first director, instituted memberships and began a whole new approach.

With a director in place, **The Smoki Museum of American Indian Art and Culture** started with a fresh, new approach and a new mission:

"To instill understanding and respect for the indigenous cultures of the Southwest"

The Board of Trustees acted and, at great financial risk, hired a second employee, a curator, to begin the process of changing the focus away from *The Smoki People* and towards a museum about Native People – not just in the past, but about today and into the future, preserving and protecting their own cultures... converting the facility into a cultural center.

Navajo Rug and Indian Art Auctions have been the museum's longest lasting fundraiser, and the Burnham Family has their fifth generation of RB Burnham & Company leading the auction crew.

AIM Founder Leonard Peltier's paintings were placed on public exhibition and sale at the museum in support of Lakota women on the Pine Ridge reservation.

First Things First for *The Smoki Museum*

The Native American Advisory Council, The Smoki People Advisory Council and a filmmaker were put into place.

A special exhibit "And Then They Danced: Cross-Cultural Reflections of The Smoki People" opened to the public. "Borrowed Dances"—a 62-minute film was produced and released in 2007. That same year the museum hired a Director of Native Heritage.

The curator brought the first public exhibition of AIM founder Leonard Peltier's paintings to the Smoki Museum for public exhibition and sale.

Michael Blake, author of "Dances with Wolves," introduced Peltier's "Warrior Elder," which became the template that other institutions used in subsequent showings of Peltier's works.

Engagement: Quest for Acceptance

Wanting and seeking to be a resource and supporter of Native culture is a noble idea. How to actually make that happen was another hurdle to overcome. Could the museum simply through programming: lectures, classes and events, make this happen? How could it become a place that was accepted? Sought out? Seen as a resource? Maybe even admired?

The American Association of Museums conducted a thorough and comprehensive Museum Assessment Program, involving all aspects of museum operations. In the end, two very important statements defined the museum, and the work that was under way.

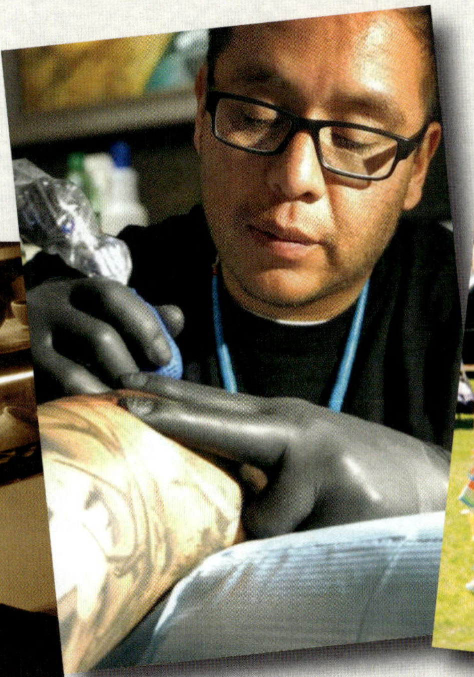

Ryan Huna Smith, Chemehuevi/Navajo, is a talented comic book artist and fine arts painter who served as director of the museum for two years. His iconic "Frybreadman" has won many awards and is known nationwide.

Among the first set of goals was to create exhibits that showed generations of Native artists in the same families to physically demonstrate the idea of Native Culture as growing—thriving on its own.

The Museum continues to present lectures, not exclusively by anthropologists and archaeologists, but by tribal members speaking of their own cultures, and engages and supports the ongoing activities of local Native organizations, including the Prescott PowWow Committee and the Granite Mountain Gourd Society, and by learning from indigenous people.

The Smoki MUSEUM
American Indian Art and Culture

147 N. Arizona Avenue • Prescott, AZ 86301
(928) 445-1230 • www.smokimuseum.org

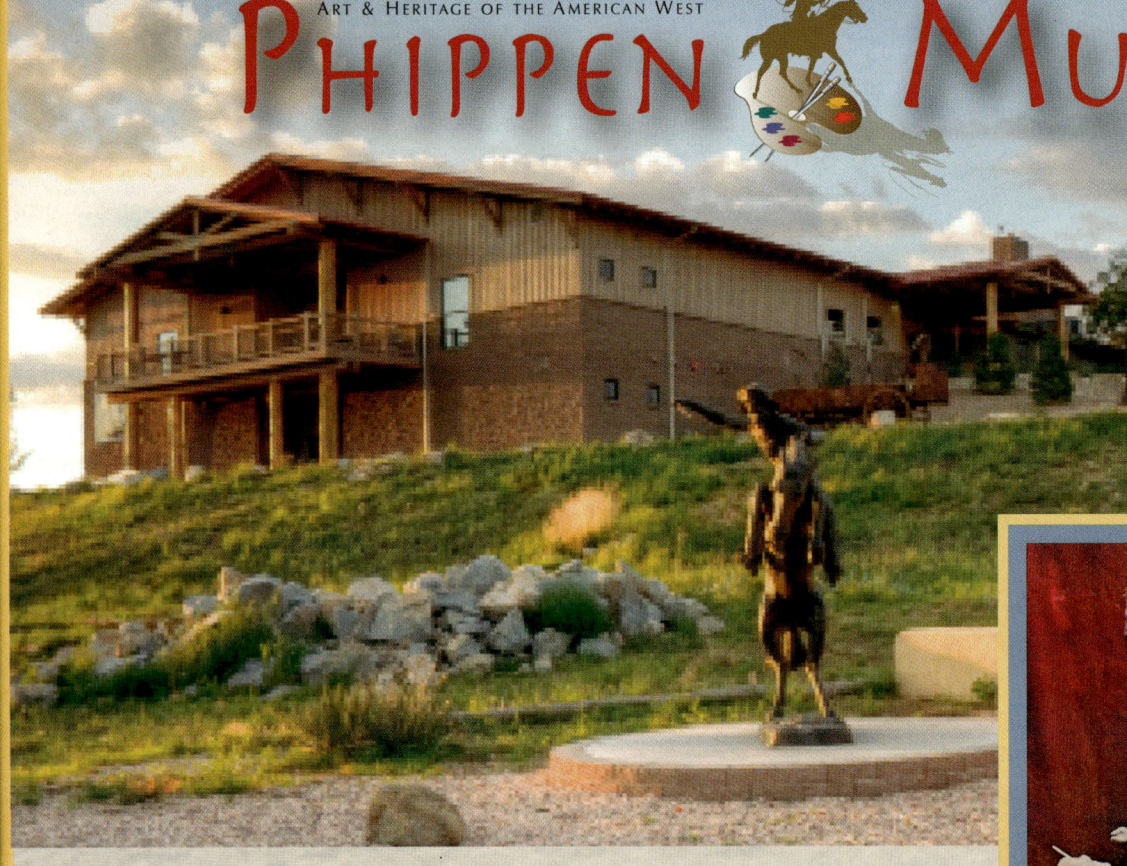

PHIPPEN MUSEUM
ART & HERITAGE OF THE AMERICAN WEST

The art, heritage, history and legends of the American West come alive at Prescott, Arizona's **Phippen Museum.** The 17,000-square-foot facility is home to two studios, replicas, four exhibit galleries, a western research library, multipurpose classroom, event space and a well-stocked museum store.

The **Phippen Museum** has numerous rotating exhibitions and permanent displays throughout the year. Exhibits include the Solon H. Borglum Collection Room, Ray Swanson Gallery, Western Heritage Gallery, including the Arizona & Rancher Hall of Fame, and an incredible collection of paintings and sculpture by the museum's namesake, George Phippen.

Following his untimely death, a memorial foundation was formed in 1974 to create a venue for western art that honored Phippen's incredible talent and character.

In the early 1980s, the Harold James Family Trust donated a parcel of land (at Deep Well Ranch) for construction of the museum, which opened Oct. 13, 1984.

On June 23, 1965, Joe Beeler, Charlie Dye, John Hampton, George Phippen and Fred Harman gathered at Oak Creek Tavern in Sedona to create a society of artists committed to making authentic, quality fine art that portrayed the cowboy of the American West. Thus, the Cowboy Artists of America was born.

George Phippen was a founding member and first President of the Cowboy Artists of America, "the longest running artist group in the nation."

...made his home in Skull Valley and was a self-taught sculptor and painter of themes from the American West.

...began his craft at a young age by sculpting figures and horses with clay he dug from nearby creek beds.

...used to cover the chalkboard of the local, one-room schoolhouse with his drawings of cattle drives and stampedes.

George passed away in 1966 at the early age of 50. During a brief career, he produced upwards of 3,000 works of art and is recognized for his bronze sculptures, including *Cowboy in a Storm*, which graces the roundabout in front of the Museum on Hwy. 89 in Granite Dells.

The rustic, hand-hewn beam above the entrance to the Museum's Western Heritage Gallery was milled from a tree taken from Prescott's local landmark, Thumb Butte. It took all day to make, at a cost of $3. Originally, it was used to build a stagecoach stop in Williamson Valley outside Prescott. That building fell into disuse and eventually collapsed in a storm. The beam was salvaged and saved by local ranchers.

At the Phippen Museum's opening in 1984, the salvaged beam had a place of honor on the front porch and local ranchers, from far and wide, took turns heating the branding irons and making their mark on the beam in a show of support for the great art and heritage of the American West and Phippen's lasting legacy. The branded beam found a final home inside with the addition of the Western Heritage Gallery in the 2012 renovation.

PHIPPEN MUSEUM

George Phippen made his home in Skull Valley and was a self-taught sculptor and painter of American West themes.

GEORGE PHIPPEN 1915·1966

Sioux Indian Buffalo Dancer by Solon Borglum

Rough Rider
Solon Borglum supervised the statue's installation at the Yavapai County Courthouse Plaza, even choosing the stone for its base.

In 1906, world-renowned sculptor Solon Borglum sought and was given the commission to create a Rough Rider statue, which now stands at the Yavapai County Courthouse Plaza.

Named "the greatest equestrian statue in the United States" as acclaimed by Theodore Roosevelt, it almost didn't make it to Prescott for the unveiling. Read the whole story and more about Borglum and this special collection at the Phippen Museum.

Galleries for exhibition include the Kemper & Ethel Marley Western Art Gallery, which was completed as part of a major expansion project in 2012, the Western Heritage Gallery, the Ray Swanson Gallery and the Borglum Collection in the Harold and Mitzie James Gallery. The large outside deck overlooks the beautiful Granite Dells.

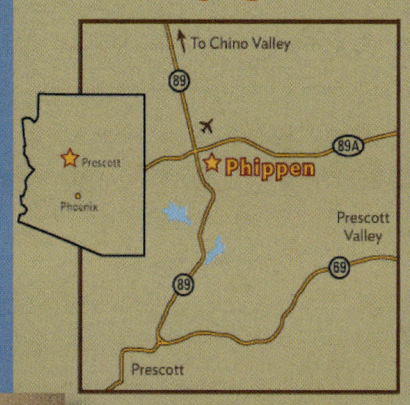

Phippen Museum
of Art & Heritage of the American West
4701 Highway 89 North
Prescott, Arizona 86301

(928) 778-1385
www.phippenartmuseum.org

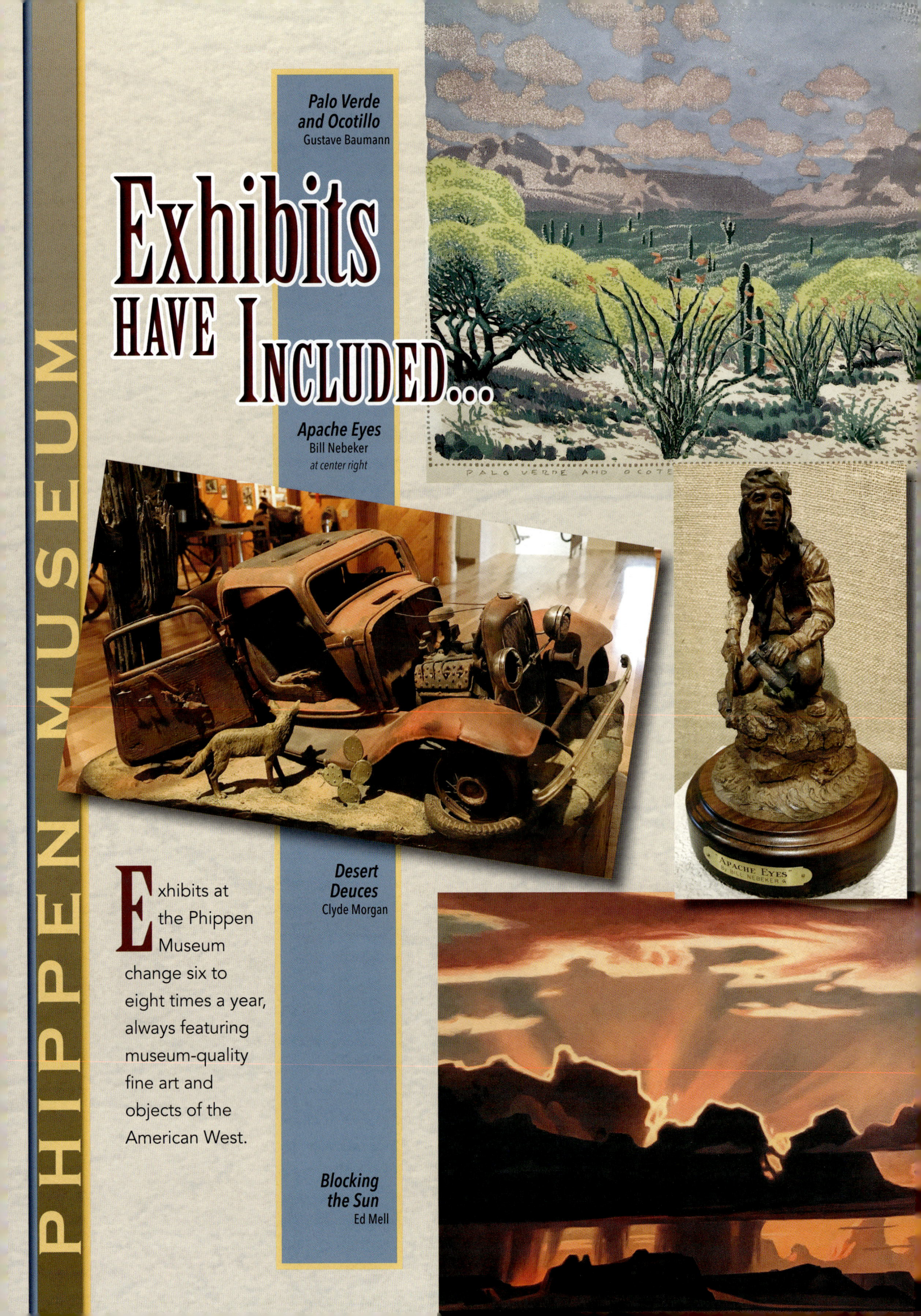

PHIPPEN MUSEUM

Exhibits HAVE INCLUDED...

Palo Verde and Ocotillo
Gustave Baumann

Apache Eyes
Bill Nebeker
at center right

Desert Deuces
Clyde Morgan

Blocking the Sun
Ed Mell

Exhibits at the Phippen Museum change six to eight times a year, always featuring museum-quality fine art and objects of the American West.

Findlay Prescott SUBARU

Service & Genuine Subaru Parts

New & Certified Pre-Owned Subarus

★

Proudly Serving the People of the Prescott / Quad-Cities Area

928-771-6900

FindlaySubaruPrescott.com

3230 Willow Creek Rd · Prescott, Az · 86305

SUBARU

Everybody's Hometown Subaru Retailer

EXPLORE PRESCOTT'S HISTORY ON THE HERITAGE TRAIL AND HISTORY HUNT ADVENTURE!

Pick up your map and booklet at the Visitor Information Center, 117 W. Goodwin Street

VISIT-PRESCOTT.COM

*It's not what you think.
It's not what you say.
It's what you do.*

- WB Dedman

Photo: Bob Shanks - Embry-Riddle Aeronautical University student landing at Prescott Airport with Flagstaff Mountains backdrop

Broberg - Photo by Cliburn

One Stage Family Theatre - Mamma Mia

Prescott Chorale

Prescott Chorale Holiday Magic

Phoenix Symphony in Prescott at Yavapai College Performing Arts Center

One Stage Family Theatre - Mamma Mia

Prescott Chorale
Holiday Magic

Music & the Performing Arts

Phoenix Symphony in Prescott at
Yavapai College Performing Arts Center

Music and Concerts

Prescott shares its many talented musicians across a few different organizations, all of which provide a wonderful selection of music genres and sounds. First up is the **Prescott Pops Symphony**, now in its 28th year. As the name implies, the Pops performs at least 5 concerts each season, with an emphasis on popular music, motion picture themes, Broadway and classical, all of which are performed at the Yavapai College Performing Arts Center. More information and concert details are available on their website at PrescottPops.com.

If you love the rousing sounds of a symphonic band, we have the **Central Arizona Concert Band** which boasts approximately 65 musicians led by Maestro Clydene Dechert and performs three free summer concerts downtown in the Yavapai Courthouse Square and 4 regular Fall/Winter season concerts at Davis Auditorium in Embry Riddle Aeronautical University. This will be their 22nd year playing for Prescott area residents. For more about the band and their concerts, visit them at CentralArizonaConcertBand.com

For those who also appreciate the beauty of vocal music entertainment, the **Prescott Chorale** under the baton of Dennis Houser has garnered a large fan base for its stunning concert performances of classical music. Entering its sixth season, this group is so talented and often brings in a few of the wonderfully talented musicians who play for the other organizations to accompany their programs. The Chorale performs four concerts each season, the dates and details of which can be found on their website at PrescottChorale.org

In their 53rd season as of October 2019, the **Yavapai Symphony** was formed by a group of community leaders committed to bringing classical music concerts to Prescott. The Yavapai Symphony contracts with the Phoenix Symphony Orchestra and other professional classical music performers to bring seven or more concerts each year. For details on upcoming concerts, please visit yavapaisymphony.org

In any given weekend, venture out and you will find a musical performance in a variety of locations ranging from the Yavapai County Courthouse Plaza to local restaurants and pubs, to performing arts centers and concert halls. All in all, Prescott music lovers can rest assured that the music scene is packed with talented singers and musicians who manage to gather together and provide exceptional concert programs throughout the year. You really can't get much better than this!

Photos: Bob Freund

Greater Prescott LIVING at Its Best! 73

Performing Arts

Photos: Lynne LaMaster, eNewsAZ

74 ANNUAL SHOWCASE EDITION 2020

Greater Prescott LIVING at Its Best! 75

Local *Art Shows*

Photo: Prescott Studio Tour

Photos: Bea Lueck

Photo: Prescott Studio Tour - Van Gogh's Ear

Photo: Prescott Studio Tour
Empty Bowls

Greater Prescott LIVING at Its Best! 77

Special Section: Parks & Recreation

Greater Prescott Parks and Recreation

Outdoor activities are enjoyable to everyone. Whether a picnic in the park, trail bike ride around town, or even a hike up a mountain, there are so many activity options. The City of Prescott and Town of Prescott Valley not only boast many options for parks, lakes and trails but also have the distinct advantage of gorgeous weather nearly year-round!

Willow Lake

Take a hike, ride a horse or bike along one of the many trails available. If fishing or boating is more your thing, visit one of the lakes in the area. Watch a baseball game or play volleyball or simply have a picnic at one of the great parks in the area.

No matter what you choose, the City of Prescott and Town of Prescott Valley have exactly the right outdoor option for you.

Photo: Blushing Cactus Photography

Photo: Prescott Parks and Recreation

Greater Prescott LIVING at Its Best! 79

Prescott Valley Parks:

Prescott Valley parks do not have entrance or parking fees. Ramadas and ballfields must be reserved to assure availability. Visit pvaz.net/parks for complete information.

- American Legion Park
- Antelope Park
- Bob Edwards Park
- Community Center Park
- Fain Park
- George Anderson Park
- Granville Park
- Mountain Valley Park
- Pronghorn Park
- Quailwood Park
- Santa Fe Station Park
- Sunflower Park
- Tonto Park – North
- Tonto Park – South
- Urban Forest
- Viewpoint Park

Parking fees are $3 per vehicle per day, valid at all five locations. Prepaid parking passes are also available:

- 10 park visits for $20
- 40 park visits for $60
- Annual pass $100 - limit one visit per day

All passes/visits expire one year from date of purchase.

Prescott Valley Chamber of Commerce
7120 Pav Way #102, Prescott Valley, AZ
(928) 772-8857

Visit the Prescott Valley Chamber of Commerce for local business information and events. The Chamber is conveniently located off of Highway 69 and open Monday thru Friday.

Monday thru Thursday 8 AM - 4:30 PM
Friday 8 AM - 4 PM

Photo: Jean Lopez - Watson Lake

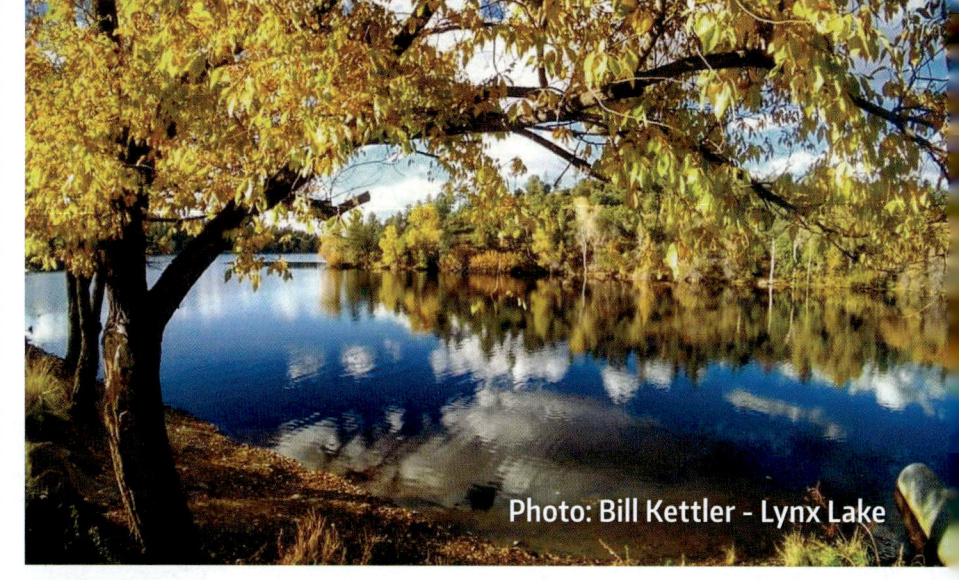

Photo: Rod Hendrick - Willow Lake

Distances (From PV)	Miles	Kilometers
Albuquerque, NM	409	657
Durango, CO	398	640
Flagstaff	88	141
Grand Canyon	217	348
Las Vegas	256	412
Moab, UT	410	660
Petrified Forest	202	324
Phoenix	93	149
Tucson	205	329

www.bestplaces.net

Photo: Bill Kettler - Lynx Lake

Climate	Av. High (°F)	Av. Low (°F)	Av. Rain (")	Av. Snow (")
January	52	24	1.4	2.5
February	55	27	1.7	3.5
March	60	31	1.6	2.9
April	67	37	0.7	0.9
May	76	45	0.5	0.0
June	86	53	0.4	0.0
July	89	60	2.3	0.0
August	86	59	2.9	0.0
September	81	51	1.7	0.0
October	72	40	1.1	0.0
November	61	30	1.1	1.1
December	52	23	1.3	1.3

Photo: Kelly Tolbert - Willow Lake

www.google.com/maps

Greater Prescott LIVING at Its Best!

Special Section: Parks & Recreation

PRESCOTT THROUGH THE EYES

by Kelly Tolbert, Recreation Services Coordinator, Prescott Parks and Recreation

Special Section: Parks & Recreation

OF THE CIRCLE TRAIL

Prescott, nestled in the Central Highlands of Arizona, is at the top of its class in geographic and biologic diversity. Encircling the City, the Prescott Circle Trail is the result of decades' long collaborations between local land managers and trail advocates.

After the City of Prescott purchased Watson and Willow lakes from the Chino Valley Irrigation District in 1998, development of recreation opportunities allowed those portions of the Circle Trail to become incorporated into the existing Prescott National Forest portions, ultimately allowing for the visionaries to reach their goal of connectivity.

From the Circle Trail, hikers, equestrians, runners, mountain bicyclists and other nonmotorized trail users can experience highlights of dense chaparral, grassland areas such as Willow Lake, amazing rock formations at Watson Lake, tall ponderosa pines strewn throughout the Prescott National Forest, as well as riparian corridors. All of this is located within miles of a bustling downtown culture that features historic Whiskey Row. Total mileage of the network of trails is now over 56 miles.

LAKES

Watson Lake, Prescott's crown jewel, is located just 4 easy miles from downtown Prescott. Nestled in the grand boulders known as the Granite Dells, Watson Lake was originally formed in the early 1900s when the Chino Valley Irrigation District built a dam on Granite Creek. The City of Prescott purchased both Watson and Willow lakes in 1998 and continues to develop recreational opportunities for this vast park.

Just 4 miles south from downtown Prescott on Senator Highway, Goldwater Lake is the perfect escape to the tall pine-filled forest where many opportunities for recreation await. Small, but quaint, the surface area of the lake is roughly 6,000 feet above sea level and measures approximately 15 acres.

For more information visit:
prescott-az.gov/recreation-events/recreation-areas.

Recreation based amenities available at Prescott area lakes and proximity to the Prescott Circle Trail

- BIRDING
- BICYCLING
- BOATING
- BOCCE BALL
- CAMPING
- CLIMBING
- DISC GOLF
- FISHING
- GEOCACHING
- HORSESHOE PITS
- LOCAL HISTORY
- NON-MOTORIZED TRAILS
- PHOTOGRAPHY
- PICKLE BALL
- PICNICKING
- PLAYGROUNDS
- VOLLEYBALL

Photo: Jean Lopez - Watson Lake

Lynx Lake

Photo: Teresa Mahan - Lynx Lake

LYNX LAKE

Nestled in the Bradshaw Mountains about 5 miles east of Prescott is beautiful Lynx Lake. The 55-acre body of water rests inside the Prescott National Forest and has much to offer any visitor. Take in the view with a tasty meal at a café or rent a boat. Hike around the lake on the lakeside trail, or try your hand at fishing. Lynx Lake also offers several camping options just a short distance from the shores of the lake. Fun for all ages just waits for you.
www.fs.usda.gov/recarea/prescott/recarea/?recid=75178

WILLOW CREEK PARK

Willow Creek Park is a fantastic facility with space for all kinds of activities. The park offers a ramada, where groups can have a picnic lunch, a parking area with access to the Willow Lake Trail, and a sports field anyone can rent. For our furry little friends, Willow Creek Park also has a dog park with separated sections for small and large dogs. Looking for a great place where your pup can get some exercise? Take them to the dog park. Your buddy will love it.
www.prescott-az.gov/recreation-area/jimmccasland-willow-creek-park/

WILLOW LAKE

About six miles from downtown Prescott, Willow Lake offers an ideal spot for many types of outdoor activities. Spend the morning hiking or fishing, or perhaps you prefer taking a canoe or kayak out on the water. Maybe you would like to explore the Granite Dells or simply have a picnic along the shore. Whatever activity strikes your fancy, Willow Lake is the perfect place just for you.
www.prescott-az.gov/recreation-area/willow-lakepark/

PIONEER PARK

Do you have a special event or a sporting event that requires the right facility to meet all your needs? Pioneer Park is just the place for you. With multiuse 4-Plex available for baseball, softball, soccer and football, plus a roller-hockey rink and pickleball courts, Pioneer Park has the right type of field for you.
www.prescott-az.gov/recreation-area/pioneer-park/

WATSON LAKE PARK

Resting on the edges of the famous Dells, Watson Lake and Park are perfect for just about any type of event. For large event seekers, the park has been home for the Prescott Fourth of July celebration, the annual Highland Festival and has hosted several auto shows. Smaller event seekers have also used the location for drum circles, meditation and parties. Looking for time on the lake, check out the rental options offered at the lake marina; perhaps try your hand at paddle boarding. There's lots to do at Watson Lake and Watson Lake Park.
www.prescott-az.gov/recreation-area/watson-lake-park/

FAIN PARK AND FAIN LAKE

Located in the Town of Prescott Valley, Fain Park and Fain Lake offer a perfect mini getaway from day-to-day life. Take a little time to try your hand at fishing or simply enjoy a picnic lunch

Photo: Ryan Closson - Watson Lake

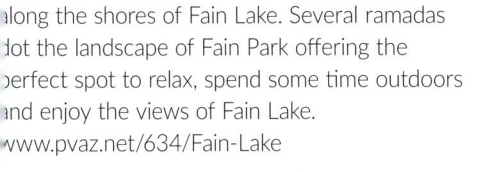

Photo: Tony Munshi - Willow Lake

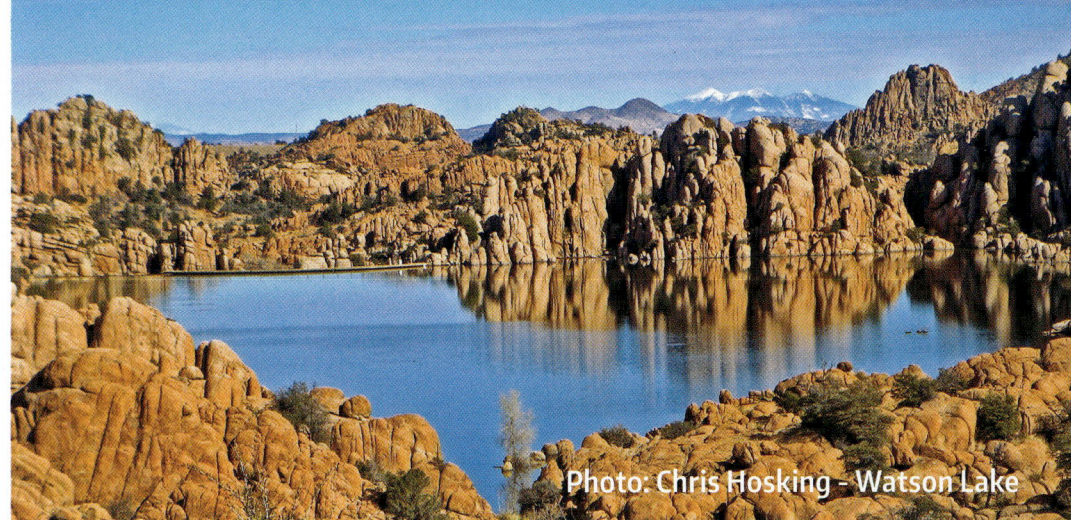

Photo: Chris Hosking - Watson Lake

along the shores of Fain Lake. Several ramadas dot the landscape of Fain Park offering the perfect spot to relax, spend some time outdoors and enjoy the views of Fain Lake.
www.pvaz.net/634/Fain-Lake

GOLDWATER LAKE

Head down Senator Highway about 4 miles to see the beauty of Goldwater Lake. Take the family and enjoy the sand volleyball court, the hiking trails and playground. Goldwater Lake is the perfect place to take a canoe or kayak out onto the water, and boat rental options are available. Three large ramadas are part of the offerings of Goldwater Lake, as well as many other fun activities for all ages. Spend the afternoon fishing or host a special event. Goldwater Lake is a special place to visit and spend a fun day.
www.prescott-az.gov/recreation-area/goldwater-lake/

Greater **Prescott LIVING** at Its Best! 85

Lower Goldwater Lake

by Kelly Tolbert

Photo: Kevin Attebery

Although smaller than Upper Goldwater Lake, Lower Goldwater Lake is charming and gives one a sense of seclusion and peace. With a maximum capacity of 351-acre feet of water, it is much smaller than the upper lake's 700-acre feet capacity.

Constructed in 1923, the Lower Goldwater Lake dam was built to retain water runoff to supply drinking water for the growing community of Prescott and has remained closed to the public since. This was mainly because of potential liabilities associated with the water treatment plant located below the dam.

In recent years, Prescott's recreation services and public works departments have worked toward the ultimate goal of opening the Lower Goldwater Lake area to the public in a safe and environmentally responsible manner.

Plans include improved parking areas, restrooms, a large ramada and day-use areas. These will all allow for recreational activities such as small boating, fishing and hiking on trails connecting the two lakes.

Hiking

Whether you are a seasoned hiker or a beginner, Prescott and Prescott Valley offer a wide variety of trail options to meet any hiker's goal.

Granite Mountain and Thumb Butte both offer beautiful vistas of the Prescott area with challenging trails. Want to hike from Prescott Valley to Prescott? The Peavine and Iron King Trails provide this option all while boasting wide-open vistas and views of the famous Granite Dells. The trail around Lynx Lake snuggles up to the shoreline as hikers make their way past fishermen and weave their way through trees. Willow Lake trail provides amazing views of the lake while traveling over a variety of terrain from flat land to boulders.

Regardless of your skill level, or if you prefer hiking in forest or over open vistas, Prescott and Prescott Valley have many trails.

For information on trails be sure to visit the City of Prescott and Town of Prescott Valley websites or make a stop into the Prescott National Forest office on Cortez Street; while you're there, you could even pick up a couple of maps.

If you're an avid hiker, you can purchase an annual parking pass from the Prescott National Forestry Service to cover the fees of many of the local area trails that fall under the care of the Prescott National Forest.

- Prescott: prescott-az.gov/recreation-events/recreation-areas/trails
- Prescott Valley: pvaz.net/373/hiking-and-trails
- Prescott National Forest Passes: fs.usda.gov/main/prescott/passes-permits

Prescott
Hiking Trails

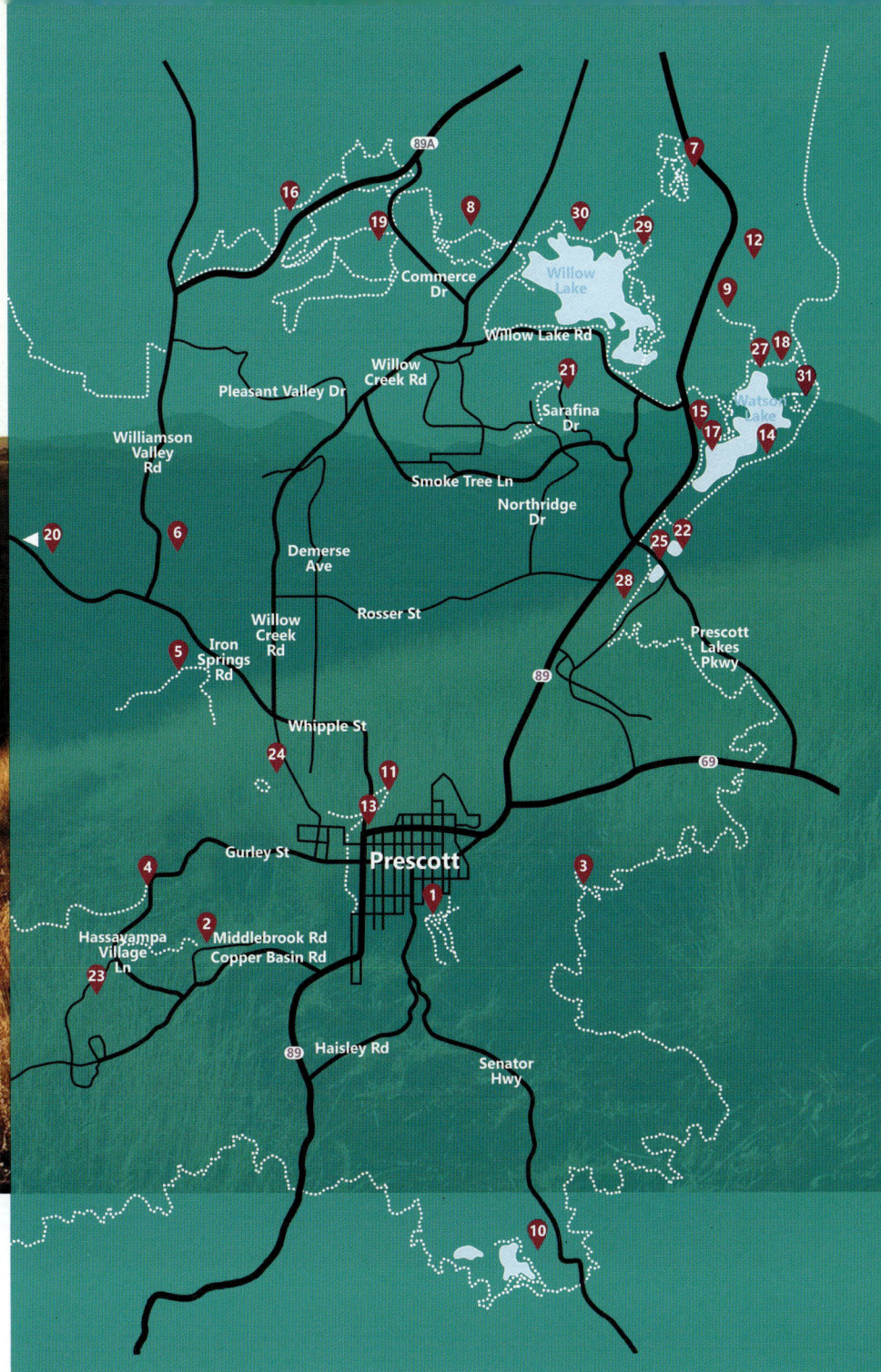

Photo: Chris Hosking

Photo: Chris Hosking

Map #	Trail Name	Miles
1	Acker Park Trails	1.5
2	Aspen Creek Trail	0.8
3	Badger Mountain	4.04
4	Butte Creek Trail	1.3
5	Centennial Trail	2
6	Community Nature	1.5
7	Constellation Trails	2.74
8	Embry Riddle - Jan Alfano Trails	2.35
9	Flume Canyon, Watson	2.4
10	Goldwater Lake Trails	1
11	Granite Creek Park	0.5
12	Granite Gardens	1.5
13	Greenways Trail System	1.5
14	Lakeshore Trail	2
15	Lakeside aka Fishing	1.1

Map #	Trail Name	Miles
16	Longview Trail	1.78
17	Lower Granite Creek	0.8
18	Over the Hill Trail	0.4
19	Pioneer Park Trails	9
20	Prescott Circle Trail	54
21	Prescott Lakes and	5
22	Prescott Peavine	6
23	Rancho Vista Trail	0.6
24	Rodeo Grounds Trails	0.5
25	Sundog to Lowes Hill Trail	
26	Turley Trail	2.65
27	Watson Lake Loop Trail	4.79
28	Watson Woods trails	1.5
29	Willow Dells Slickrock	3
30	Willow Lake Loop Trail	5.7
31	Storm Trails	6.26

Greater Prescott LIVING at Its Best! 87

Fishing

Photo: Dave Suggs - Goldwater Lake

Spending the day at the lake can be a great way to spend your time, and spending that time fishing can be loads of fun.

The City of Prescott and Town of Prescott Valley have several options for anyone wanting to try his or her luck and skill at catching the big one. Lynx, Goldwater and Fain lakes, just to name a few, are some great places to go, spend some time and catch some great fish.

Anyone can have their own experience fishing at the different lakes, but be sure to take a little time to get to know the rules. Get yourself a fishing license before you go.

The Arizona Game and Fish Department website has lots of information for anyone wishing to learn more about fishing licenses, lake-stocking schedules and fishing conditions at the different lakes.

Going to the websites for Prescott and Prescott Valley also will give you plenty of information about the lakes and also provide links to the game and fish department so you can get signed up for that necessary fishing license.

So good luck out there, have fun trying your hand at fishing. At the very least, if you don't catch the big one, perhaps you will have your own fish tale about the one that got away.

- City of Prescott: prescott-az.gov/recreation-events/recreation-areas
- Town of Prescott Valley: pvaz.net/634/fain-lake
- Arizona Game and Fish: azgfd.com/fishing

Special Section: Parks & Recreation

Boating

by Staff Reports

Does the idea of spending your day on a lake sound like fun? Prescott and Prescott Valley both have lakes where you can spend a day out on the water.

Many of the lakes offer boat ramps to launch your small craft out onto the water. Take a boat out onto Watson Lake or Willow Lake and enjoy the beauty of the granite boulders. Launch out into waters of the forested shores of Lynx Lake or Goldwater Lake.

No boat? No problem. Lynx, Watson and Goldwater lakes all offer boat or kayak rental options.

Before you go out onto the water, if you are taking your own craft, be sure to take a little time to become informed about the rules of safe boating in Arizona by checking out the Arizona Game and Fish website at azgfd.com/boating. There's tons of great information and even a fun little quiz to test your knowledge of boating safety.

The Town of Prescott Valley and City of Prescott both proudly share information about the lakes in the area on the city websites. Be sure to check them out. You may not have been considering it before, but just take a look at the lakes in these two cities and you'll just be itching to get out on the water.

- Prescott: az-prescottvalley.civicplus.com/325/parks-facilities
- Prescott Valley: prescott-az.gov/recreation-area/goldwater-lake

Photo: Kialana Duenas

Cycling

Whether you prefer street, mountain or gravel, the City of Prescott and Town of Prescott Valley have all kinds of options for cyclists who want to get out and ride. Miles of bike paths line the roads of the city streets, and bike friendly trails dot the landscape throughout the area.

Prescott Valley boasts trails such as the Iron King Trail or the Glassford Hill Summit Path, as well as several multiuse paths. Prescott has great trails like the Greenways Trail System and the Embry Riddle-Jan Alfano Trails. For the adventurous rider there is also the Willow Dells Slickrock Loops.

Cycling of any type is popular among residents of Prescott and Prescott Valley and is growing even more so. There are two major cycling groups who specialize in organizing group rides for fun and also can support a cause. Bike Prescott's mainstay is road cycling but also includes gravel biking and mountain biking. Prescott Mountain Bike Alliance (PMBA) largely focuses on mountain biking and use trails.

Check out the exciting trails offered in the Prescott and Prescott Valley areas by visiting the city websites. If you are looking for a great group to ride check out one of the local groups. No matter what choice you make, when choosing to spend time on your bicycle in Prescott or Prescott Valley, you're going to have a great day.

- Prescott Rides: prescott-az.gov/recreation-events/recreation-areas/trails
- Prescott Valley Rides: az-prescottvalley.civicplus.com/182/Prescott-Valley-Trails
- Bike Prescott: bikeprescott.com
- PMBA: prescottmtb.com

Special Section: Parks & Recreation

Horseback Riding

Images of Westerns and cowboy life might go through your head when thinking about horseback riding in Prescott and Prescott Valley. For the horse enthusiast, though, riding here can be the real deal. A day spent on the back of a horse while enjoying the beauty of the area is a day well spent.

Several trails including Aspen Creek Trail, Pioneer Park Trail and Longview Trail, just to name a few, permit horseback riding. Also, the ever popular Iron King Trail of Prescott Valley and Peavine Trail of Prescott connect, offering the seasoned rider a chance to ride from Prescott to Prescott Valley while taking in the open spaces and Granite Dells.

To learn more about rider-friendly trails, be sure to visit the websites for the City of Prescott and the Town of Prescott Valley. No matter how you look at it, horseback riding in the area is just part of the fabulous life that Prescott and Prescott Valley have to offer.

- City of Prescott: prescott-az.gov/recreation-events/recreation-areas/trails
- Prescott Valley: pvaz.net/373/hiking-and-trails

Photo: Jody Miller

Geocaching

Take technology, an adventure and a treasure and put them together. What do you have? Geocaching!

Using GPS-enabled devices, participants navigate to a specific set of GPS coordinates with the goal to find the cache hidden at the location coordinates. Tech-savvy adventure seekers would be hard pressed to find a better location of geocache sites than the ones offered in the Prescott and Prescott Valley areas.

If you are new to the area or looking for places of geocaching sites in the area, be sure to check out the TrailLink website traillink.com/stateactivity/az-geocaching-trails to see the many offerings in the area.

Never done geocaching before but have always wanted to? Check out Geocaching 101 at geocaching.com/guide; a great way to start.

Novice or expert, local resident or the adventure seeker just passing through, the City of Prescott and Town of Prescott Valley both have so many options for that treasure hunter in you. Get out there and start your hunt.

Fain Park

Prescott Valley's Fain Park offers rich history, outstanding recreational opportunities

Photos: Town of Prescott Valley

by Heidi Foster, Communications Relations Coordinator, Town of Prescott Valley

Of Prescott Valley's 28 public parks, Fain Park is perhaps the most iconic, combining the rich history of the area with a myriad of recreational opportunities. Fain Park first opened to the public Aug. 16, 1997. The Fains — one of the area's original frontier families — donated the 100-acre parcel of land to the residents of Prescott Valley.

The Town of Prescott Valley is developing this park in two phases. The western half is open to recreational activities such as picnicking, hiking, fishing and gold panning. The lake is stocked with fish by the Arizona Game and Fish Department. An Arizona fishing license is required to fish for trout and catfish; children younger than 12 fish for free.

Occupation of the Fain Park site dates as far back as 200 B.C. The Prescott Tradition People lived in primitive earthen homes and prospered off the water supply from Lynx Creek. They hunted for deer and antelope and farmed around the Clipper Wash area, two miles south of this site.

As the civilization grew, the Prescott Tradition People chose to live in a more compact fashion, which gave birth to the most significant archeology site in Central Yavapai County — the Fitzmaurice Ruins. The University of Arizona was the first, in the 1930s, to excavate the site and later, with Yavapai College conducted a second archeological dig. Many of the artifacts recovered are now on display at the Smoki Museum in Prescott.

The first Anglo occupation came with the Walker Party in 1864. This group of miners found gold in the adjacent Bradshaw Mountains. As the search for gold continued, the miners followed Lynx Creek to Fain Park and found considerable quantities of the precious metal.

As news quickly traveled, the Fain Park area also attracted a Chinese colony, an English partnership, and a variety of sophisticated gold mining efforts that included extensive hydraulic and dredging operations. Records show in excess of $100 million worth of gold was removed from this area.

Greater Prescott LIVING at Its Best! 93

Special Section: Parks & Recreation

Visitors can enjoy 1.6 miles of easy-to-moderately difficult hiking trails through beautiful scenery, birdwatch and sight wildlife, or simply bring a picnic and enjoy the shade of numerous ramadas. A mining exhibit at the west end of the park gives visitors a view of times past.

For more information on Fain Park or any of Prescott Valley's other fine parks, visit pvaz.net/parks.

Photos: Town of Prescott Valley - Fain Park

Photo: Chris Hosking

Special Section: Parks & Recreation

The Barlow-Massicks Victorian House

Barlow-Massicks House

Photos: Town of Prescott Valley

The eastern half of the park, when opened, will include Massicks, a rebuilt 1890s gold town, a restored Fitzmaurice Ruin archeology site, the restored Barlow-Massicks Victorian house and a regional museum.

English entrepreneur Thomas Gibson Barlow-Massicks arrived in the area in 1890 and began to buy land and mines. He completed construction on the Victorian house in the park in 1891. He also founded a town adjacent to and north of the house, along with the U.S. Post Office that bore his name. His enterprises ended in 1899 when he died from an accidental pistol shot.

Fain Park features an expanse of green lawn, a fishing dock and swinging bridge, and an overlook from which visitors can get a spectacular view of the more than 100-year-old dam built by Thomas Gibson Barlow-Massicks and the Lynx Creek below the dam.

Fitzmaurice Ruins 1936

Thomas Gibson Barlow-Massicks

reflection
/rəˈflekSH(ə)n/

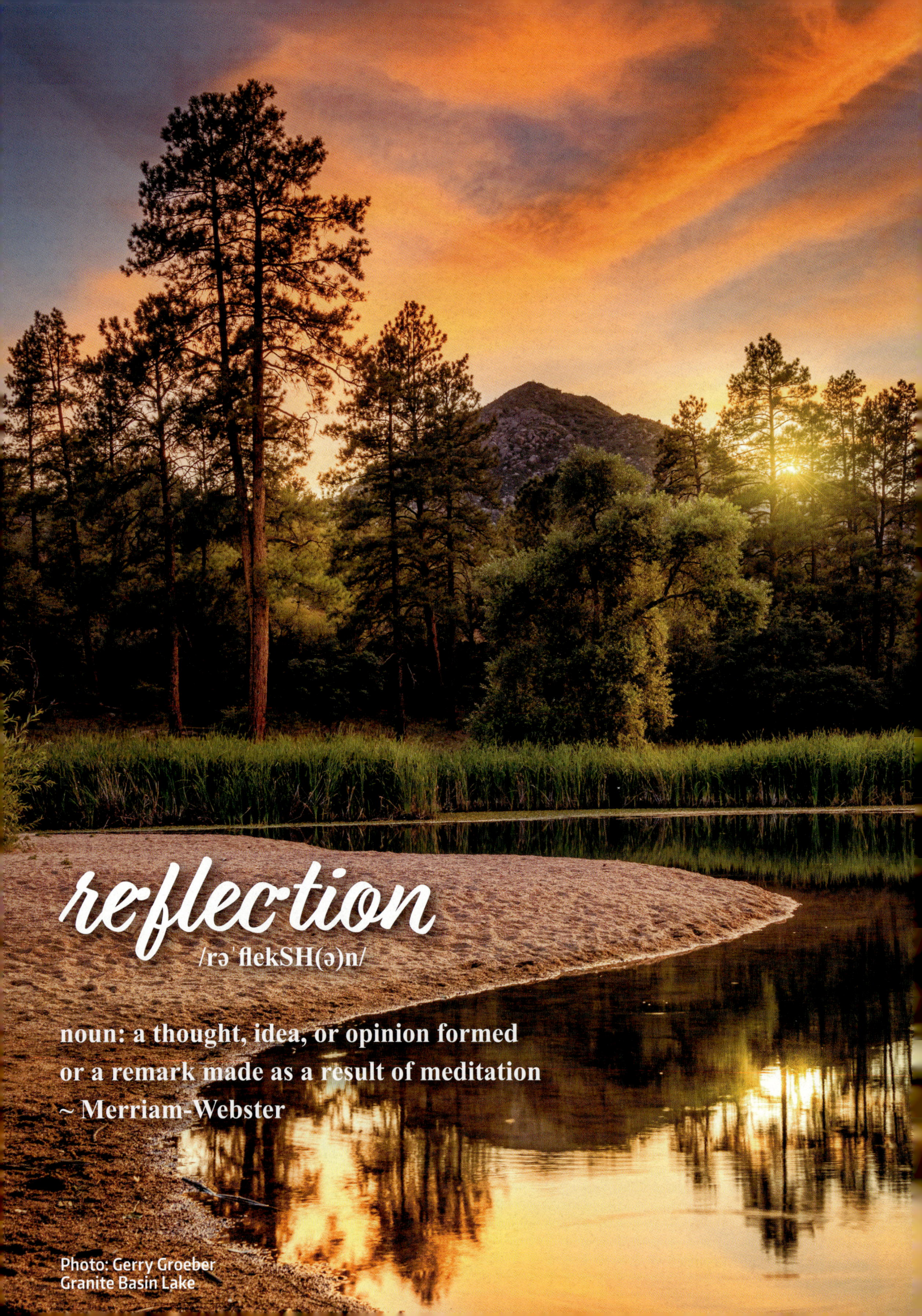

noun: a thought, idea, or opinion formed or a remark made as a result of meditation
~ Merriam-Webster

Photo: Gerry Groeber
Granite Basin Lake

PRESCOTT VALLEY
TALKING GLASS MAGAZINE
PV

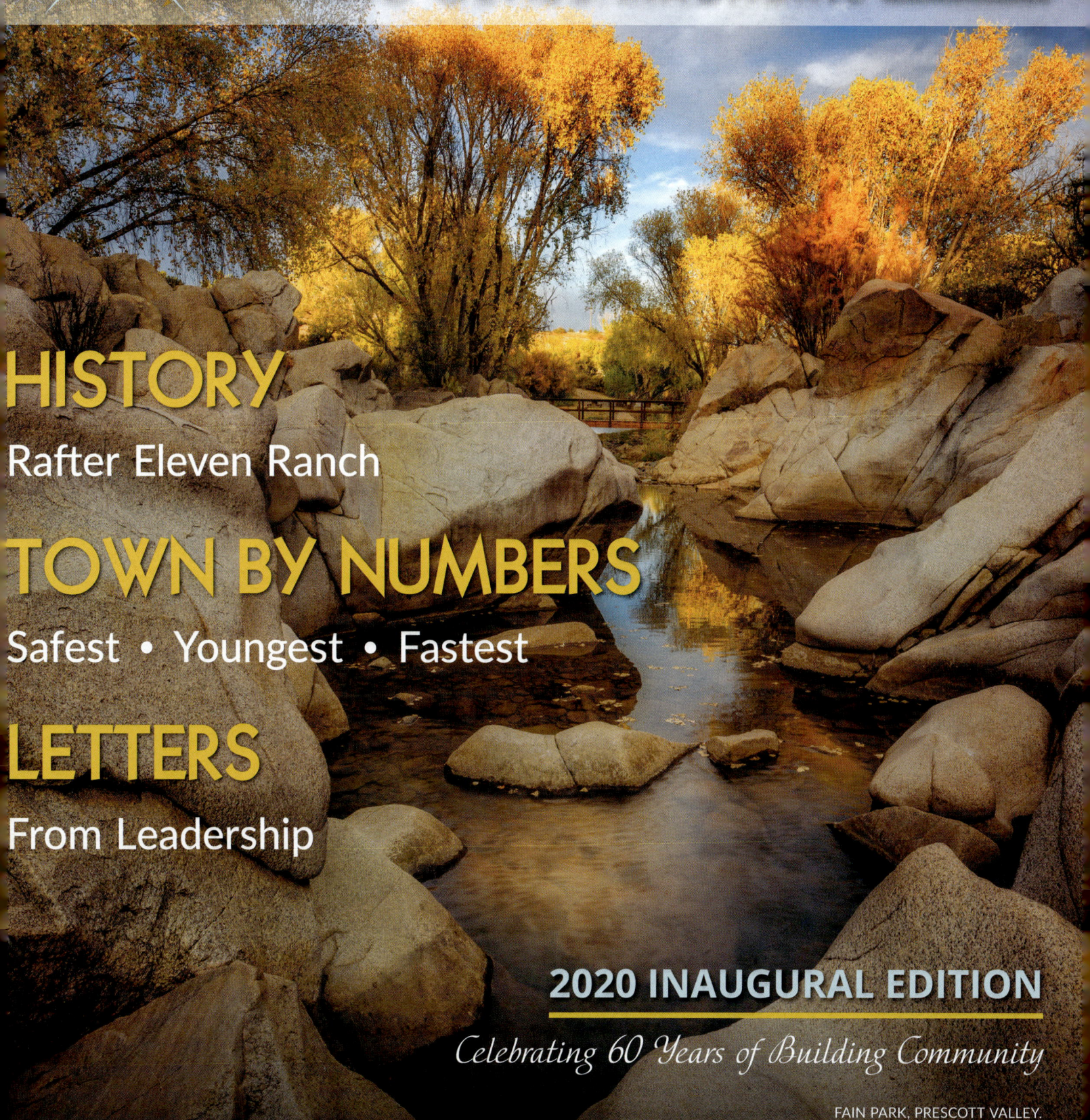

HISTORY
Rafter Eleven Ranch

TOWN BY NUMBERS
Safest • Youngest • Fastest

LETTERS
From Leadership

2020 INAUGURAL EDITION

Celebrating 60 Years of Building Community

FAIN PARK, PRESCOTT VALLEY.
PHOTO BY TREEROSE PHOTOGRAPHY.

PRESCOTT VALLEY | DEWEY-HUMBOLDT | CHINO VALLEY | PRESCOTT

From The Editor

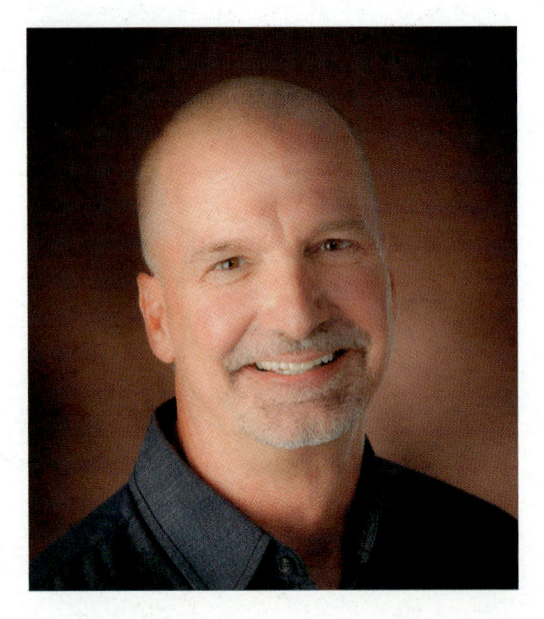

During my early childhood and throughout my teens, my family owned a small vacation spot at Katherine's Landing on Lake Mohave, AZ. We'd spend our summers water skiing, taking outside showers during the magical monsoon season, and traveling throughout the great state of Arizona visiting incredible destinations like Sedona, Flagstaff, Lake Powell, the Grand Canyon and the Petrified Forest to name just a few. My love of the outdoors, Arizona's impeccable sunrises and sunsets, that Northern Arizona breeze against my skin all led me to this place. Northern Arizona never stopped enchanting me and the dream to have a rural, outdoor lifestyle became a reality in 2004 when I chose to call this region home.

I grew up playing outside all day. No mobile phones, no internet, no big screen TVs. I rode my first horse at the age of 10, the same year my dad handed down to me his 1940s' era wood-stock Red Ryder BB Gun. I may have grown up in a city, but so many of my experiences whispered to me I was a cowboy, of sorts. I've always preferred the outdoors, dreaming of having a patch of dirt to call my own and working the land with my hands. Today, my partner and I are living that dream with horses, goats, dogs and yes, chickens. Now, I realize how I got here and why we do what we do at Talking Glass Media.

We are working the land by sharing positive, feel good stories about a place we call home. Instead of shovels, hoes and plows, we leverage storytelling tools and positive mindsets to plant solutions while helping others create great memories. A place that was seeded and revered by homesteaders and cowboys in the 1800s is now loved by a family of community builders and stewards of the land, the Fain family, who are still homesteaders and ranchers to this day. It is because of this family that we are able to do what we do at Talking Glass Media.

This Inaugural Edition of Prescott Valley Talking Glass Magazine is a celebration of 60 Years of Building Community in Prescott Valley and working the land to create a place for families and success. This first edition is just a small start as we build the publication and work with the community to share its voice and vision.

Welcome to Prescott Valley.

Sincerely,

Guy C. Roginson

Executive Editor
Talking Glass Media, LLC.
Prescott Valley Talking Glass Magazine & SignalsAZ.com

Contents

WINTER 2020

2020 Inaugural Edition
Celebrating 60 Years of Building Community

Features

Pages 3-4
Letters from Leadership

Page 5
History of Rafter Eleven Ranch and Birth of a Town

Page 11
Town Directory, Civic Center, Restaurants & More

Pages 12-13
Town by Numbers - Prescott Valley: Northern Arizona's Fastest Growing Community.

Page 14
Humboldt Unified School District

Talking Glass Media, LLC

Prescott Valley Talking Glass Magazine, Talking Glass Media Studios, &
SignalsAZ.com

PUBLISHING | ADVERTISING | MARKETING

3001 N. Main St., Ste #2-B
Prescott Valley, AZ. 86314
Tel: 928-257-4177
Email: Editor@SignalsAZ.com

Reflecting on the legacy of those who came before, I draw upon the values, beliefs and traditions that have been bestowed upon our family through the generations. We enjoy collaborating with our friends and neighbors both as a company and as a family to work the land and produce opportunity for all. We do so with a commitment to community, family and the environment.

As we approach our 60th year of building community at Fain Signature Group (FSG), I am humbled to lead the next generation forward in harmony with the legacy and traditions that have been passed down from one generation to the next. These traditions have been formed over 140+ years in the Arizona Territory and 100+ years in cattle ranching in an area once called Lonesome Valley, home to the historic Rafter Eleven Ranch, our family's brand that is still in operation today under the leadership of my brother Ron. Looking toward the next 60 years, FSG is committed to creating opportunities in which families, businesses and visitors can all come together to enjoy life, make a difference and produce their future.

I want to thank the community and region for the decades past and the decades to come for the support and trust in which each of you invest and become a part of Prescott Valley: Tradition, Entrepreneurialism, Integrity and Leadership.

Brad Fain
CEO, Fain Signature Group
Publisher, Talking Glass Media, LLC

Congratulations on the inaugural edition of Prescott Valley Talking Glass Magazine. A new voice for the Town of Prescott Valley that is now recognized as the fastest growing community in Yavapai County.

The vision and leadership of Bill Fain helped create jobs and industry, build schools, hospitals and institutions of higher education. What is most amazing is how one man created so much opportunity in a single generation. His accomplishments are a true testament to his grit, determination and good will.

Congratulations on the 60th anniversary of Building Community by the Fain Family. I look forward to reading the first edition of Prescott Valley Talking Glass Magazine in January 2020.

Best wishes and continued success!

Karen Fann (R)
Senate President, LD1
Arizona

Prescott Valley, Northern Arizona's fastest growing community, boasts mild weather, four distinct seasons, and amazing scenery in a high plains environment. In North Central Arizona, Prescott Valley is located in the "middle of it all." Since being incorporated in 1978, Prescott Valley has become the "hidden gem" of Northern Arizona.

The 2020 Census is expected to show that Prescott Valley has grown to a population of almost 50,000, and yet Prescott Valley is the safest town in all of Northern Arizona, highlighting an outstanding police force. Our residents, however, are vested in keeping the "small town feel" that brought so many of them here while still enjoying the amenities of much larger communities.

The 5,500-seat Findlay Toyota Center, Northern Arizona's premier indoor event arena, is home to the Northern Arizona Suns G-League franchise, along with sold out concerts, championship rodeos like the PRCA and PBR, monster truck shows and many more exciting events catering to all ages.

The Town boasts 27 parks, sports fields, ramadas, inclusive playgrounds, and walking — hiking trails. One of the Town's premier hiking trails is the Glassford Hill Summit Trail, which will take you 900 feet above the Town for spectacular views.

Our business and education opportunities are growing with the community. Our children can receive a great education, including the ability to earn an associate's degree while still in high school. More of these talented young people are choosing to stay here after graduation to begin a career, start their own businesses and raise their families. Manufacturing, retail, restaurants and service establishments also are finding Prescott Valley a great place to do business.

The Town of Prescott Valley truly is the place "Where Opportunity Lives!"

Kell Palguta
Mayor
Town of Prescott Valley

Celebrating 60 Years of Building Community

Dear Friends,

On behalf of Yavapai Regional Medical Center's Board of Trustees, medical staff, employees and volunteers, it is my privilege to recognize a true Arizona success story. Prescott Valley is a thriving community where integrity, visionary leadership and strong family values combine to create a symbol of the new American West.

I had the privilege of knowing Bill Fain, and I always respected Bill for his integrity, commitment and accountability – the very same values that guide us today at Yavapai Regional Medical Center.

While some might be intimidated by the challenge of building a great community, Bill Fain was a man who had a vision for the future and believed in the potential of people.

YRMC is proud to be part of such a vibrant community – growing alongside the people and families we serve with an eye on the future and a deep respect for our rich heritage.

We look forward to the next 60 years and beyond of working together for the benefit of this incredible region.

Warm regards,

John Amos
President and CEO
Yavapai Regional Medical Center

Innovation, courage and community are what bring ideas to life. Just as the Humboldt Unified School District instills these values into our students, the Fain family has also built a community on these same values. They have built a community through their vision that incorporates their ranch history, business aptitude, perseverance and partnerships.

It is said that there are four pillars of any community. These include the people (our families), our posterity (manifested through civic service), commerce (the businesses), and governance (as displayed through town councils and school boards). While the growth of our community can be traced back to these integral pillars, it is our schools that serve as evidence of any community. Public schools are about educating, but they are also about community building. There is a sense of community that our public schools foster. It is the public schools that often bring these four pillars together.

Through the growth of our community, the Humboldt Unified School District has welcomed our families, and we continue to provide a world-class education for all students. The vision of the Humboldt Unified School District is not much different from the vision of the Fain legacy. Our district's success depends on the families who live and work here. When a community comes together and sees the benefits of a strong economy, world-class education and opportunities, the successful building of a town is achieved. The success of this town depends on leaders who have foresight and vision. This vision is what the Fain family has used to help grow this community and we are proud to be their partners and proud of the wisdom they bring to the table.

Dan Streeter
Superintendent
Humboldt Unified School District

So many of us in the community have said that Bill Fain was known as a man of his word. Many contractors in our community had the privilege of Bill Fain's handshake – that was all that was needed to seal a business deal. To this day, we have generations of contractors in our communities that follow in Bill Fain's way of doing business – with a hand shake. The Yavapai County Contractors Association, which has been serving Yavapai County for over 60 years, and its 300+ members celebrate the remarkable achievement of 60 years of building community in Prescott Valley.

Bill Fain was one in an "gazillion," however his wisdom and trust is a legacy that lives within Fain Signature Group.

Sandy Griffis
Executive Director
Yavapai County Contractors Association

HISTORY OF RAFTER ELEVEN RANCH AND THE BIRTH OF PRESCOTT VALLEY

In 1874, William and Cary Fain set out from Missouri on their journey west ending at a Cavalry post in Camp Verde, Arizona. It is said they arrived with 50 cents to their name, a buffalo calf and two milk cows pulling their cart. William began cutting hoe grass for stock feed and Cary sold milk and butter to the military outpost. Soon hired on to take care of the animals at the fort, William began buying and selling cattle as the pioneering couple built up their holdings.

The Rafter Eleven has been in the Fain Family since 1918 and is still a working cattle ranch located near the intersection of Fain Road and HWY 69. 1920 – At its largest, the Rafter Eleven Ranch covered almost 50,000 acres and ran from the west side of Granite Mountain, east to Mingus Mountain, and from the Bradshaws to the south, to north of the Jerome Highway in Lonesome Valley. Granville Dan Fain invested in both cattle ranching and sheep ranching, amassing one of the largest herds of sheep in the territory with over 70,000 ewes.

Mildred Back Fain, Norman Fain and Granville Dan Fain.

16 Ranch, Bar 16.
The first Fain Ranch established by William and Cary Fain.

1948 Norman, Johnie Lee and Bill Fain.

The Rafter Eleven cattle ranch has been in the Fain family since 1918 and is still a working ranch.

For More History; go to: www.FainSignatireGroup.com/Fain-Family-Legacy/

Celebrating 60 Years of Building Community

HISTORY CONTINUED

Granville Dan Fain King of the Range

1936 Railroad

Prescott Regional Airport

Bill Fain, Johnie Lee Parsons Bill's Mother and Bill's Sister Donna Fain

1874

In 1874, William and Cary Fain set out from Missouri on their journey west ending at a Cavalry post in Camp Verde, Arizona.

1879

William and Cary established the first Fain Ranch on the east side of the Verde River called the 16 Ranch, Bar 16 brand. William and Mary sold livestock feed, milk and eggs to Ft. Whipple in Prescott and began to make a life for themselves.

1880s

William "Marion" Fain became involved in the establishment of roads throughout Central/Northern Arizona as an "Overseer" and road builder. In fact, sections of road that he built are now a part of the I-17 leading from Camp Verde to Flagstaff.

1890

Granville Dan Fain, fifth son to William and Cary Fain, and first generation of Arizona Fains, was put in a saddle very early in life and eventually became known as one of the last free ranging cowboys and "King of the Range." It is said that six horses died under him.

1907

In 1902, Granville Dan Fain married Mildred Back. They worked the Back family Montezuma Well Ranch – now part of the National Monument. In 1907, Norman Fain was born on the ranch.

1914

Granville Dan Fain and Arthur Heath purchase OK and Bloody Basin Outfits, which took in the whole Verde Valley. Granville Dan Fain owned or managed at least 65 different outfits in the Verde Valley. This was the beginning of Dan Fain Land and Livestock Company.

1918

The Rafter Eleven has been in the Fain family since 1918 and is still a working cattle ranch.

1928

Philanthropy in the Fain family began with Dan Fain donating a prime piece of ranch land to the City of Prescott, which is now known as the Prescott Regional Airport. These years were also the years of the Great Depression through which the Fains lost well over half of their ranchlands.

Barlow-Massicks home

Arizona State Senator, Norman Fain

The beginnings of HWY 17 and SR 69

Bill Fain

Granville Dan Fain

Bill and Nancy Fain Circa 2000

1936

Dan and Norman Fain jump into debt to rebuild the ranch. With strong belief in the family, the Valley National Bank helped. Through hard work, ingenuity and vision, the Fains rebuild and acquire vast tracts of land in Lonesome Valley owned by the Santa Fe Railroad.

1938

Late January, 1938, Norman William II (Bill Fain, Founder of Prescott Valley) was born in Cottonwood.

1940s

Arizona State Senator Norman Fain played an integral role in getting the I-17 HWY and 69 HWY built, making it safer and quicker to get travelers and commerce through to Prescott and Prescott Valley. He was a graduate of Prescott High School and Stanford University.

1956

Bill Fain entered University of Arizona and studied finance and business economics to make sure the Rafter Eleven Ranch remained viable. His grandfather Dan Fain told him, "Come home after you finish college. You might make more money doing something else, but you'll find a good living in ranching and have a lot of satisfaction doing it."

1957

Norman and Dan Fain purchase the Fitzmaurice and Savage Properties assuming the rock and gravel business for building needs, damming of the creek upstream to create 55-acre Lynx Lake and the preserving the Barlow-Massicks home, "The Castle," and the Fitsmaurice ruins dating back to 200 A.D.

1959

By the age of 83, Granville Dan Fain was one of the best known and well respected cattle ranchers, dubbed the "King of the Range." He roped his last wild stray on Mingus Mountain and passed two years later.

1960

While at UofA, Bill Fain met his future wife Nancy Williams, an experienced horsewoman whose family was in the feed lot (livestock) business. Graduating in 1960, Bill and Nancy married and spend the next nine years living at the Rafter Eleven Ranch, planning for the birth of a town now called Prescott Valley..

Celebrating 60 Years of Building Community

EARN RESPECT
AND A $40K BONUS

#GOARMYARIZONA

U.S. ARMY

TO REQUEST INFORMATION
TEXT ACGU TO GOARMY (462-769)

2982 N. PARK AVE, STE H
PRESCOTT VALLEY, AZ 86314
(928) 443-8958

FAIN SIGNATURE GROUP

TALKING GLASS. | FAIN LAND & CATTLE CO. | HOMESTEAD | SIGNALS

Residential | Commercial | Industrial | Build to Suit | Publishing

www.FainSignatureGroup.com

Celebrating 60 Years of Building Community.

Fain Signature Group Properties, Inc.
Ron Fain, Designated Broker

SIGNALS
signalsaz.com

EVENTS | ENTERTAINMENT | GOOD NEWS

I have been in the U.S. Army (Active Duty) over 16 years; 10 years as an infantryman with the 101st Airborne Division (AASLT), deployed four times (Iraq and Afghanistan) and have worked with countless community leaders, communities, and Warriors, foreign and domestic, across the globe. All which have been working with parallel goals. To make this world a better place!

I've been in Prescott Valley since November 2017 and have never worked with another organization (Fain Signature Group) who gives so much back to the people and have never had such an opportunity to interact with such high caliber citizens, who truly care about where they live. This is a true "Hand Shake Agreement" type of community, where your word is your bond.

Prescott Valley and the Fain Signature Group have welcomed me and my team with open arms. What this community has done for us will echo through eternity, and I assure you, it'll be heard forever! We will be forever grateful to this town and all of our Community Partners.

Sergeant First Class
Matthew C. Vinson,
Station Commander
U.S. Army 101st Airborne Division (AASLT)

You're Retired. Your Money Isn't.

To learn why consolidating your retirement accounts to Edward Jones makes sense, contact your Edward Jones financial advisor today.

Danny Pruhs, CRPC®
Financial Advisor

7025 E Florentine Rd Suite 105
Prescott Valley, AZ 86314
928-772-5474

www.edwardjones.com
Member SIPC

Edward Jones
MAKING SENSE OF INVESTING

Celebrating 60 Years of Building Community

YAVAPAI REGIONAL MEDICAL CENTER

Inspired.

YAVAPAI REGIONAL MEDICAL CENTER

Proudly Caring for Western Yavapai County

Life's precious moments.

YRMC wants you to have more moments like this. That's why innovation is so important to our team. A new heart procedure for people whose health is too fragile for surgery ... a non-surgical way to repair dangerous aneurysms ... a painless therapy for vein disease—just a few of our latest innovations.

INSPIRED BY YOU.

YRMC.org   YRMCHealthConnect.org

Entertainment District & Downtown Directory

APARTMENTS

Homestead Talking Glass Luxury Apartments
3131 N. Main Street
Prescott Valley, AZ 86314
(928) 277-0184

BEAUTY – HEALTH – SPA

Cosmopoliton Salon
2982 N. Park Avenue, Suite A
Prescott Valley, AZ 86314
(928) 759-3397

Fantastic Sam's
6301 Baja Cir., Suite A
Prescott Valley, AZ 86314
(928) 759-3550

Great Clips
3298 N Glassford Hill Rd Ste 106
Prescott Valley, AZ 86314
(928) 775-9952

Lynn's Nail & Spa
7025 Florentine Rd.
Prescott Valley, AZ 86314
(928) 775-4339

DINING – FOOD

BAJA FRESH
3088 N Glassford Hill Rd Ste 104
Prescott Valley, AZ. 86314
(928) 772-1705

CASA PEREZ
3088 N Glassford Hill Rd Ste 104
Prescott Valley, AZ. 86314
(928) 772-7777

Chili's
7281 Pav Way,
Prescott Valley, AZ 86314
(928) 775-6918

Gabby's Grill
2982 N. Park Avenue, Suite B
Prescott Valley, AZ 86314
(928) 277-1787

Garcia's Restaurant
2992 Park Ave # B
Prescott Valley, AZ 86314
(928) 759-9499

Buffalo Wild Wings
2985 N. Centre Court
Prescott Valley, AZ 86314
(928) 759-9800

Rafter Eleven
2985 N. Centre Court # B
Prescott Valley, AZ 86314
(928) 227-2050

Robeks Juice
3140 N Glassford Hill Rd #102
Prescott Valley, AZ 86314
(928) 227-0535

Flour Stone Café – NEW!
2992 N. Park Avenue, Suite C
Prescott Valley, AZ 86314
(928) 277-8197

Firehouse Subs
3088 N Glassford Hill Rd
Prescott Valley, AZ 86314
(928) 227-0557

Panda Express
3140 N. Glassford Hill Rd., #105
Prescott Valley, AZ 86314
(928) 775-5612

Papa Murphy's Pizza
3298 N Glassford Hill Road, # 105
Prescott Valley, AZ 86314
(928) 710-8755

Streets of New York
Fry's Shopping Center
7025 Florentine Rd
Prescott Valley, AZ. 86314
(928) 759-9877

Starbuck's
Glassford Hill Road
Prescott Valley, AZ.
(928) 642-7505

MOD Pizza
3007 N. Glassford Hill Rd,
Prescott Valley, AZ 86314
(928) 212-1980

Dunkin' Donuts
3015 N. Glassford Hill Rd.
Prescott Valley, AZ. 86314
(928) 458-5600

Baskin-Robbins
3015 N. Glassford Hill Rd.
Prescott Valley, AZ. 86314
(928) 458-5600

EDUCATION K-12

Humboldt Unified School District
6411 N Robert Rd
Prescott Valley, AZ 86314
(928) 759-4000

EDUCATION UNDERGRAD

Yavapai College, Prescott Valley Campus
6955 E Panther Path
Prescott Valley, AZ 86314
(928) 717-7911

Northern Arizona University
2982 N. Park Avenue, Ste F
Prescott Valley, AZ 86314
(928) 775-9877

FAMILY ENTERTAINMENT

Findlay Toyota Center
3201 N, Main St, Prescott Valley, AZ 86314
(928) 772-1819

Harkins 14 Theaters
7202 Pav Way
Prescott Valley, AZ 86314
(928) 775-2284

In The Game – Family Entertainment Group
2992 Park Avenue, Suite A
Prescott Valley, AZ 86314
(928) 775-4040

FINANCES – BANKING – LOANS – PROFESSIONAL SERVICES

Allied Cash Advance
3140 N. Glassford Hill Rd., #104
Prescott Valley, AZ. 86314
(928) 772-1290

Colt Cleaners
1042 Willow CreekRd, #A101-433,
Prescott, AZ 86301
(928) 775-0599

One Main Financial
2982 N. Park Avenue, Suite C
Prescott Valley, AZ 86314
(928) 772-0240

BMO HARRIS BANK
7221 Florentine Rd
Prescott Valley, AZ 86314
(928) 775-7600

Scott A. Smith Insurance Agency
3298 N. Glassford Hill Rd # 103
Prescott Valley, AZ 86314
(928) 772-7100

Edward Jones
7025 Florentine Rd Suite 105
Prescott Valley, AZ 86314
(928) 772-5474

Foothills Bank
3322 N. Glassford Hill Road
Prescott Valley, AZ. 86314
(928) 460-4211

Post Net
3298 N. Glassford Hill Rd # 104
Prescott Valley, AZ 86314
(928) 759-3700

HEALTH CARE – IN-HOME CARE & COUNSELING

Mountain Valley Rehabilitation Hospital
3700 N Windsong Dr.
Prescott Valley, AZ 86314
(928) 759-8800

ResCare Home Care
3001 North Main St., Suite 1B
Prescott Valley, AZ 86314
(928) 717-9981

Sage Counseling
3001 North Main St., Suite 1D
Prescott Valley, AZ 86314
(928) 237-9089

Yavapai Pediatrics
3001 North Main St., Suite 1C
Prescott Valley, AZ 86314
(928) 458-5470

YRMC – EAST
Yavapai Regional Medical Center
7700 Florentine Rd, Prescott Valley, AZ 86314
(928) 445-2700
yrmc.org

IN SERVICE OF COUNTRY

US Armed Forces Recruitment Offices
2982 N. Park Avenue, Suite D & G
Prescott Valley, AZ 86314
(928) 443-8958

LOGISTICS

Global Tranz
3001 North Main St., Suite 1E & 1F
Prescott Valley, AZ. 8631

MISCELLANEOUS

AZ Dept of Corrections
3001 North Main Street, Suite 2C
Prescott Valley, AZ 86314
(928) 277-2786

REAL ESTATE

Fain Signature Group Properties, Inc.
Real Estate Development
Residential – Commercial – Industrial - Build to Suit
Ron Fain, Designated Broker
Terry Marshall
(928) 772-8844
www.FainSignatureGroup.com

RETAIL – HOME – GARDEN

Boot Barn
7321 Pav Way
Prescott Valley, AZ 86314
(928) 772-6665

Kohl's
3280 N Glassford Hill Rd
Prescott Valley, AZ 86314
(928) 772-0989

Mattress America
8004 N Sunset Ridge
Prescott Valley, AZ 86314
(818) 428-9155

Peddler's Pass
6201 E State Rte 69
Prescott Valley, AZ 86314
(928) 775-4117

Queen Esther's Closet
9100 N Poquito Valley Road
Prescott Valley, AZ 86315
(928) 899-5516

Walmart
3450 N Glassford Hill Rd
Prescott Valley, AZ 86314

TELECOMMUNICTIONS

Sprint / Connectivity Source
3140 N. Glassford Hill Rd., #101
Prescott Valley, AZ 86314

TOWN RESOURCES

Town of Prescott Valley, AZ.
7501 Skoog Blvd.
Prescott Valley, AZ. 86314
Switchboard: (928) 759-3000
Water Billing: (928) 759-3120

Prescott Valley Civic Center – Recreation Area
7501 Skoog Blvd.
Prescott Valley, AZ 86314
(928) 759-3000

Prescott Valley Economic Foundation (PVEDF)
7120 Pav Way # 106,
Prescott Valley, AZ 86314
(928) 775-0032

Prescott Valley Police Department
7601 Skoog Blvd.
Prescott Valley, AZ 86314
(928) 772-9261

Prescott Valley Public Library
7401 Skoog Blvd
Prescott Valley, AZ 86314
(928) 759-3040

Central Arizona Fire and Medical (CAFMA)
8603 E Eastridge Dr
Prescott Valley, AZ 86314
(928) 772-7711

Prescott Valley Chamber of Commerce
7120 Pav Way #102,
Prescott Valley, AZ 86314
(928) 772-8857

TRANSPORATION

GROOME TRANSPORTATION – Shuttle Service
Pick-up location at:
3001 N. Main Street
Prescott Valley, AZ. 86314
(800) 888-2749

Maverick Gas Station & Convenience Store
3576 N Glassford Hill Rd
Prescott Valley, AZ 86314
(928) 772-1126

VETERINARIAN – PET CARE

Premier Pet Hospital
3322 N Glassford Hill Rd
Prescott Valley, AZ 86314
(928) 460-4211

Celebrating 60 Years of Building Community

TOWN BY NUMBERS

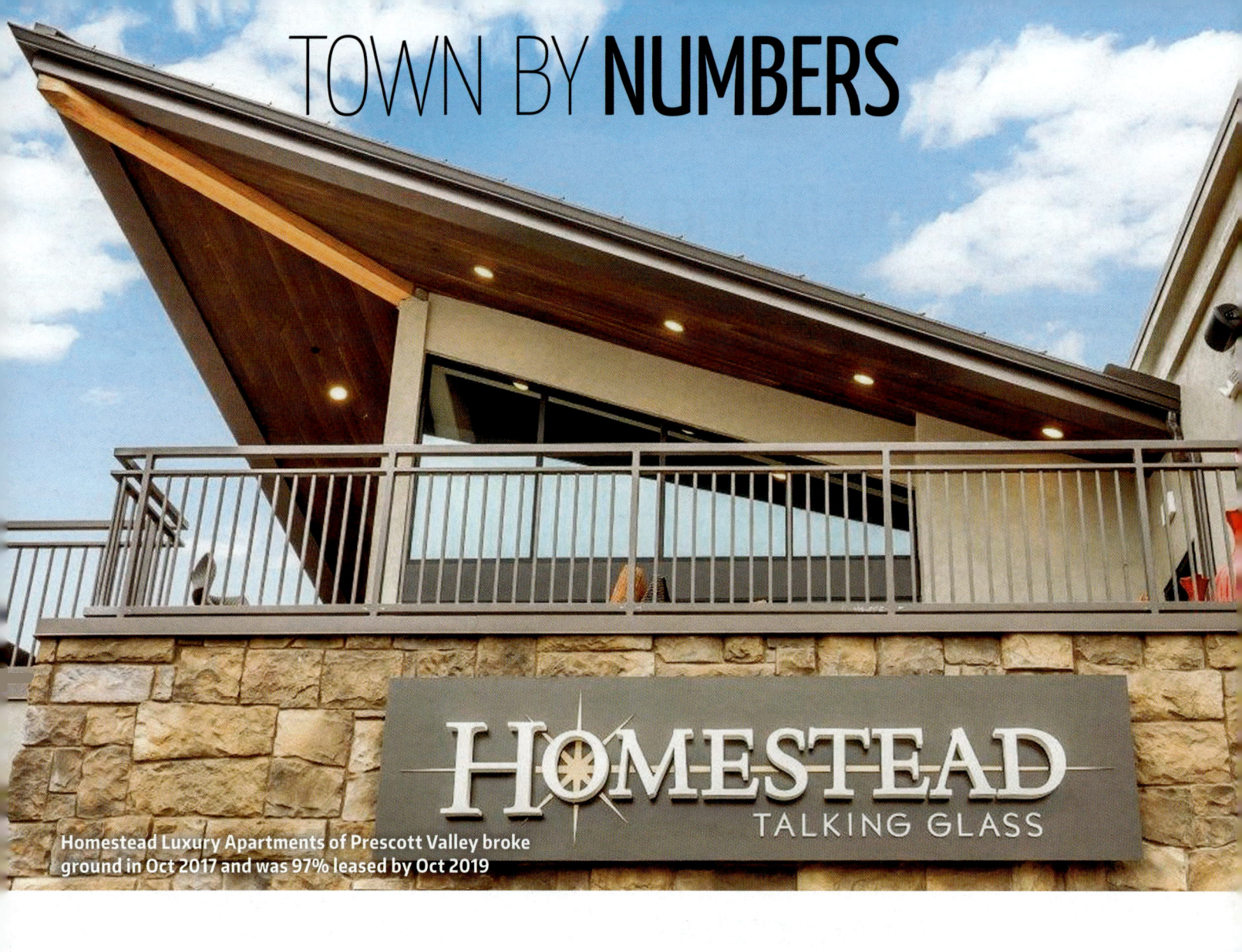

Homestead Luxury Apartments of Prescott Valley broke ground in Oct 2017 and was 97% leased by Oct 2019

The area's economy is composed of industry, manufacturing, retail and service businesses. A strategically planned new downtown with a state-of-the-art indoor events arena, regional shopping center, brand new 214 unit luxury apartment community and crosstown highway offer new development opportunities. The Town's $61 million regional medical center and a $15 million regional rehabilitation hospital is complemented with a downtown Civic Center complete with Council Chambers, Police Department and Public Library. All within a ¼ mile of downtown are Harkins 14 Theatres, Safeway, Fry's, Walmart and Kohl's. The county's largest school district Humboldt Unified is headquartered only blocks away from the Town's center.

Population
45,751, 2018 current census estimate. Estimates for 2020 Census are near 50,000.

Largest, Fastest Growing and Youngest Municipality in Yavapai County with a 3-5% population growth rate.

Industry –
Prescott Valley's industrial centers are centrally located in the state, adjacent to major highways including the I-17, SR69 and I-40, complete with transloading terminals – "Truck to Train."

PRESCOTT VALLEY TALKING GLASS MAGAZINE

Prescott Regional Airport (KPRC) Expanding –

The Prescott Regional Airport is the third busiest airport in the state of Arizona and is only a 16-minute drive from downtown Prescott Valley, offering daily non-stop commercial flights to both Los Angeles (LAX) and Denver (DIA).

ERAU's Prescott's College of Security and Intelligence (CSI), located adjacent to the Prescott Regional Airport, is the first of its kind in the U.S., training future security and intelligence professionals.

ERAU Cyber Lab

Mountain Valley Splash Aquatic Center, Prescott Valley, AZ

25 Community Parks!

American Heart and Lung Association Says –

Our region is ranked as having the cleanest air in the United States, according to a 2015 American Heart and Lung Association survey of the air and particulates.

FBI Crime Statistics Say –

Prescott Valley Is the safest town in Northern Arizona.*

*FBI Uniform Crime Report statistics, National Council for Home Safety and Security

Yavapai Regional Medical Center, East, Prescott Valley

Top Employers in Prescott Valley –

- Humboldt Unified School District K-12*
  (Largest School District in Yavapai County)
- Yavapai Regional Medical Center*
- MI Windows and Doors*
- Walmart*
- Town of Prescott Valley*
- Mountain Valley Regional Rehabilitation Hospital*
- Ace Hardware Retail Support Center
- Fry's Food and Drug*
- Yavapai College – Prescott Valley Campus*
- Print Pak Inc
- Home Depot
- Superior Industries
- Safeway*

*In downtown or within a 1.5 miles of downtown Prescott Valley.

Celebrating 60 Years of Building Community 13

HUMBOLDT UNIFIED
Best Kept Secret in Quad-City Area

by Kelly Lee, Family and Community Engagement Coordinator, Humboldt Unified School District

In Arizona, parents choose their neighborhood public school over 88% of the time. The Humboldt Unified School District (HUSD) is the largest school district in Yavapai County. Located in Prescott Valley, Arizona, HUSD provides a comprehensive, world-class education to over 5,700 students. HUSD encompasses more than 300 square miles and serves the Prescott Valley and Dewey/Humboldt communities.

HUSD offers a preK-12 educational program with many opportunities and experiences available to students throughout their educational journey.

Bright Futures Preschool
- 3- and 4-year-old classrooms
- certified teacher and two paraprofessionals for each class
- TELL curriculum offered in partnership with ASU, Eureka Math
- full-time PT and OT staff
- early childhood hands-on science curriculum in partnership with the Arizona Science Center
- two outdoor playground areas with equipment, play structures
- half and full-day programs

Coyote Springs Elementary
- 21st century teaching and learning
- embedded 5 C's into our teaching and learning
- problem-/project-based learning
- co-teaching
- PBIS school (Positive Behavior System)
- physical education, music, coding, gardening, media, accelerated math and gifted students recently presented at a conference to a national audience of educators

iChoose Academy at Glassford Hill Middle School
- for seventh- and eighth-grade students
- located within the Glassford Hill Middle School campus; focused on personalized learning
- competency-based curriculum delivered with a blended, flipped and online learning strategy
- 1:1 computing environment that transforms the learning environment beyond the walls of a traditional classroom

Bradshaw Mountain High School AP Academy
- BMHS offers 19 AP courses, the most in Yavapai County
- Advance Placement tests are paid for; $93 savings to our families
- eligible for AP Capstone diploma
- AP Map class for student support; only AP Academy school to offer this
- one of few schools nationwide to offer AP seminar and research

Tel: 928-759-4000 | Web: www.humboldtunified.com

YAVAPAI COUNTY
CONTRACTORS ASSOCIATION
PROUDLY SERVING YAVAPAI COUNTY FOR 58 YEARS

LEADING THE WAY TO RELIABLE CONSTRUCTION PROTECTING THE CITIZENS OF YAVAPAI COUNTY

YCCA PROVIDES THE BEST SERVICE AT YOUR SERVICE

SANDY GRIFFIS
EXECUTIVE DIRECTOR

HERE TO HELP
LOCAL RELIABLE REFERRALS

DON'T START WITHOUT US!

928.778.0040 • WWW.YCCA.ORG • YCCA@CABLEONE.NET

FAIN SIGNATURE GROUP

TALKING GLASS. | FAIN LAND & CATTLE CO. | HOMESTEAD TALKING GLASS. | SIGNALS signalsaz.com

Residential | Commercial | Industrial | Build to Suit | Publishing

Celebrating 60 Years of Building Community.

SIXTY YEARS OF BUILDING COMMUNITY 1960-2020

Fain Signature Group Properties, Inc.
Ron Fain, Designated Broker

www.FainSignatureGroup.com

Photo: Blushing Cactus Photography
"Only the Brave"

Western Heritage Center

Photos: Western Heritage Center

Sam Hill - Model Ts

Western Heritage Center can be found on historic Whiskey Row within a structure built in 1901 after the great Prescott fire of 1900. It is a one-of-a-kind showcase for Yavapai County's many museums, organizations and exhibits that preserve and present the area's unique history and culture. It makes that history even more accessible to its residents and visitors through multiple displays, and the foundation that sustains it also supports other programs and events. These include a guide to local museums and resources at www.VisitWHC.org, the Heritage Keeper scholarship program, outreach to elementary schools and the Western Heritage Banquet, which honors those who contribute to preservation of the area's history and heritage.

156-C S. Montezuma Street
Prescott, AZ 86303
928.910.2307

Visit www.visitWHC.org for seasonal hours of operation

Prescott Western Heritage Foundation is a charitable 501(c)(3) all volunteer, nonprofit organization.

116 ANNUAL SHOWCASE EDITION 2020

Smoki Museum Exhibit

Sharlot Hall Museum Exhibit

Phippen Museum Exhibit

Greater Prescott LIVING at Its Best! 117

Photo: Laura Zenari - A heron enjoying lunch in Watson Lake

Photo: Rod Hendrick
Great Blue Heron

Photo: Daryl Weisser — Winter at Goldwater Lake

Photo: Rod Hendrick – Baby ducks at Lynx Lake

Photo: Rod Hendrick Blue Heron at Watson Lake

Photo: Rod Hendrick - Great Blue Heron at Lynx Lake

Greater Prescott LIVING at Its Best! 119

How about a walk in the woods?

The story of the Highlands Center for Natural History, Prescott's nature center, begins on a lush, wooded, 22-acre biologically diverse site among ancient boulders. In the early 1970s, far-sighted community members and Prescott Unified School District leadership recognized the value of outdoor science-based education and created the community nature center.

Members of the Youth Employment Program built a log cabin, and the dream for the center grew. Sadly, in 1989, after 13 years of operating, the gates closed. But the idea of an outdoor classroom where students of all ages could learn about the natural world, particularly that of the Central Arizona Highlands, was too good to let go.

The center's first director Nichole Trushell, together with a band of supporters and volunteers, reshaped the Nature Center and forged the way toward the center's future. In November 1995, after many, many meetings with good baking and much coffee, the Highlands Center for Natural History was incorporated and the search for a new site began.

Stroll along the creek through Learning Circles that illustrate the natural history of the Central Highlands.

In April of 2001, a Special Use Authorization gave the Highlands Center permission to establish operations on a beautiful 80-acre parcel in the Prescott National Forest for a 25-year term. By partnering with the national forest, the center created a unique partnership between a governmental agency and a private nonprofit. Even though there were no buildings on the site, it was immediately used for educational purposes with several programs making use of the location.

The campus opened to the public in 2004 and included trails, restrooms and the Kiwanis Amphitheater. In January 2007, staff moved into their new offices in The James Learning Center, and life as we now know it began. With this prime location on Lynx Creek near the Lynx Lake Recreation Area, the Highlands Center was poised to meet the needs of a rapidly growing region. With a unique Gold Certified LEED building and an experienced staff, the center was perfectly placed to provide education and recreation for residents and visitors of Central Arizona.

Bring the kids and play on the boulders, sand box and web in a natural Forest Play area.

Currently, the center serves over 10,000 children a year through on-site school programs and nature camps and off-site at our Schoolyard Habitats. Nature Camps for preschool through middle-school students include multiple sessions in the fall, spring and summer. An Adult Naturalist Certification program was developed in 2015, and a high school internship program was added in 2016.

Special events and programs include family nature festivals throughout the year; the Grow

Native! Plant Sale in late spring; adult travel trips; Shakespeare in the Pines in June and adult Insights to Outdoors programs. In 2017, more than 30,000 visitors from throughout the country enjoyed the Highlands Center.

Listen to birds and sounds of the forest or relax in the shade on a comfortable bench.

In 2017, we opened The James Family Discovery Gardens. The goal of the Gardens is to make nature more accessible to everyone. The Gardens are also a regional botanical garden, interpreting the unique biological habitats of the Central Arizona Highlands.

Over the years the Highlands Center has continued to expand and grow while adhering to its core mission of an outdoor classroom where students of all ages could learn about and explore the natural world.

Highlands Center for Natural History
1375 S. Walker Road, Prescott, AZ 86303
(928) 776-9550
highlandscenter.org

Photo: Nancy Lyon Maurer

Photo: Martha Court

Bottoms Up!

Prescott
Everybody's Dog Town

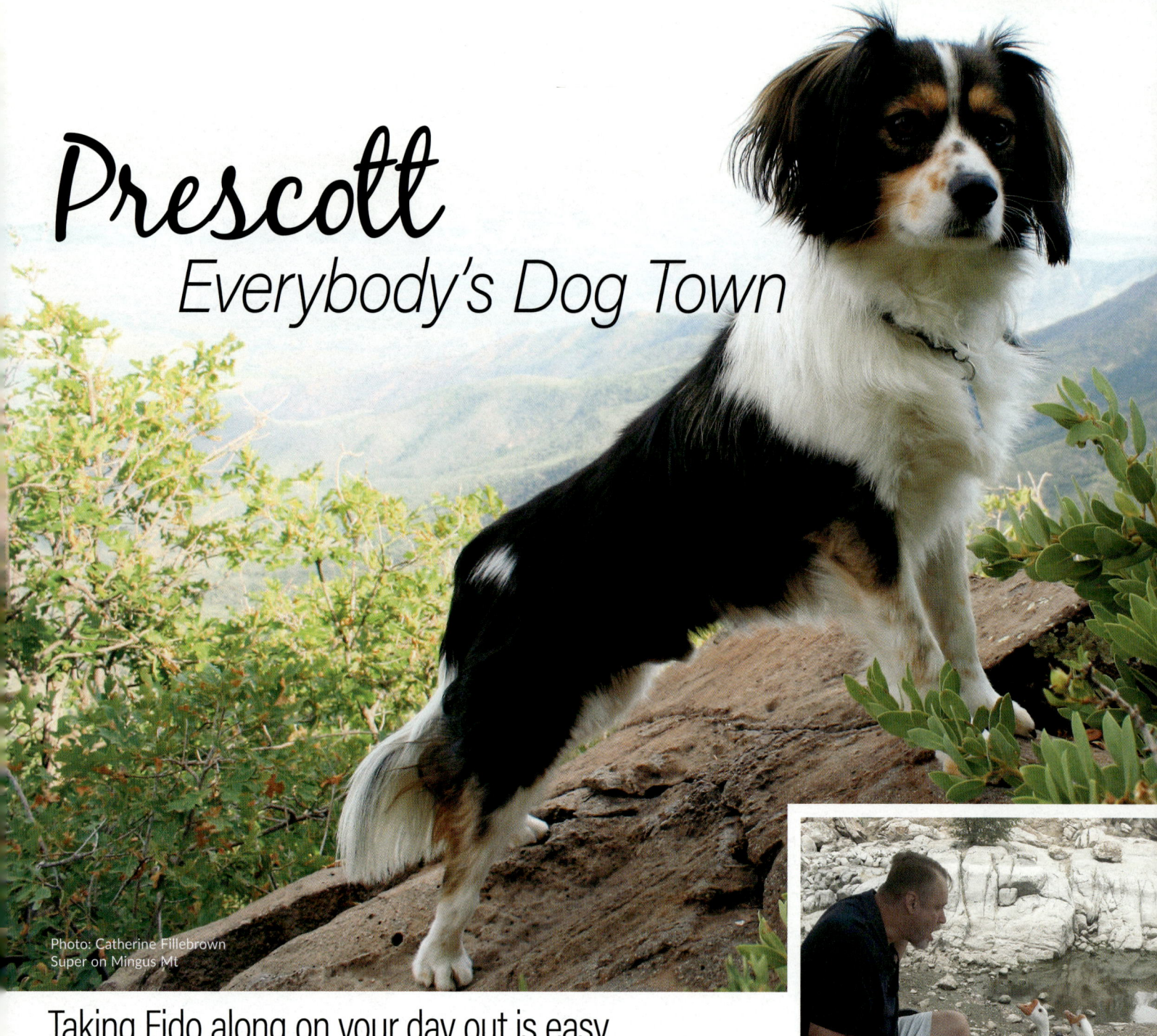

Photo: Catherine Fillebrown
Super on Mingus Mt

Taking Fido along on your day out is easy
by Robin Layton

Spending a day wandering around the Prescott area doesn't mean your puppy gets stuck alone at your house.

Our four-legged companions are welcome to come along while we hike, grab a meal, enjoy area events and more.

Gabrielle, the owner of Draco, a 1-year-old German Shepherd, said, "As a pet owner I have never lived in a place that has opened its arms so wide to include my dog as Prescott has. The city and its people are so welcoming. They've made us feel right at home. We love Prescott."

The Yavapai County Courthouse Plaza is a popular and dog-friendly central spot in downtown Prescott.

"Besides being a beautiful place to walk, it's a great place to meet the wonderful people and their dogs of Prescott. We also go to all the vendor events as well. The Yavapai County Courthouse Plaza is a great place to socialize Draco," said Gabrielle.

Just for Doggie

Prescott dogs have their own downtown store, Whiskers Barkery, where they are encouraged to walk through with their owners and pick out snacks and toys. They also have their own locally famous park, Willow Creek Dog Park.

"Our favorite times in Prescott are all the events that are put on in town specifically meant for the dogs. We love the Dog Easter Egg Hunt," Gabrielle said. "We went into 19 different stores to find Easter eggs and were given treats for the dogs. What a fun event. We also did the Walk for the Animals and the Woof Down Lunch, too. I can't wait for DOGtoberfest."

Don't miss the Bark For a Cure Walk by the American Cancer Society the same day.

Check out Woof Down Lunch next summer, held annually by the United Animal Friends. The event features vendors, live music, dog obedience, agility and K-9 unit demonstrations,

Photo: Elaine Earle
Rock Earle with the geese

raffles, dog contests, kid activities, adoptable dog introductions and more. Learn about it at unitedanimalfriends.org.

Another popular fundraiser is the Yavapai Humane Society's Walk for the Animals. Every dollar raised provides medical treatment, behavior programs, and compassionate care to the more than 3,000 animals who come through YHS each year. Check out yavapaihumane.org for the next event.

Photo: Martha Court - Sage at Watson Lake

Photo: Alexandra Rhody with Kevin & Kooper at Watson Lake

Photo: Helen Schmeck Nugget 7 month OLD Pomchi at Granite Gardens

Greater **Prescott LIVING** at Its Best! 125

Eating Out

Restaurants in downtown Prescott with patio seating often welcome our furry friends. Farm Provisions, Bill's Pizza, The Palace, Cuppers, Augie's, Hassayampa Inn, Two Mamas' Gourmet Pizzeria, Wild Iris, Prescott Station and the Barley Hound are a few, according to Trip Advisor and bringfido.com. Just to be sure, though, give your favorite restaurant a call to check on its dog-dining status.

Skyler Reeves of the Barley Hound said, "We love it when guests bring their well-behaved dogs to our restaurant and dog-friendly patio. We offer hooks for leashes at each table, water to each dog (we have our own dog bowls, so no need to have to carry your own), and we even have a dog menu. Our dog food items on our menu are chicken and rice or steak and rice. We serve the dog food on a Barley Hound Frisbee that you are free to take home with you."

"Having the restaurant dog friendly was always part of our concept from the very beginning. It has really blossomed and become a more central part of who we are. Guests really love bringing their dogs with them and with websites like BringFido.com more people search us out because we are dog friendly and not just as an added value," said Skyler.

The Barley Hound supports dog-related charities.

"We love the way that dogs can create a more social atmosphere. Often we witness tables sitting near each other strike up a conversation because their dogs are being friendly or are the same breed, etc. The social aspect of dining out is a big part of going out to restaurants and having a friendly pooch there simply adds to that social experience," Skyler said.

Photo: Michelle Haynes at the Barley Hound

Photo: Barley Hound

Greater **Prescott LIVING** at Its Best! 127

Remembering the Granite Mountain Hotshots

Photos: Martha Court - Granite Mountain Hotshot Memorial

"Permanent Half Mast"

"Chains that Bind"

Greater Prescott LIVING at Its Best! 129

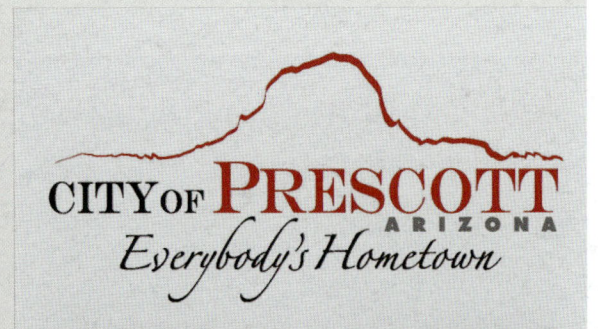

top reasons to VISIT PRESCOTT!

#1 City in the Southwest
Sunset Magazine

Top 13 Happiest & Healthiest Cities
Time Magazine

One of the Coolest Downtowns in N. America
Expedia Viewfinder

Top Visitor Destination in Arizona for Nature Lovers
Expedia Viewfinder

Five 'Must-See' Towns in Arizona
USA Today

Bicycle Friendly Community - Bronze Status
League of American Bicycles

One of the Top 10 Cities for Well-Being
Gallup

One of the Most Charming Small Cities in Arizona
Travel Magazine

13 Adorable Small Towns in Arizona You Need to Visit
Narcity.com

America's Top 25 Best Small Towns for Christmas
Country Living Magazine

Best Place to Live Like an Old West Cowboy and Best Old West Town to Live In
True West Magazine

Top Ten True West Towns - #4
True West Magazine

19 Cities that Must be Seen in 2019
Expedia Viewfinder

Top 56 Best Places to Visit with a Dog
Reviews.com

50 Most Beautiful Towns to Visit in Each U.S. State
TheCultureTrip.com

Seven Best Arizona Cities to Visit for Christmas
TravelAwaits.com

Reprinted with permission of Prescott Mariott Hotels

Prescott
ARIZONA

True West. Real Adventure.
866.878.2489 · VISIT-PRESCOTT.COM

Outdoor Lovers' Paradise

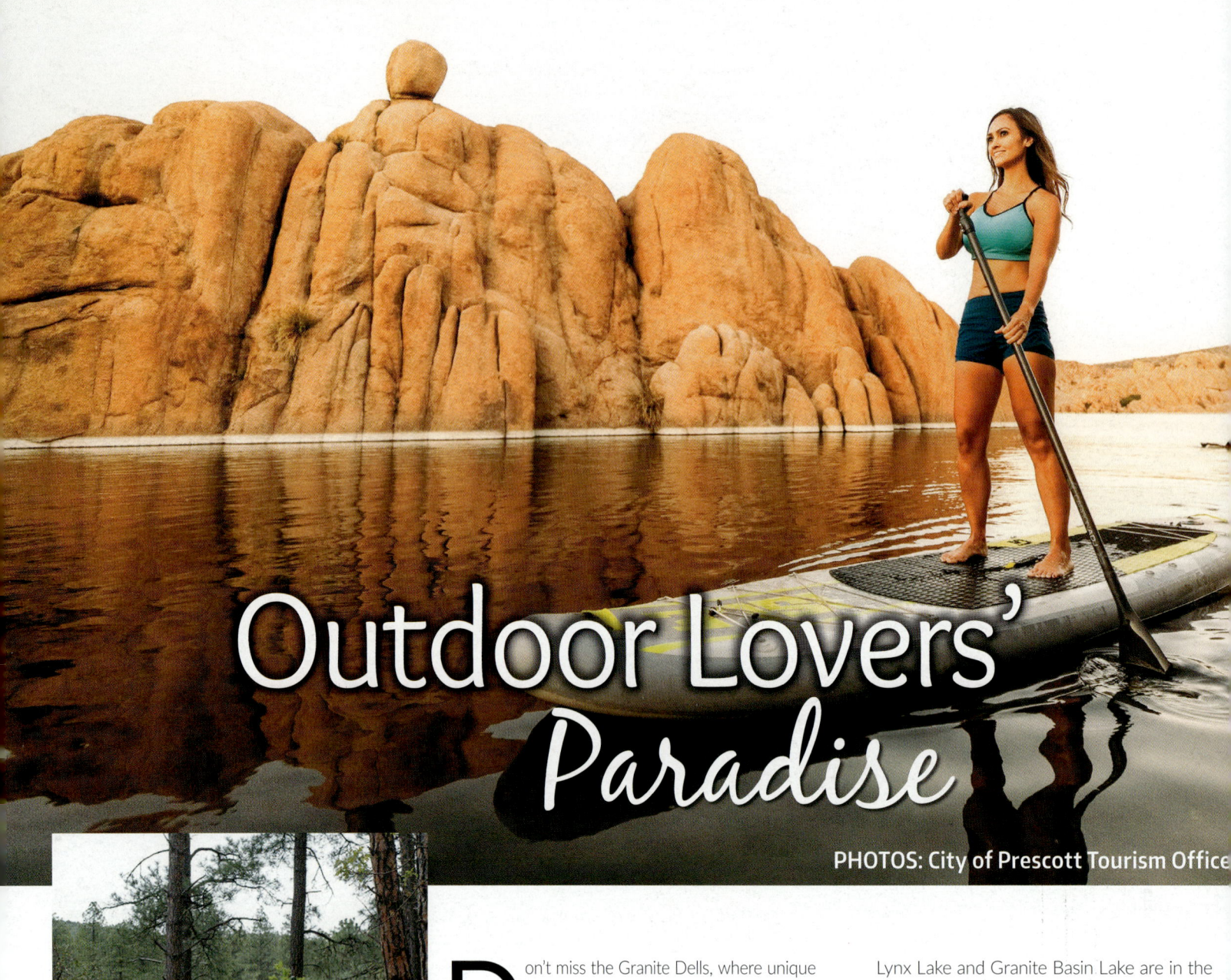

PHOTOS: City of Prescott Tourism Office

The 57-mile Prescott Circle Trail will challenge you. A complete list of the Mile High Trail System - 106 miles of it - is available at the Chamber of Commerce Visitor Center on Goodwin Street south of Courthouse Plaza. prescott.org.

Don't miss the Granite Dells, where unique rock formations thrust out of the ground and tempt hikers and rock climbers.

Watson Woods Riparian Preserve is the remaining 126-acre portion of what was once a 1,000-acre riparian forest of cottonwood and willow trees. Since the Preserve was established in 1995, it has become an oasis for wildlife.

If you're into birding, Prescott's the place. Designated as an Important Birding Area (IBA) by the Audubon Society, Prescott is home to more than **360 species of birds**. The Prescott Audubon Society **prescottaudubon.org** can provide full details about where to go and when.

EXPANSIVE PARKS & BREATHTAKING LAKES

If you like water activities, you'll enjoy the three local lakes - Willow, Watson and Goldwater lakes. Maintained by the City of Prescott, the **15-acre** Goldwater Lake is located in lush pine forests surrounded by rugged mountain areas. The City of Prescott has kayak and canoe rentals available **prescottoutdoors.com**.

Lynx Lake and Granite Basin Lake are in the Prescott National Forest. Here you can enjoy kayaking, canoeing and fishing.

Willow Lake is home to examples of prehistoric pithouses. The unique site is an example of the Hohokam influence on the people living in the area around A.D. 900-1100. Petroglyphs are found throughout the region, with several areas accessible via the trail system.

Want to spend time in a park? The city boasts **16 of them**, all with amenities that guarantee memorable times. Some are purely recreational - walking and exercising and picnicking. Some are athletic parks - softball, Pickleball, baseball, soccer, tennis, basketball, skateboards, a skating rink and the like. One in particular - McCasland Willow Creek Park - features one of only four custom created dog parks in the U.S. Canines are the most welcome visitors.

A complete list with locations is available on the city website **prescott-az.gov/services/parks**.

EVERYBODY'S HOMETOWN
Prescott
ARIZONA
CHAMBER of COMMERCE

Located in Historic Downtown Prescott
117 W. Goodwin St.
Across from the Courhouse Plaza

Membership - *join today!*
Visitor Information Center - *visit us!*
Special Events - *year round!*
Calendar of Events - *website and printed!*

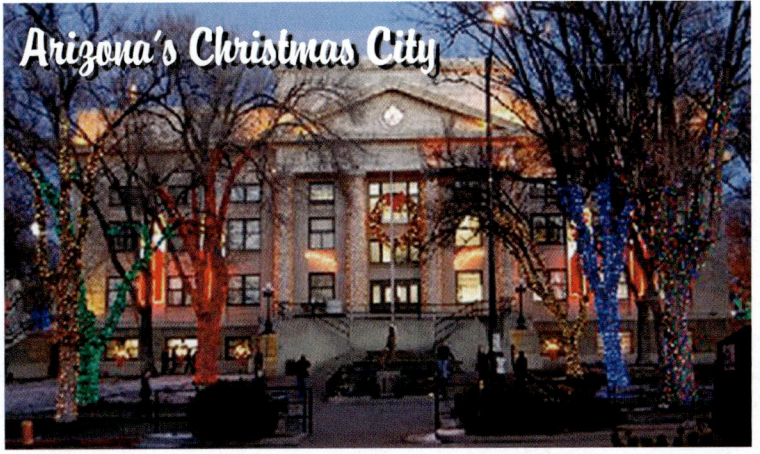

Arizona's Christmas City

Lakes and Hiking Trails

Prescott Bluegrass Festival

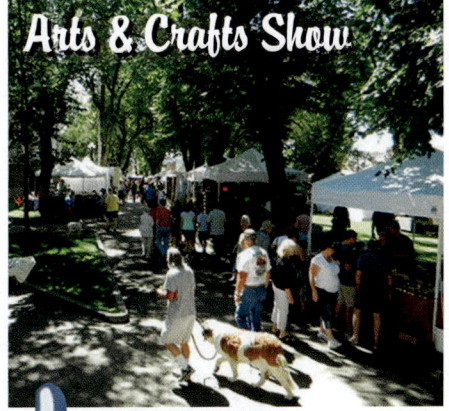

Arts & Crafts Show

World's Oldest Rodeo

Photos by Bob Shanks

Like us on facebook

Photo by Miller Photo
Facebook.com/PrescottChamber

Prescott.org | 928-445-2000 | 800-266-7534

Prescott Offers

Old West Charm, Outdoor Adventures and Vibrant Arts, Culture and Entertainment

Unparalleled hospitality, exceptional outdoor activities, a variety of entertainment venues and rich history attract tens of thousands of visitors to Prescott every year – many returning again and again.

There's always something drawing out-of-towners and international guests to "Everybody's Hometown," and it goes well beyond the beautiful, moderate summer weather. It might be the annual Frontier Days Rodeo Parade occurring around the Fourth of July, where thousands of people don Western wear, whoop and applaud. Sometimes they join the Frontier Days cowboys and cowgirls in town for the World's Oldest Rodeo® – the second-largest in Arizona. Or it might be one of the two Christmas parades. One is during early evening, featuring lighted floats; the other is midday and has nearly 100 entries, which all celebrate the city that is officially designated "Arizona's Christmas City."

Visitors enjoy a range of entertainment options, such as the sold-out Prescott POPS Symphony Orchestra to the classical programs performed by the Phoenix Symphony, brought to town by the Yavapai Symphony association. They delight in outdoor summer concerts by the Central Arizona Concert Band on the iconic Courthouse Plaza and stand in awe of history at the restored century-old Elks Theatre. And they can wash down all of the fun with a night out on the town in the vibrant Whiskey Row nightlife area.

The City of Prescott Recreation Department organizes programs throughout the year. Competitors from throughout the Southwest come to "Arizona's Softball Capital" for tournaments almost every month. Same is true for Little League and adult baseball, soccer, basketball, and a growing favorite, pickleball leagues.

VISITORS MAKE A POSITIVE IMPACT

The most recent Prescott Chamber of Commerce count of visitors who walk through its doors showed that more than **30,000 guests registered** this past year. That figure doesn't begin to tell the true number of tourists, as only a small number of those who visit sign in.

A better gauge might be the ever-increasing transient tax collection numbers (based on the citywide bed tax). Those numbers are up the past year by **13.8%**, and represent more than **630,200 receipts**.

In sum, Prescott is not just a "pass-through" community on the way to somewhere. It is a destination, one gaining national and international recognition as the place to go for a "True West Real Adventure."

Prescott
Venues

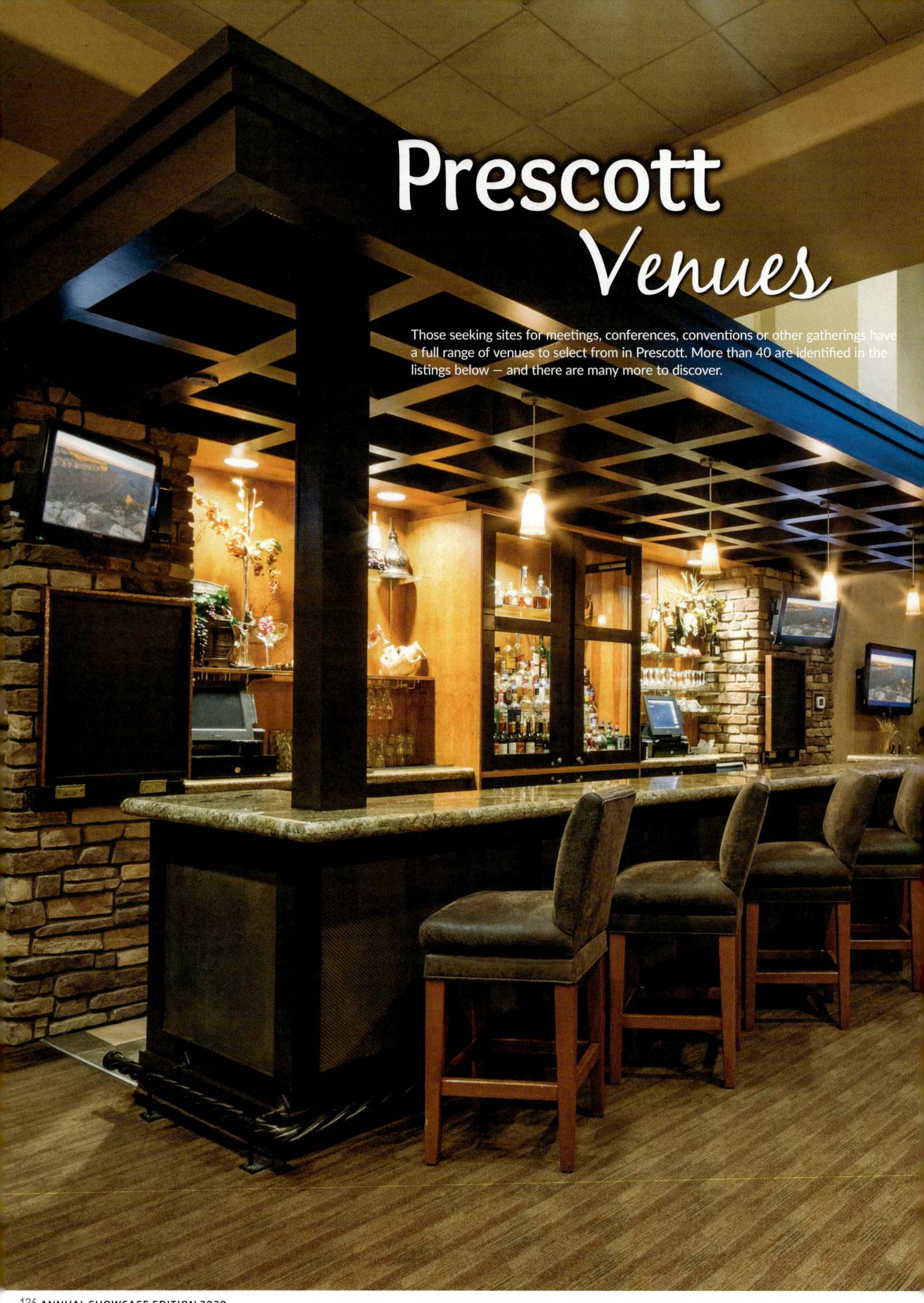

Those seeking sites for meetings, conferences, conventions or other gatherings have a full range of venues to select from in Prescott. More than 40 are identified in the listings below — and there are many more to discover.

Special Section: Prescott Tourism

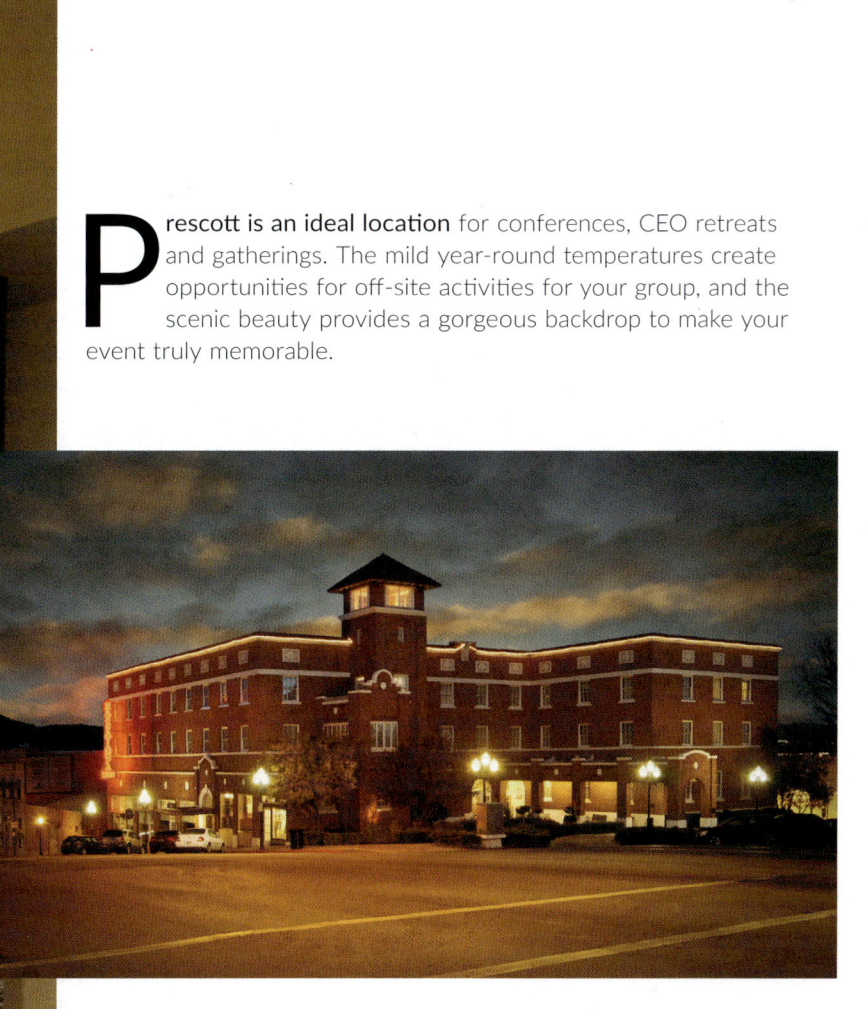

Prescott is an ideal location for conferences, CEO retreats and gatherings. The mild year-round temperatures create opportunities for off-site activities for your group, and the scenic beauty provides a gorgeous backdrop to make your event truly memorable.

HOTELS WITH MEETING, BANQUET, EVENT SPACE

- Best Western Prescottonian
- Forest Villas
- Grand Highland Hotel
- Gurley Street Lodge Bed & Breakfast
- Hampton Inn
- Hassayampa Inn
- Hotel St. Michael
- La Quinta Inn & Suites & Convention Center
- Prescott Pines Inn
- Prescott Resort and Conference Center
- Residence Inn by Marriott Prescott
- SpringHill Suites by Marriott Prescott

OTHER VENUES

- Capital Canyon Club
- Elks Theatre & Performing Arts Center
- Embry-Riddle Aeronautical University: Davis Learning Center; Jim and Linda Lee Planetarium at STEM Center; The Hangar at Jack L. Hunt Student Center; Student Activity Center
- Finn at Touchmark
- Grace M. Sparkes Activity Center
- Heritage Park Zoo
- Holiday Courtyard
- Prescott Adult Center
- Prescott Centennial Center at Antelope Hills Golf Course
- Prescott Chamber Visitor Information Center
- Prescott College Crossroads Center
- Prescott Vibes Event Center
- Sharlot Hall Museum Gardens
- Talking Rock
- The Barley Hound
- The Club at Prescott Lakes
- 'Tis Art Center & Gallery
- Yavapai College—Performing Arts Center; Boyd Tenney Library Community Room

OUTDOOR

- The Highlands Center for Natural History
- Prescott Parks and Lakes – Goldwater, Watson, Willow
- Granite Creek Park
- County Courthouse Plaza

For additional information and help planning your next event in Prescott, contact:
Ann Steward,
Sales & Marketing Coordinator,
City of Prescott
201 S. Cortez St., Prescott AZ 86301
928.777.1259
ann.steward@prescott-az.gov
www.visit-prescott.com

Top Attractions

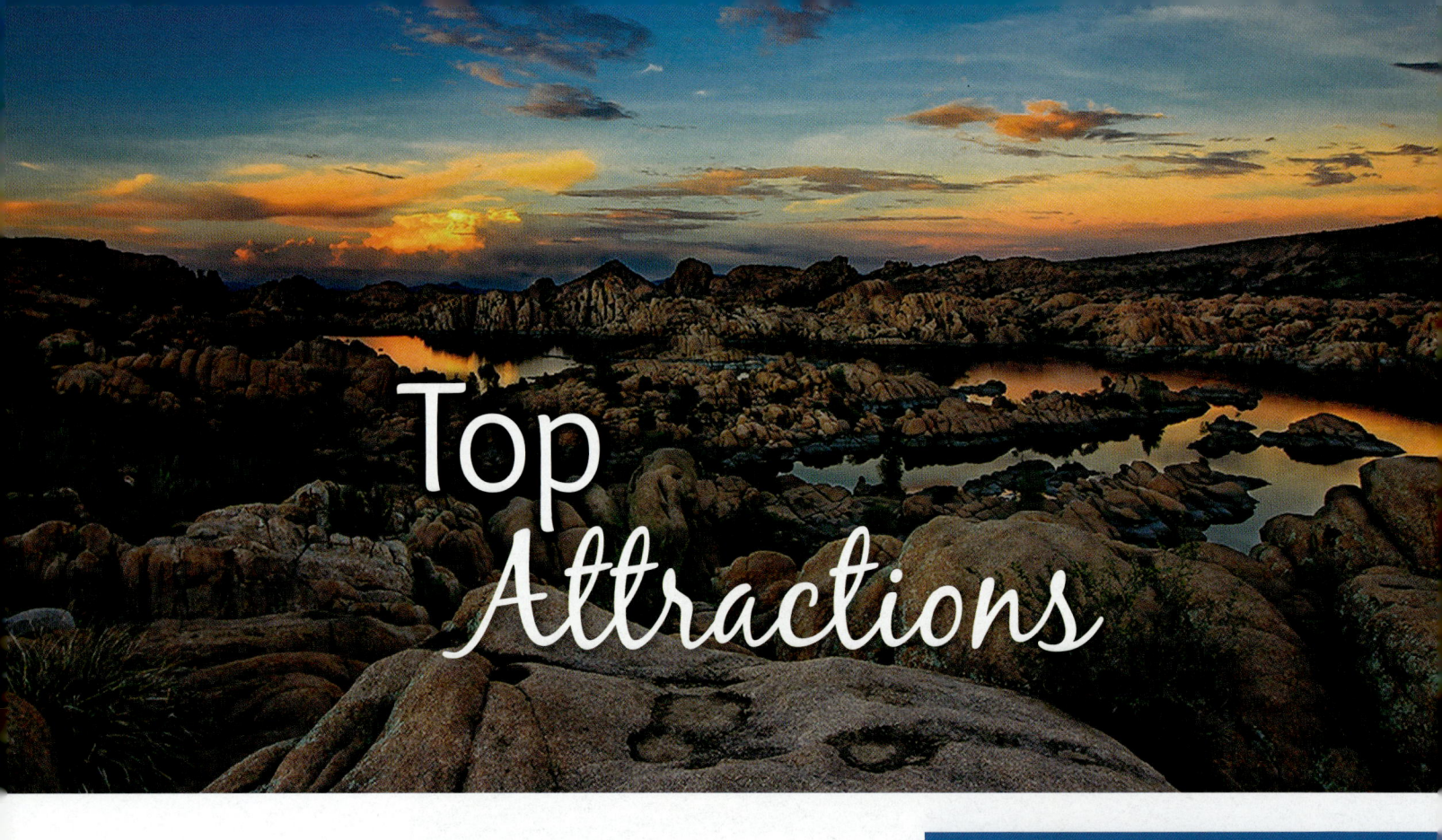

First-time visitors to Prescott come here for a whole host of reasons, but most often they are lured by the historic, romantic appeal of Western heritage coupled with the area's breathtaking beauty. No place more embodies the Old West than Whiskey Row, where saloons, restaurants, boutique shops and hotels look straight out of a Western movie set. Stroll the street, and it's a cinch that someone in a cowboy hat will look at you, smile and offer a sincere, warm greeting.

Prescott offers outdoor enthusiasts unlimited adventure and beauty. Known locally and nationally for having the state's best and most extensive opportunities for hiking and biking, Prescott lays claim to more than 450 miles of well-maintained and developed trails. Sixteen city parks round out these offerings, while five area lakes (Goldwater Lake, Willow Lake, Watson Lake in Prescott, and Lynx Lake and Granite Basin Lake in the adjacent Prescott National Forest) provide ample opportunities for boating and fishing. Five golf courses are immediately available, too.

Guests enjoy the Sharlot Hall Museum, where the history and culture of Central Arizona has been preserved. They can visit Smoki Museum, where the history and culture of Southwestern Native American tribes are on display. The Phippen Museum of Western Art on the north side of the city features exceptional Western arts exhibits. The world's largest model airplane display is open to the public at the Christine and Steven F. Udvar-Hazy Library on the campus of Embry-Riddle Aeronautical University. The Highlands Center for Natural History is a contemporary scientific and ecological center for the region.

So, while it might be true that the tens of thousands of visitors to Prescott come every year for the Wild West, they often stay and return for the arts, culture and abundance of recreational opportunities.

Special Section: Prescott Tourism

A full range of social organizations serve various roles within the community. Some cater to military and veterans (VFW, DAV, American Legion and others). Others include Habitat for Humanity, People Who Care, Coalition for Compassion and Justice and Prescott Area Women's Shelter. Several non-denominational and religious or spiritual organizations reach out to assist the needy. Still others provide food and necessities (among them Community Cupboard, Yavapai Food Bank and Catholic Social Services) to children and those in need.

The same is true of service organizations that volunteer to assist the community, such as Lions International, Kiwanis International, Rotary Clubs, Prescott Elks Club, Soroptomists and PEO, a philanthropic educational organization.

SPORTS OPPORTUNITIES

Some are sponsored, such as recreational leagues for both youth and adults in soccer, softball, baseball, bowling, tennis, pickleball, golf, biking and swimming. Many of the foregoing are supported through the city's recreation department, which provides dozens of facilities designed for such activities.

ARTS, CULTURE AND ENTERTAINMENT

Recently, the Prescott City Council designated a multiblock sector area in the center of town as the official Entertainment District. The result is a well-defined and quite walkable area that is replete with educational, cultural and entertainment experiences to match almost every interest at any time of year.

Scattered throughout the greater community are venues and attractions designed to educate, entertain and provide pleasure.

The following list cites just a few:

- Arizona Softball Hall of Fame Museum
- Elks Theatre and Performing Arts Center
- Fort Whipple Museum
- Granite Mountain Interagency Hotshot Crew Learning Tribute Center
- Heritage Park Zoological Sanctuary
- The Highlands Center for Natural History
- Jim and Linda Lee Planetarium at ERAU Natural History
- Mountain Arts Guild and Gallery
- Phippen Museum of Western Art
- Prescott Chamber Orchestra
- Prescott Film Festival
- Prescott Center for the Arts
- Prescott POPS Symphony Orchestra
- Prescott Western Heritage Center
- Sharlot Hall Museum
- Smoki Museum of American Indian Art and Culture
- Western Heritage Center
- Yavapai College Performing Arts Center and Art Museum
- Yavapai Symphony Association

COUNTY COURTHOUSE A FOCAL POINT

Year-round, the more than a century-old iconic Yavapai County Courthouse Plaza has been a gathering spot for individuals, groups, organizations and visitors.

Visitors and residents alike enjoy the annual Christmas Courthouse Lighting. Linked to the designation given to Prescott by the late Gov. Rose Mofford - "Arizona's Official Christmas City" - the event is preceded by a colorful Christmas parade the first week of December.

The rest of the year is equally as busy, providing educational, cultural and entertainment experiences to match almost any desire. Among them:

- Arts and crafts shows
- Car shows and exhibits
- Musical concerts
- Patriotic events
- Historical commemorations

GIVE ME A SIGN

Alleys
Photos: Gerry Groeber

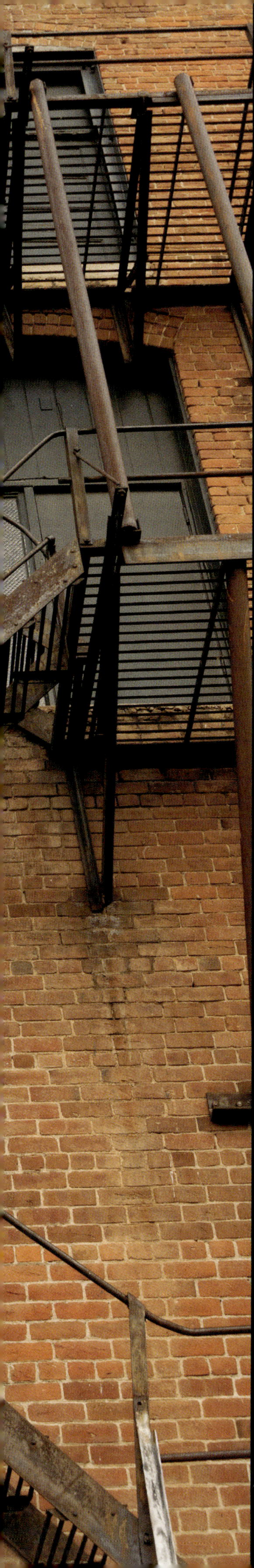

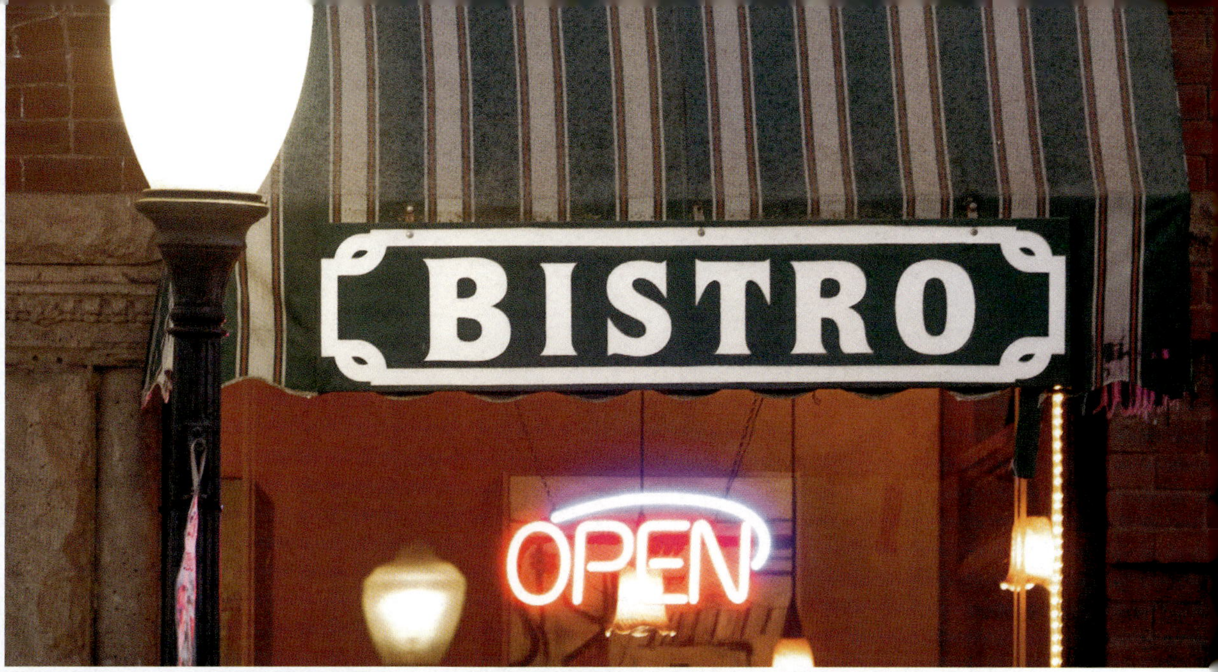
BISTRO
OPEN

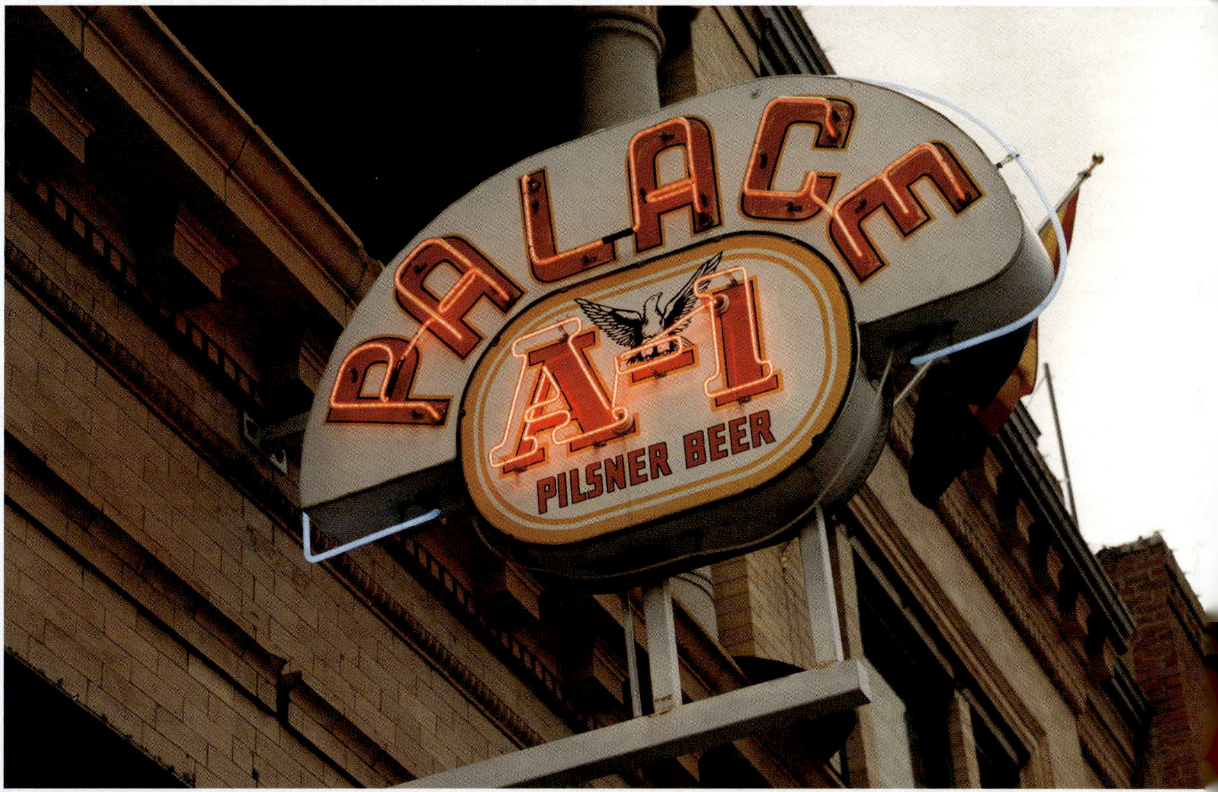
PALACE
A-1
PILSNER BEER

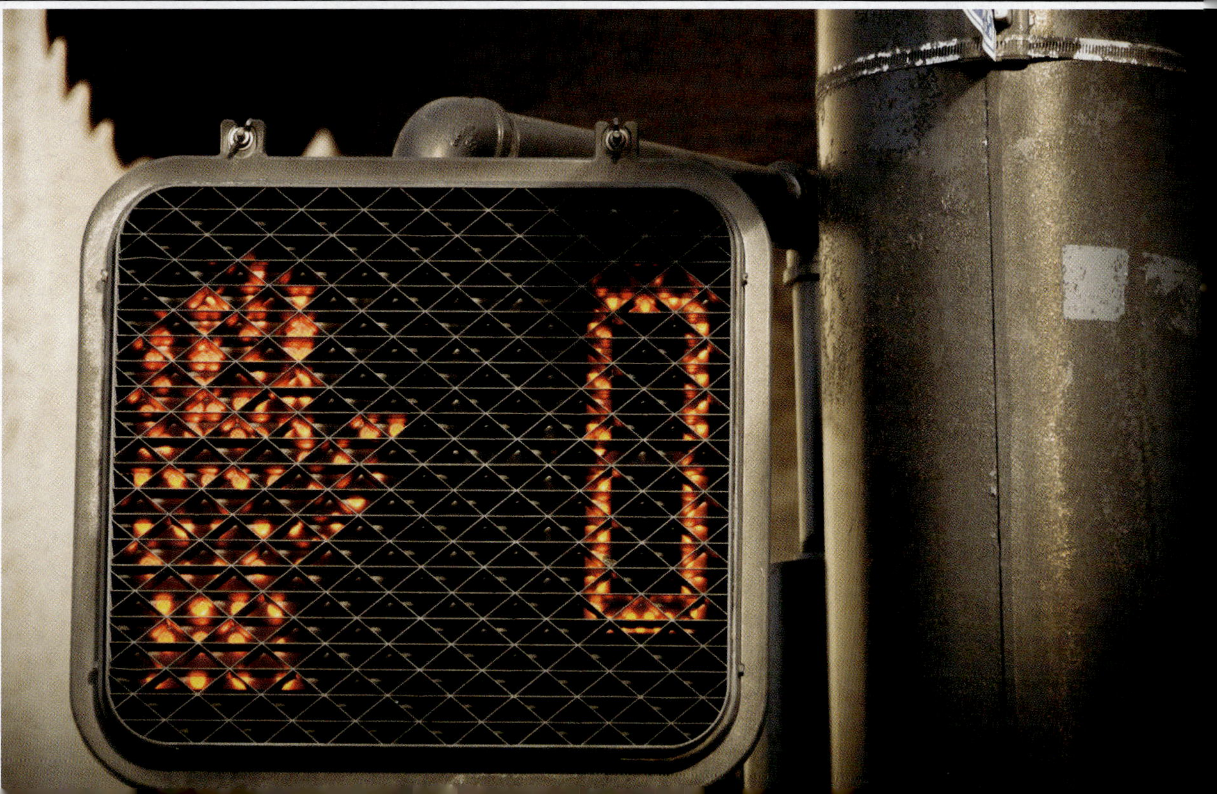

Arizona's *Christmas City*

Photo: Blushing Cactus Photography

Photo: Rod Hendrick

142 ANNUAL SHOWCASE EDITION 2020

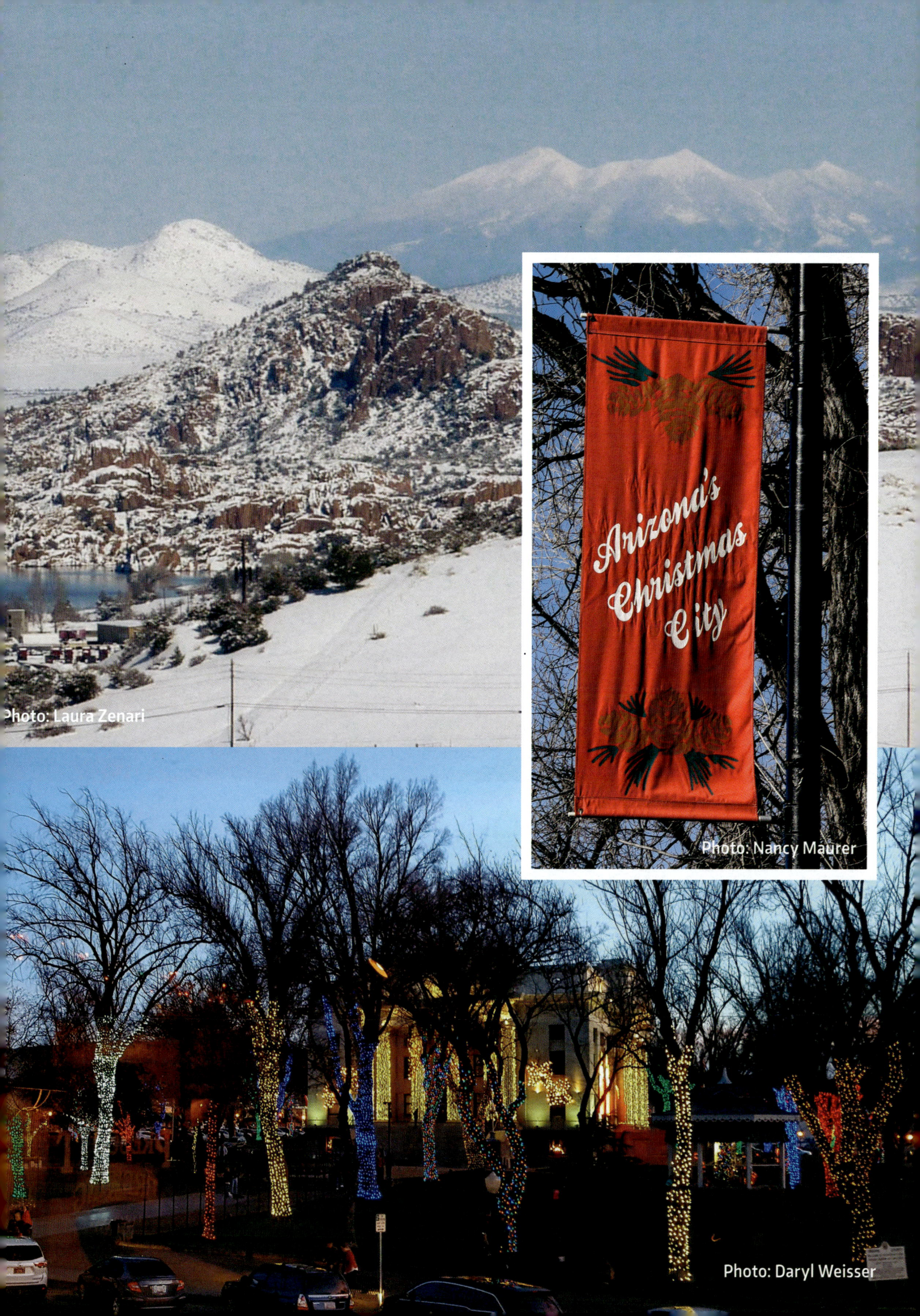

Photo: Laura Zenari

Arizona's Christmas City

Photo: Nancy Maurer

Photo: Daryl Weisser

Elks Continues to Drive Growth in Prescott Performing Arts Community

by Trevor Odom, Assistant Marketing and Program Manager, Prescott Elks Theatre & Performing Arts Center

Hello all! It is hard to believe the Elks Theatre and Performing Arts Center is now two years past its renovation. A lot has happened in the past couple of years, so much that one article cannot do it justice.

The Theatre now shows movies almost every Wednesday, playing a variety of titles from *Gone with the Wind* to *Top Gun*. The second-floor dance halls have been filled with dance and movement instructors in a variety of disciplines. We have also had huge success with our Top of the Elks Jazz concerts.

Partnerships also have begun with The Folk Sessions, Mile High Comedy Theater and the Arizona Philharmonic to bring you more diverse music and entertainment. Additionally, the Elks Theatre and Performing Arts Center was able to donate $6,000 to students of Prescott High School for scholarships in the performing arts.

One of the most exciting things that has happened in the last year is the addition of our new state-of-the-art audio-recording and mixing studio. The completion of this studio represents two years of work from the Elks' team. Its purpose is

Prescott LIVING 2020 Annual Showcase

to provide a low-cost, professional audio-recording option accessible to a larger segment of the performing arts community.

We have been fortunate enough to contract with multiple experienced and well-trained recording engineers to help local artists take their talents to the next level. This studio includes Wenger sound isolation recording booths with eight input channels. Powered by a Logic X software interface, the studio includes all of the mixing software to service any of your audio-recording desires.

The new recording studio is open to the public and will operate 24 hours a day, seven days a week. Our engineer specializes in a variety of genres including bluegrass, hip hop, rap, metal, rock and roll, blues, country and Latin, among others. Using our Wenger sound booth technology, the engineers are able to simultaneously record different musicians in isolation, creating crisp and clean sound for professional recordings.

The recording studio is representative of the Elks Theatre and Performing Arts Center's mission to enhance the performing arts community in Prescott and the surrounding area. We take pride in being able to offer these types of subsidized services to the great performers here in the Prescott area. We are truly blessed to have such a great and supportive performing arts community here, and it is an honor and privilege for the Elks to be able to make a positive impact.

The hope is that the Elks Performing Arts Center can recreate the success that has been seen in the second-floor dance studios, which now accommodate dozens of instructors in 18 different dance, exercise and movement disciplines. We have been able to create this success by supplying professional resources at subsidized prices to give all community members access to space. One of the major draws for our dance studios is the fact that we have the only permanently installed sprung Marley floored studio in the Prescott area.

In our continual drive to provide top quality resources for performers, the recording studio is meant to enhance the music community in the same way as the dance studios have been able to enhance the dance community. We are confident that the quality of the equipment and personnel will ensure that our hope becomes a reality.

It is through participation from community members that we are able to provide the entertainment and services we do, and we are extremely thankful to be living in such a responsive and engaged community.

In addition to supporting the maintenance of one of the oldest historical buildings in Yavapai County, a portion of every dollar spent in the Theatre or Performing Arts Center goes to our community outreach programs benefiting youth in the Quad Cities. Without Prescott's caring support, along with the donations and patronage of the community, we would not be able to do what we do.

Those interested in receiving tours of any of the spaces can contact the Theatre at 928-777-1359 or the Performing Arts Center at 928-756-2844. On behalf of all of the staff and volunteers at the Elks Theatre and Performing Arts Center, we thank you for your support. Whether you catch a movie, enjoy a class, attend a show or join us for Acker Night, it's always a great time at the Elks.

Elks Theatre & Performing Arts Center
117 E Gurley St #115, Prescott, AZ 86301
(928) 777-1370
https://prescottelkstheater.com

Embry-Riddle Aeronautical

Photos: Embry-Riddle Aeronautical University

University's
Wings Out West Airshow

Greater **Prescott LIVING at Its Best!** 147

CAPITAL CANYON
CLUB

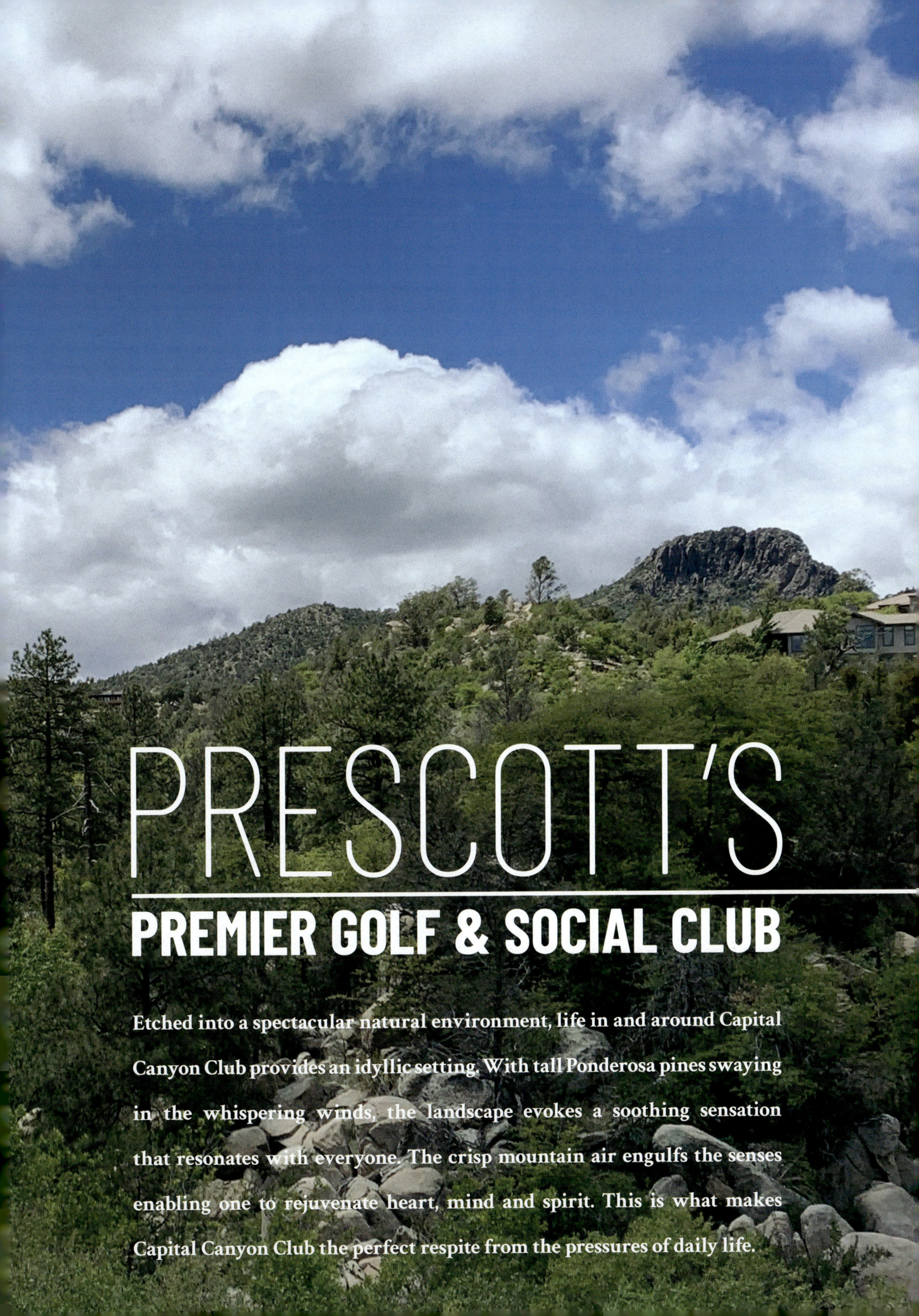

PRESCOTT'S
PREMIER GOLF & SOCIAL CLUB

Etched into a spectacular natural environment, life in and around Capital Canyon Club provides an idyllic setting. With tall Ponderosa pines swaying in the whispering winds, the landscape evokes a soothing sensation that resonates with everyone. The crisp mountain air engulfs the senses enabling one to rejuvenate heart, mind and spirit. This is what makes Capital Canyon Club the perfect respite from the pressures of daily life.

Situated into the site occupied in 1919 by Hassayampa Country Club, both the land and traditions of the game have been honored by Capital Canyon Club's course designer, Tom Weiskopf. Weaving through dramatic granite boulder outcroppings, the impeccably manicured, 18-hole, 6,660-yard Par 71 course is embraced between a margin of towering Ponderosa pines. A testament to Weiskopf's skill and artistry, multiple tee positions cling to hillsides, while generous fairways ribbon through the forested landscape toward greens that present their own distinct personality.

The layout is almost three courses in one. The first six holes wrap around the higher elevation of the Hassayampa Community with the highest point at 5,800 feet. As you descend into the valley, holes seven through fourteen *(where the original nine hole course laid)* are considered the flat lands where errant shots are a bit more forgiving. The last four holes feature a number of canyons and multiple creeks, while back to back par 3's on holes 16 and 17 showcase the true beauty of the course.

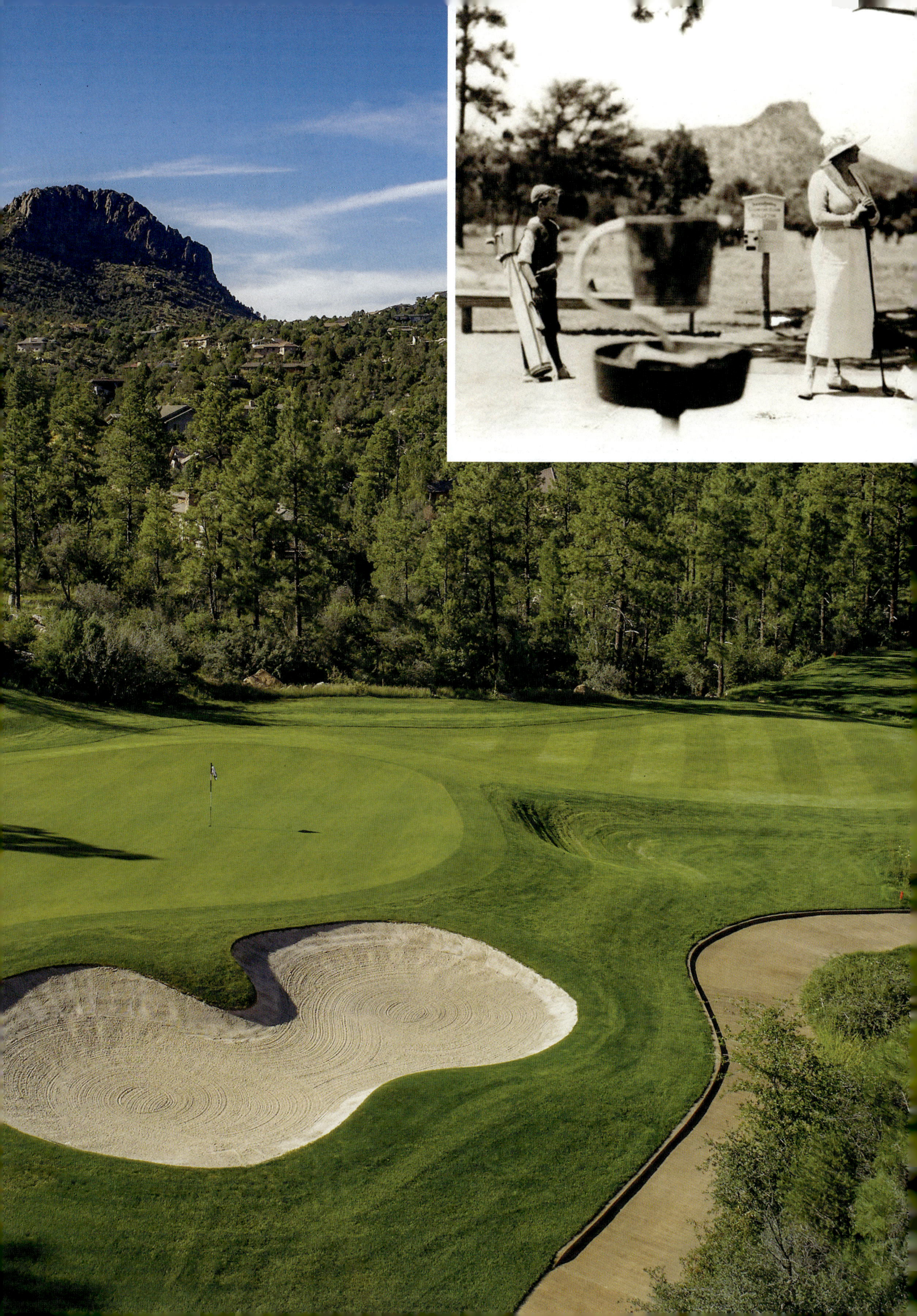

CAPITAL CANYON
CLUB

The club provides incomparable amenities for every member of the family. The rustic exterior of the Clubhouse sets the stage for country ambiance, but inside the modernized clubhouse combines a fresh new look with historic lodge style architecture, native stone accents and refreshing finishes which make everyone feel right at home. Casual get-togethers with family and friends over a fantastic meal and at club events create memories to last a lifetime.

Prescott's Premier Golf & Social Club entices families from the neighboring community to as far as Scottsdale to join the Club. Choose a family membership which fits your lifestyle best, ranging from our Pioneer Membership, tailored toward young professionals, or our Maverick or Frontier Memberships with monthly dues or our Prospector or Founder Membership which provide an all-inclusive long-term alternative, If golf isn't your game, the 1864 Social Membership is just for you.

Capital Canyon Club is proudly managed by Troon Privé, the private club division of Troon – the world's largest third party club operator. Qualified members enjoy reciprocal play at private clubs around the world through the Troon Privé Privilege program, as well as discounts of up to 50% off at resort and daily fee courses around the globe through the Troon Advantage program.

Capital Canyon Club
Prescott's Premier Golf and Social Club
928.350.3155

Celebrating 100 Years of Golf
Discover Capital Canyon Club

CAPITAL CANYON CLUB

info@capitalcanyonclub.com | CapitalCanyonClub.com

Troon Privé
PRIVATE CLUBS OF DISTINCTION

weather

ˈwe-thər

noun: disagreeable atmospheric conditions
~ Merriam-Webster

Photo: Gerry Groeber
Monsoon

HASSAYAMPA INN
PARKING GARAGE
WELCOME TO
Historic Downtown Prescott!
EveryONE's Hometown!
REALTYONEGROUP
(928) 440-2522
www.RealtyONEGroupPrescott.com
Sales Center

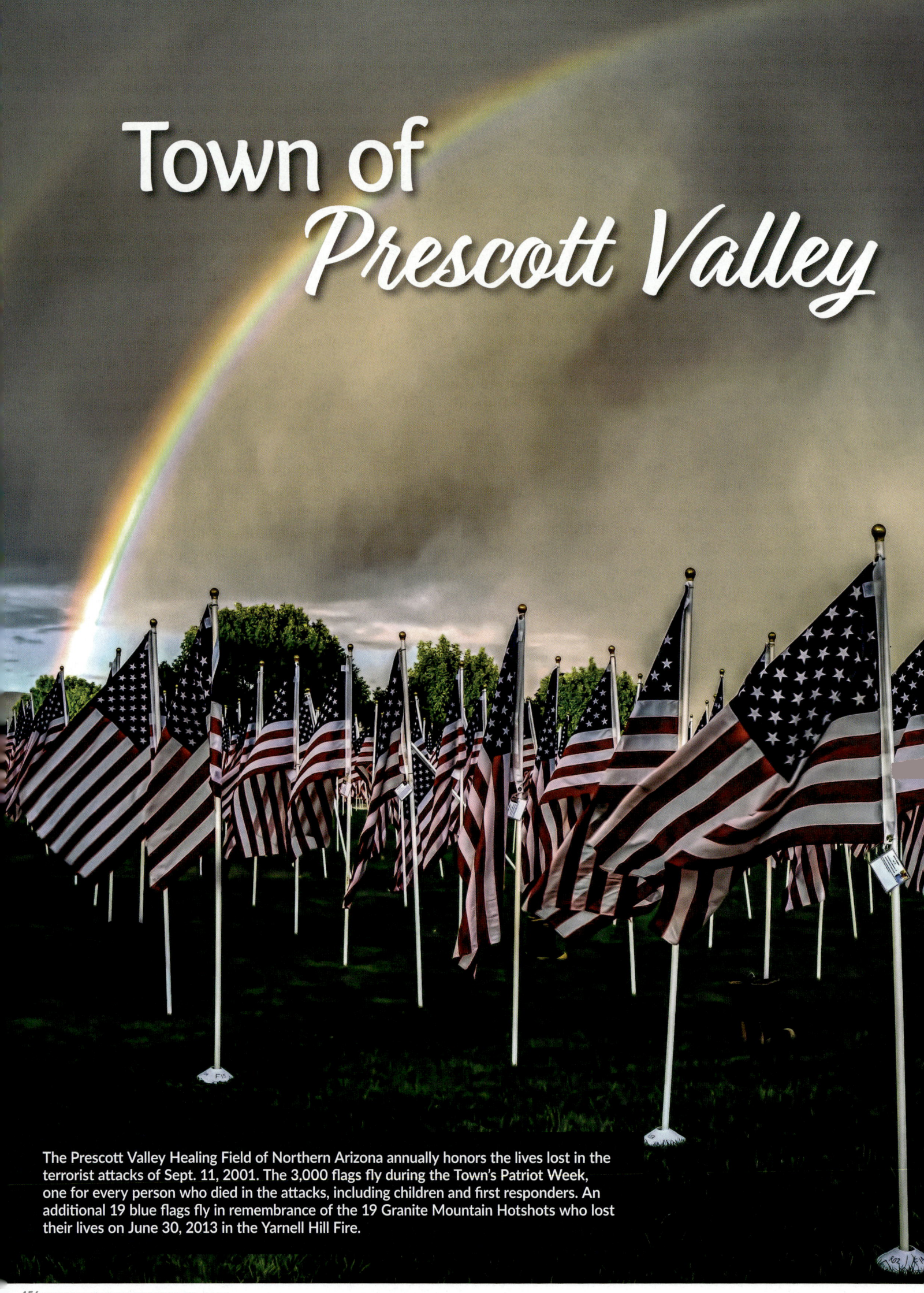

Town of Prescott Valley

The Prescott Valley Healing Field of Northern Arizona annually honors the lives lost in the terrorist attacks of Sept. 11, 2001. The 3,000 flags fly during the Town's Patriot Week, one for every person who died in the attacks, including children and first responders. An additional 19 blue flags fly in remembrance of the 19 Granite Mountain Hotshots who lost their lives on June 30, 2013 in the Yarnell Hill Fire.

Prescott Valley is the largest, fastest growing and youngest municipality in Yavapai County, with a population approaching 50,000 residents.

Located at an elevation of 5,100 feet in the high desert of Central Arizona, the community is about 85 miles north of Phoenix. The area enjoys four mild seasons with temperatures generally about 20 degrees cooler than the Valley of the Sun. Growth of the region was first driven by the discovery of gold in nearby Lynx Creek in the 1860s, and shortly thereafter, by ranching. The Fain family owned and operated the Rafter Eleven Ranch and continues to have working ranching operations to this day in addition to a property development firm. With the connection of Interstate 17 to Prescott via State Route 69, the Fain's saw an opportunity to create the Town that grew in size and popularity, incorporating in 1978. In just 40 years, Prescott Valley has established itself as an economic driver for the region and a wonderful place to live, work and play.

Photo: Charles Ables

Events List:

There is never a shortage of fun, family-friendly events in Prescott Valley! Please check out the list of some of our most popular annual events.

*These events are sponsored by the Prescott Valley Chamber of Commerce.

January
Polar Bear Splash

March/April
Eggstravaganza

April
Gold Fever Days Festival & Badges and Bobbers

May
Prescott Valley Days Festival*

May/June
Movies Under the Stars

May-September
Spring and Summer Concert Series

July
4th of July Celebration

September
Patriot Week

October
Run for the Hill of It 5K

December
Festival of Lights *
Valley of Lights *

Town Parks and Recreation contact information: 928.759.3090 | pvaz.net/292/parks-recreation
Prescott Valley Chamber of Commerce contact information: 928.772.8857 | PVChamber.org

Findlay Toyota Center

The Findlay Toyota Center (FTC), located in Prescott Valley is a 6,200-seat multipurpose facility that opened its doors in November 2006. The FTC leads the field among venues in north and central Arizona and is home to the Northern Arizona Suns, the NBA G-League affiliate of the Phoenix Suns. With 165,000 square feet of extended floor space, the Findlay Toyota Center is ideal to host concerts, sporting events including basketball and hockey, family shows, conferences, banquets and cultural programs. The arena features a single concourse and has 22 suites and two party suites, as well as a large club lounge for dinners and parties. The technical expertise and dedication of the FTC staff ensure audiences will be dazzled and entertained with shows they will never forget.

NAZ Suns Game

The Findlay Toyota Center is owned by the Town of Prescott Valley and managed by Spectra Venue Management. The arena has hosted such headlining acts as Heart, Dierks Bentley, Stevie Nicks, Miranda Lambert, Jeff Dunham, Godsmack, Eric Church, Chicago, Willie Nelson, ZZ Top, WWE, Blue Man Group, PBR, Harlem Globetrotters and Cirque du Soleil.

For information on upcoming events, please visit FindlayToyotaCenter.com

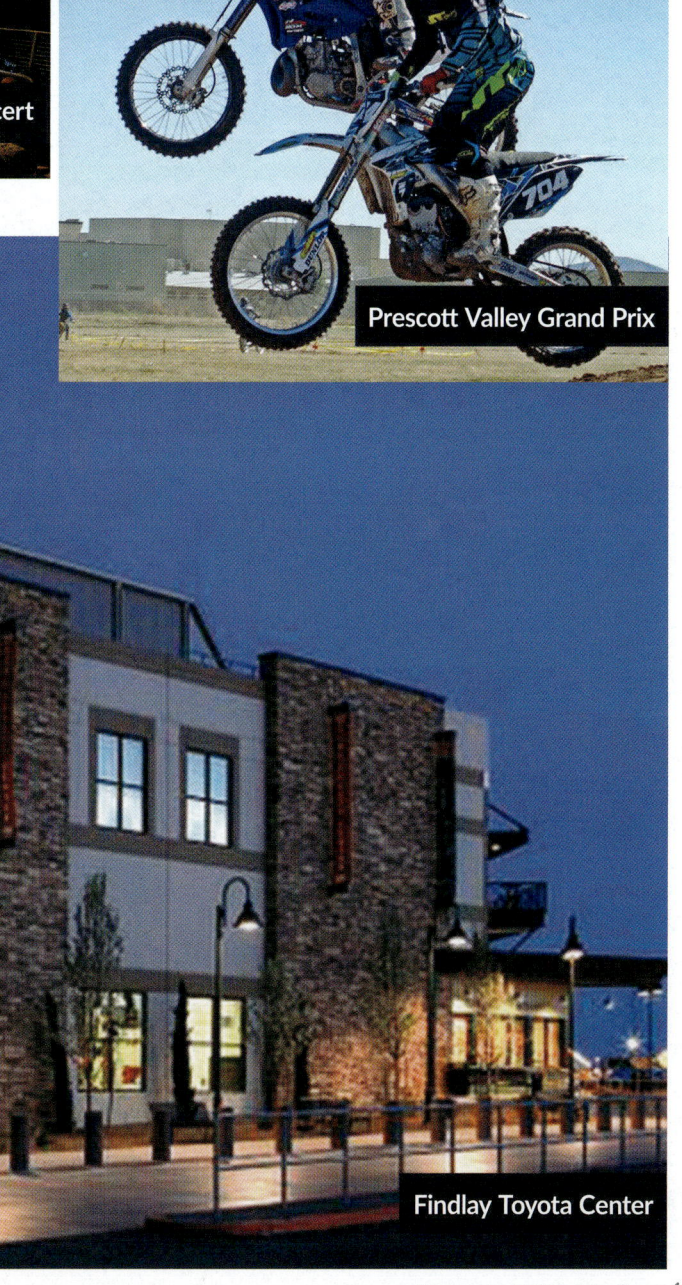

Turquoise Circuit Rodeo

Willie Nelson Concert

Prescott Valley Grand Prix

Findlay Toyota Center

Greater **Prescott LIVING** at Its Best! 161

Family Friendly

"La Puente de la Comunidad" Celebration

Eggstravaganza

Polar Bear Splash

As the youngest community in the region, it comes as no surprise that many families find Prescott Valley a great place to call home. The public, nonprofit and private sectors all look to promote festivals and other events that are fun and affordable (or free) for the entire family. The Town offers 28 parks for resident and visitor enjoyment, many including playground areas, athletic fields, walking paths and trails; and at our flagship Mountain Valley Park, a skate park and enclosed off-leash dog park. With nationally recognized public and private schools available in the area, parents to children of all ages can find a school that will help set their children up for academic success.

Badges and Bobbers

Greater Prescott LIVING at Its Best! 163

Live Here

StoneRidge Subdivision

With median home values in the mid $200,000s, Prescott Valley is the most affordable community in Yavapai County that also offers drive times of 15 minutes or less to most amenities. A wide range of housing options are available, including golf course estates and homes closer to the median price contained in master-planned subdivisions, single-family lots and existing homes outside of HOAs in the traditional Town core, and apartment and condo products for rent or sale. Future residents who desire a larger plot of land can find large acreage properties and homes north of Town in unincorporated areas of the county. A home is available in Prescott Valley to fit every budget and lifestyle.

Granville Subdivision

A partial view of Prescott Valley taken atop the award winning Glassford Hill Summit Trail

Photo: Chris Kissling

Contact Info

Town of Prescott Valley
928.759.3000
comrel@pvaz.net
7501 E. Skoog Blvd.
Prescott Valley, AZ 86314

Prescott Valley Chamber of Commerce
928.772.8857
Gloria@pvchamber.org
7120 Pav Way, Ste. 102
Prescott Valley, AZ 86314

Prescott Valley Economic Development Foundation
928.775.0032
Info@pvedf.com
7120 Pav Way, Ste. 106
Prescott Valley, AZ 86314

One plus one is waaaaay more than two.

\- WB Dedman

Photo: Gerry Groeber - Lynx Lake

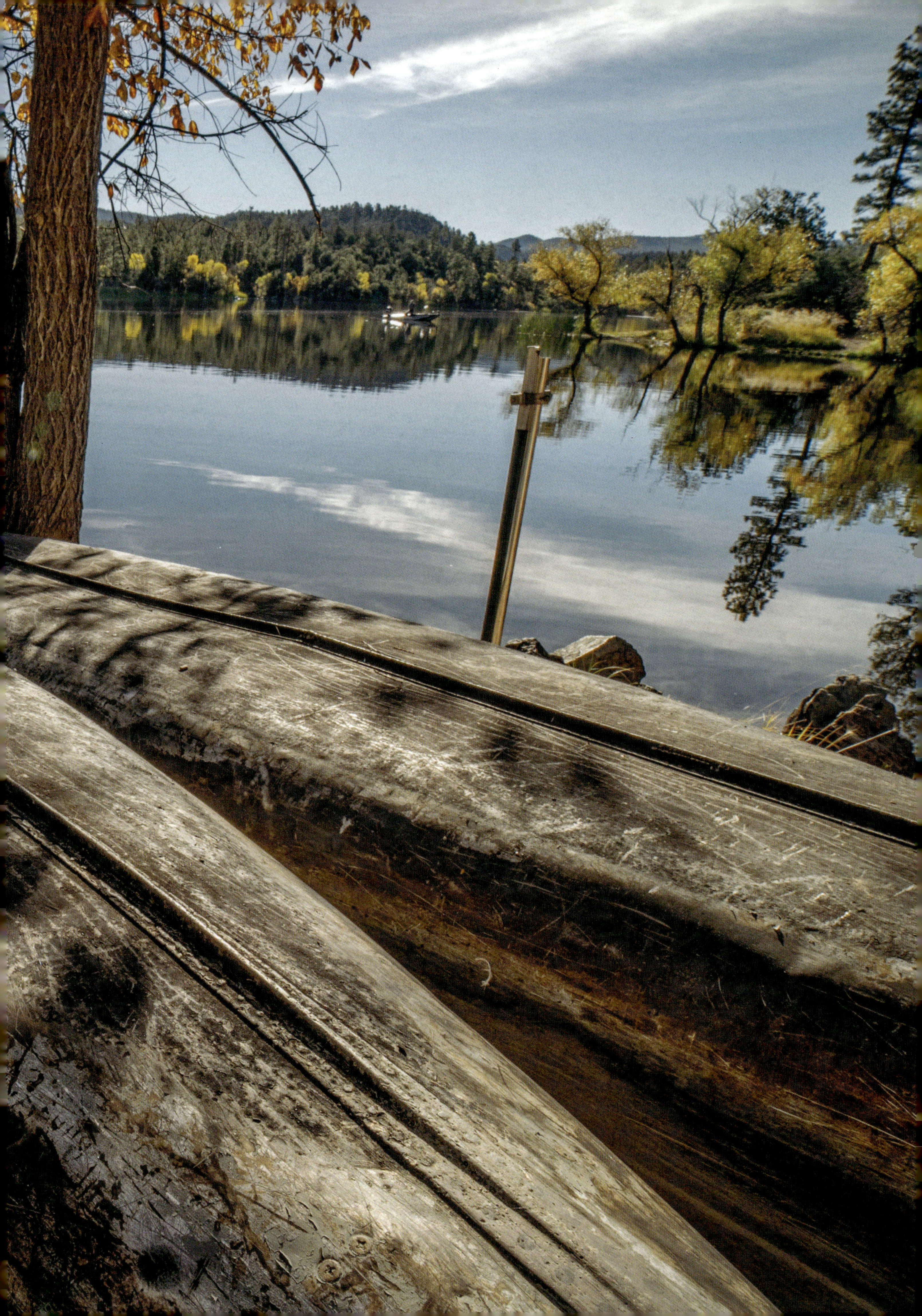

Chino Valley

The Town of Chino Valley, AZ has a long and rich history as the first Territorial Capital of Arizona in the 19th Century. Chino Valley is known for its abundant farmland that fed generations of indigenous cultures as well as sprawling vistas and beautiful scenery.

Incorporated September 1970, Chino Valley will host a year-long celebration to mark their 50th Anniversary in 2020.

The celebration begins with various events in 2019 culminating in a Golden Jubilee Celebration on their Territorial Days Labor Day Event in September 2020.

Chino Valley is **Open** for Business

50 GOLDEN JUBILEE
TOWN OF CHINO VALLEY, ARIZONA
1970 – 2020

The town is seeking help from the community to share your memories, family history, photos, home movies, and other milestone events that connect everyone together to make Chino Valley a great place to live.

Please email 50th@chinoaz.net with your comments, suggestions, and submissions to include in the celebration.

My attention is very narrowly micro-focused ... on the BIG PICTURE.

- WB Dedman

Photo: Michael Wilson - "Eruption"

Talking Rock Ranch

The exclusive private community centers around the Jay Morrish designed, 18 hole championship golf course and Ranch Compound complete with fine dining, swimming pool, bocce courts, coffee shop, bar and grill, golf shop and so much more. The golf course weaves naturally through the terrain offering views of the surrounding Granite Mountains.

Life is better at Talking Rock Ranch.

talkingrockaz.com   928.858.7000

TALKING ROCK

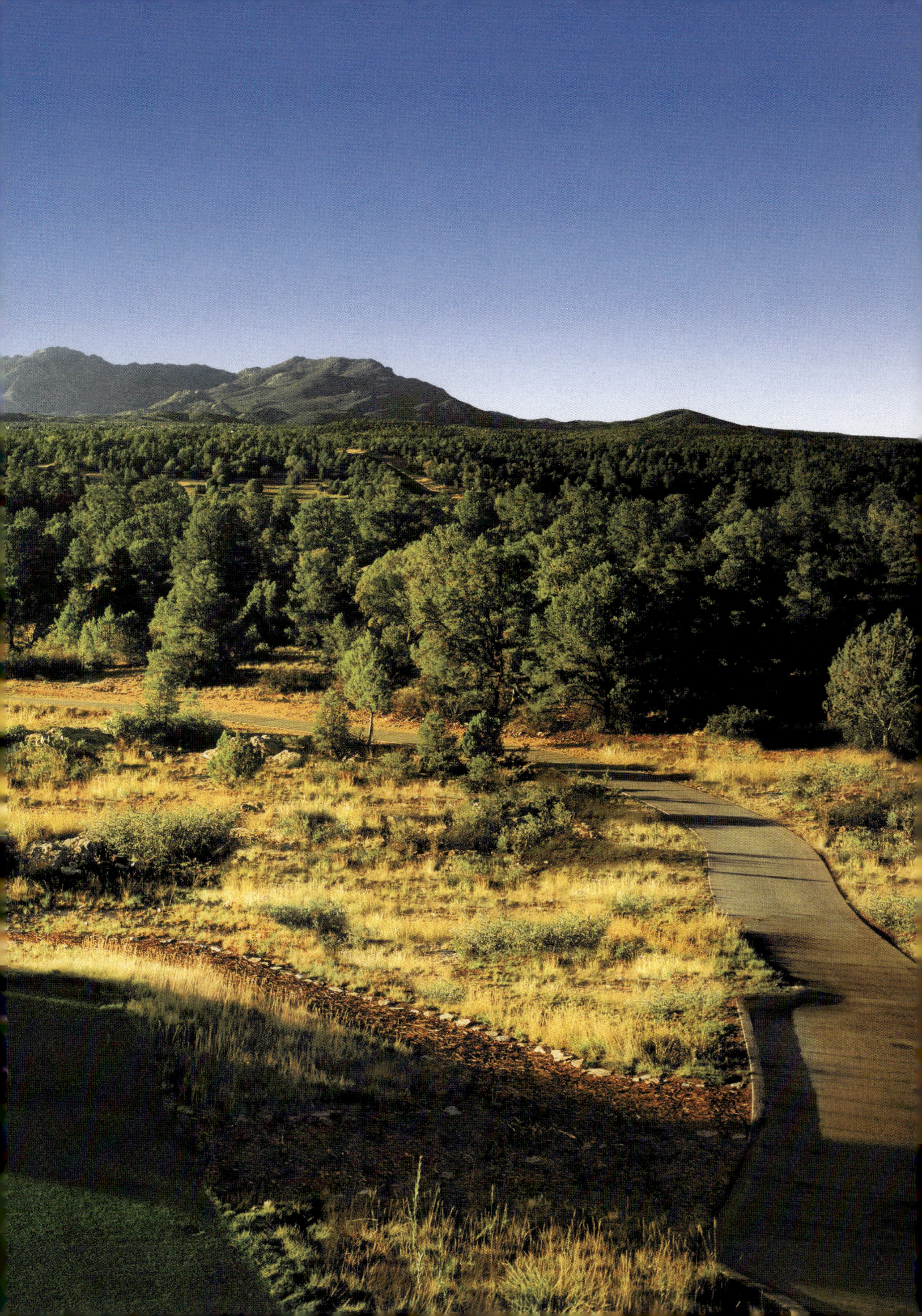

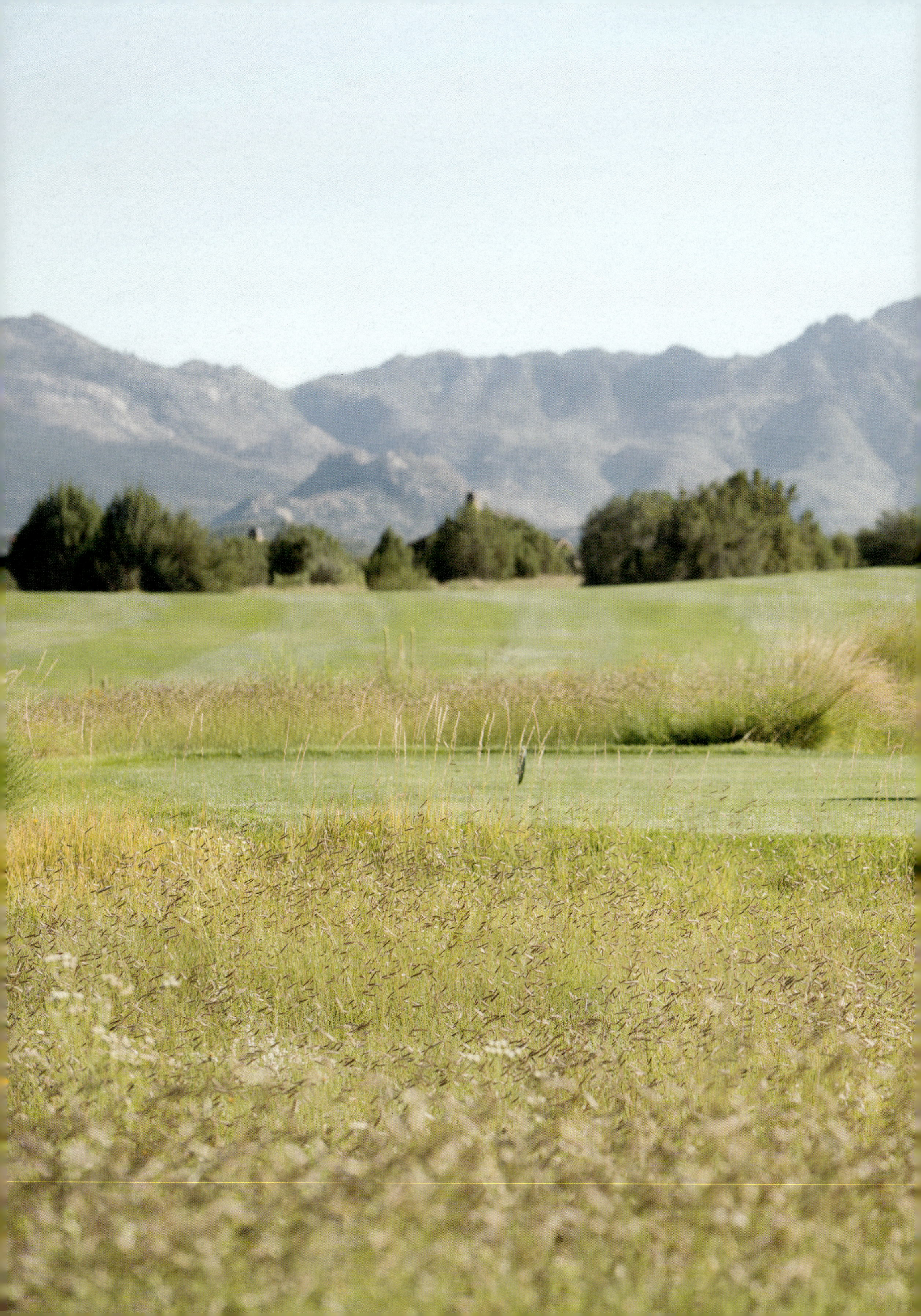

TALKING ROCK

Talking Rock Ranch   talkingrockaz.com   928.858.7000

gan·der
/ˈɡandər/

noun: a look or glance
~ Merriam-Webster

Photo: Michael Wilson

A Look Back in Time
Prescott Frontier Days

Photos: Prescott Frontier Days Archives

Greater Prescott LIVING at Its Best! 179

Special Section: Worlds Oldest Rodeo

Prescott's 'cowboy contests' more than 130 years ago developed into today's modern rodeo

by Jim Anderson & Danny Freeman

Photos: Prescott Frontier Days Archives

The name, Prescott Frontier Days®, originated with a committee of the Yavapai County Fair Association, came into being in 1913, the year the July 4th celebration began at its present location — then called the Yavapai County Fairgrounds, today called the Prescott Rodeo Grounds. Participation by the likes of Tom Mix and attendance by celebrities such as Will Rogers increased the awareness and popularity of the event.

"Rodeo" is a Spanish word meaning "to roundup," and the word "rodeo" for cowboy contests wasn't used anywhere until 1916. It was first used in Prescott in 1924.

Whereas the Yavapai County Fair ceased operation from 1933 until 1947, the rodeo continued uninterrupted and has never missed a year since 1888. In the mid '30s, the grandstand, the two rock buildings (today called the Pardee and the Freeman buildings), and the stone "fish pond" were built at the existing site with the help of federally funded Works Progress Administration (WPA) and the Civilian Conservation Corps (CCC) projects.

Recovered artifacts from that construction are on display at the Smoki Museum today, along with other rodeo artifacts and

July 4, 1888, became the birthday of professional rodeo when a group of Prescott merchants and professional businessmen organized the first formalized "cowboy tournament" and offered cash prizes.

A cowboy named Juan Leivas walked off with rodeo's first professional title and was documented in the subsequent edition of the Arizona Journal-Miner. These "cowboy contests" continued and were planned, promoted and carried out by a committee of local merchants.

From then on, rodeo has grown into a multimillion-dollar enterprise with more than 700 professional rodeos in 50 states.

The act of rodeo is as old as cattle raising itself. Stemming out of the Spanish traditions of the vaquero, it has become a worldwide phenomenon. But only in America has rodeo reached its zenith.

Of all the sports we the viewer or the participant have to choose from, no other is directly related to the natural world like rodeo. And unlike any other sport, rodeo is a reflection of the skills used in real life. The knowledge, tenacious spirit and athletic ability are inherent in the ranching world and are exemplified in the competitive arena of the rodeo.

The earliest editions of Prescott's rodeo were mostly appealing to the local cowboys and ranchers because it gave them the chance to bring their ranch-bred skills to town for people to see. The fancy rodeo arenas we know today were nonexistent in the late 1800s and early 1900s. Prescott's rodeo "arena" was merely a tract of land in what was called Forbing Park, off of what today is Iron Springs Road; very much unimproved and roped off to keep the broncs from running away after they unseated their riders. Exact numbers of total contestants were often confused, but total purses of less than $1,000 were common.

memorabilia at the Sharlot Hall and Phippen museums. A weeklong celebration marking 50 years of Prescott rodeo was held in 1937. Several locals participated in the gala event, and many former rodeo contestants helped put on festivities that also attracted thousands of Arizonans from around the state.

In the early '40s, a group of locals called the 20-30 Club decided to lend a hand to help produce Prescott's rodeo. In those days, problems of a financial nature were pressing on the producers of the rodeo so much there was talk of postponing or canceling it entirely, but they didn't! The 20-30 Club, composed of young men from 20 to 30 years of age was led by local historian Lester "Budge" Ruffner.

These men decided to promote the "working" cowboy concept of rodeo, and any professional cowboy was banned from 1941-1946. World War II took many men and contestants from the rodeo ranks during this period, but with the help of local ranchers and volunteer workers the show went on.

During the late '40s and '50s, Prescott saw the rodeo tradition continue with the help of die-hard supporters such as Gordon Koch, Danny Freeman, Fred Schemmer and Andy Jauregui. These men garnered considerable support from rodeo lovers from around town and Yavapai County.

Rodeo grew as a spectator and contestant sport continually for a period of years. Purses grew to compete with rodeos in the West that sprung up to compete with Prescott's crowds. Purses grew to astronomical sums for those days, often exceeding $20,000. With the competition for the rodeo spectator came the increases in charges for quality livestock. No longer could the local rancher provide enough calves, steers and broncs to fulfill the needs of the larger number of cowboys coming to Prescott.

The 1960s saw the transition of rodeo production change hands until 1968 when the Prescott Jaycees took control. The Jaycees made many changes, perhaps the most important being to hire a stock contractor named Harry Vold in 1972. The Harry Vold Rodeo Company continues to furnish some of the best stock available today to the World's Oldest Rodeo® in Prescott, attracting top cowboys to compete on top stock. That same year, the Hollywood movie, "Junior Bonner" with Steve McQueen was filmed around the actual rodeo and parade and thrust the Prescott Rodeo into the national and worldwide spotlight.

In the 1970s, the Prescott Jaycees ran the celebration. In between, the Yavapai County Fair Association, a nonprofit organization, was always there to keep the rodeo going. In 1978, the present organization, the nonprofit Prescott Frontier Days®, Inc., was organized and conducted its first 4th of July celebration in 1979. The Prescott Jaycees folded in 1979 due to internal problems, but Prescott Frontier Days®, Inc. kept the rodeo going.

In 1984, a number of the Rodeo Committee members signed notes on their own houses to guarantee the perpetuation of the World's Oldest Rodeo®. The Prescott Frontier Days®, Inc. has continued ever since, with the main event being the World's Oldest Rodeo®. This name was approved and registered by the U.S. Patent Office in 1985, based upon five separate criteria to which it qualified.

The Prescott Frontier Days®, Inc. exists today as the backbone of Prescott's rodeo. This group is composed of hundreds of hard-working members and volunteers dedicated to the preservation of Prescott Frontier Days® and the World's Oldest Rodeo®. In 2004, Prescott Frontier Days®, Inc. hired JC Trujillo, 1981 Bareback World Champion, five-time Prescott Champion and 1994 Pro Rodeo Hall of Fame inductee, as its general manager.

In July 2008, the Prescott Frontier Days®, Inc. Committee was inducted into the Pro Rodeo

Photo: Milller Photo

Hall of Fame in Colorado Springs, Colorado as one of only 30 rodeo committees in the U.S. ever to have this honor bestowed upon them.

Prescott Frontier Days®, Inc., is an organization of people of all ages from the Prescott area. They give their time and talents as volunteers to put on a number of events each year. There are currently over 200 active members, and during the peak period, around the 4th of July, that number swells with an additional 700 volunteers, who typically stage a golf tournament, Arizona's second largest parade — the Prescott Frontier Days®, Inc. Rodeo Parade — a Happy Hearts event for exceptional children, an Old-Timers gathering, a rodeo dance, and of course, the eight performances of the World's Oldest Rodeo®. The organization has a nine-member board of directors, including the president, and some 40-plus chairmen of as many committees.

Prescott Frontier Days®, Inc. serves people and is a major economic engine for the surrounding communities. Annually, Prescott Frontier Days®, Inc. draws more than 35,000 rodeo spectators and an additional 30,000-plus in the other 11 months of the year that hold events at the Prescott Rodeo Grounds.

Photos: Milller Photo

Watson Lake Car Show

Photo: Daryl Weisser

All Other Photos: Rod Hendrick

184 ANNUAL SHOWCASE EDITION 2020

Greater **Prescott LIVING at Its Best!** 185

Concerts

Photos: Blushing Cactus Photography

The Black Moods

Roger Clyne & The Peacemakers

Sean McDermott

The Palace

Justin Moore

Walt Richardson

Day Trips From *Prescott*

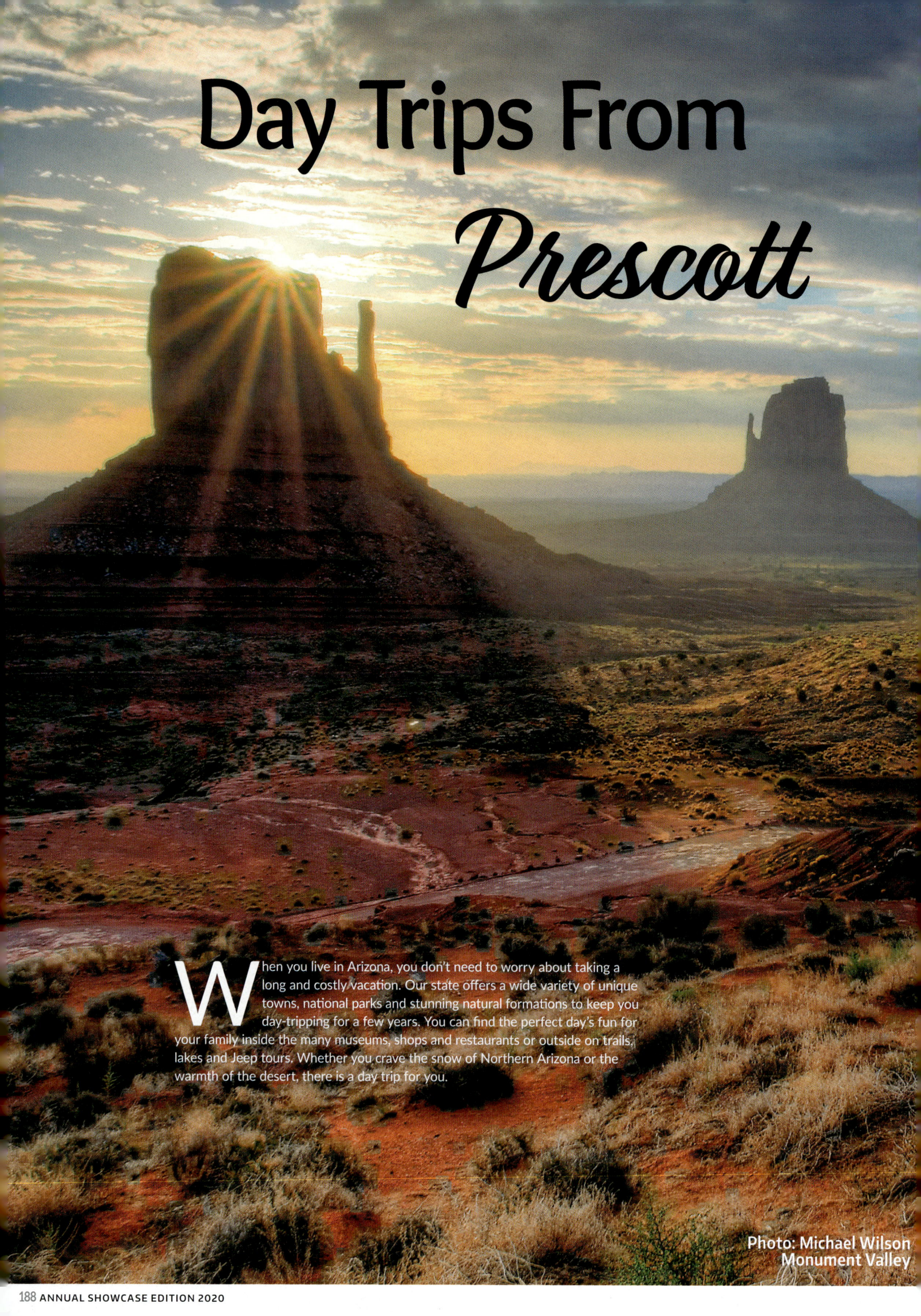

When you live in Arizona, you don't need to worry about taking a long and costly vacation. Our state offers a wide variety of unique towns, national parks and stunning natural formations to keep you day-tripping for a few years. You can find the perfect day's fun for your family inside the many museums, shops and restaurants or outside on trails, lakes and Jeep tours. Whether you crave the snow of Northern Arizona or the warmth of the desert, there is a day trip for you.

Photo: Michael Wilson
Monument Valley

Jerome (35 miles)

This historic copper mining town caters to the ghost hunter, art lover, wine or beer connoisseur and history lover. After each member of your family finds something entertaining to do in the more than two dozen galleries and eclectic shops, you can meet up on the hill at the Haunted Hamburger for your choice of nine burgers or many options on the "Not The Burgers" menu.

Williams (69 miles)

Yes, you can find your kicks right here on Route 66! Williams offers six blocks of historic advertisements, shops, motor lodges and eateries. The "Gateway to the Grand Canyon" gives you a glimpse into what life on the road was like decades ago. Mountain biking, hiking and fishing are waiting for the outdoor enthusiast. Animal lovers will embrace the Bearizona Wildlife Park. Love trains? The Grand Canyon Railway leaves Williams daily.

Wickenburg (59 miles)

Thick with the atmosphere of the Old West, Wickenburg is set alongside the Hassayampa River. Its quaint downtown offers shopping and a variety of restaurants including Anita's Cocina, where you can get authentic Mexican food. You can bring your inner cowboy and let him play on the many guest ranches or soak in some Western culture at the Desert Caballeros Western Museum.

Greater Prescott LIVING at Its Best!

Sedona

Sedona (67 miles)

Outdoor lovers flock to the Red Rocks of Sedona for mountain biking and hiking. Enjoy the cool waters of Slide Rock State Park or the majestic natural wonders in Red Rock State Park. Many New Age shops will give you the information for visiting Sedona's famous vortexes, or you can take the official Vortex Tour from the several Jeep tour groups. If unique shopping venues are your thing, visit Tlaquepaque Arts & Crafts Village, as well as the Main Street shopping district.

Verde Valley Wine Country (59 miles)

Take the winding Page Springs Road between Cornville and Sedona to experience several vineyard tasting rooms or horseback riding under the cool trees. For something completely different, visit the two fish hatcheries for a family educational experience. Red Rock State Park is just a few miles down the road with a museum and several easy-to-walk trails.

Pine (83 miles)

Cruise into Pine and feel your temperature drop under the tall trees. Saunter through the quaint downtown area to visit an art gallery or two and small specialty shops. Don't forget the Honey Stand or the Trident Winery. Ready for dinner? Swing into THAT Brewery & Pub and kick back on the patio to enjoy some delicious food and one of its in-house, hand-crafted micro-brewed beer selections.

Montezuma's Castle, Camp Verde (45 miles)

Spend the day with the family learning about the cliff-dwelling Sinagua culture at this national monument. Tours offer insights into the local reptiles and medicinal plants. After your day outside, head into the cool air of the Cliff Castle Casino Hotel to pick from several restaurant choices, including the Mountain Springs Buffet.

Photo by: Michael Wilson

Lake Pleasant (86 miles)

With 116 miles of shoreline, this recreation area offers boating, swimming, fishing, camping, picnicking, hiking ... everything your outdoor warrior craves. Open all year, it boasts two marinas where you can even rent a houseboat for that daylong party.

The Grand Canyon

South Rim Grand Canyon

Grand Canyon (123 miles)

Hiking trails, shopping, gorgeous hotels and cabins, shopping, restaurants and more are awaiting the visitor to the Grand Canyon Village on the South Rim of the Grand Canyon. See historical buildings, hear stories of former residents, and learn about the designs of trailblazing architect Mary Colter. Trailheads for Bright Angel and South Kaibab trails start near the village. Tour more of the South Rim on the shuttlebuses to see even more views before heading back to one of the numerous restaurants for a tasty meal with views that can't be beat.

Payson (98 miles)

"The Heart of Arizona" brings it all together with rodeos, swimming, hiking, fishing and camping. The historic downtown offers dining and shopping. Visit the Zane Grey Museum and see the Rim Country through the famous author's eyes. Swing by Western Village Art & Antique Corral for some unique finds. Tonto Natural Bridge offers hiking trails, the natural bridge and the park's cavern. Fossil hunting and Indian ruins will keep the history buff enthralled. The area is also a popular destination for "rock hounds" looking for geodes and "Arizona diamonds" (gemstone-quality quartz crystals). After a full day of Payson touring, the Buffalo Bar and Grill will set your toes to tapping with the band and the petite dance floor will call your name.

Kingman/Grand Canyon West (148 miles)

Along the historic Route 66 you can find a city with a storied history. Check out the Powerhouse Visitor Center, the Mohave Museum of History or Locomotive Park before stopping at one of the many restaurant options offered in this wonderfully historic city.

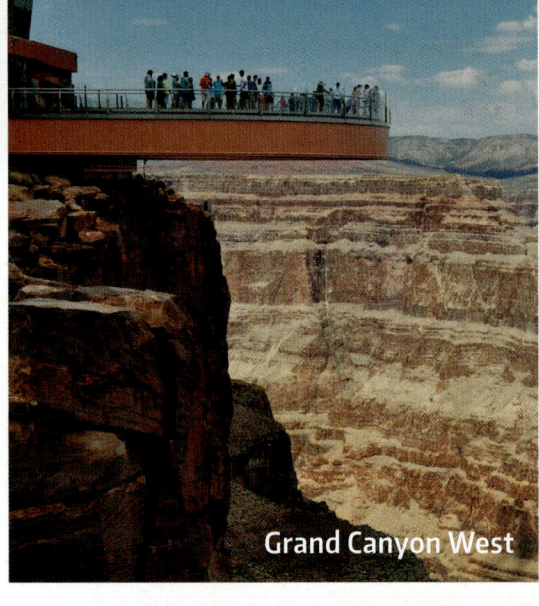

Grand Canyon West

Horsehoe Bend

Goldfield Ghost Town, Apache Junction (137 miles)

This is a very active ghost town! Boasting a gunfight show, mine tours, railroad, reptile exhibit, museum, Mystery Shack, stables, shops and more, the entire family will be immersed in the Old West, Arizona flavor. You can even try your luck at gold panning at the Prospector's Palace. A full-service steak house and saloon will help you refuel, and the town's bakery will satisfy your sweet tooth.

Antelope Canyon (228 miles)

On Navajo land just east of Page, Antelope Canyon offers two separate and scenic slot canyons known as Upper Antelope Canyon and Lower Antelope Canyon. Both slot canyons offer amazing views of sandstone rock and red sandy floors. Photography buffs would be hard pressed to take a bad picture here. Traveling unguided into the slot canyons is not permitted so be sure to sign up for one of the many tours of Antelope Canyon where a guide will share history, amazing stories and show you the best angles for legendary pictures.

Photo: Bea Lueck

Meteor Crater (137 miles)

Fifty thousand years ago a meteor hit earth with more energy than 20 million tons of TNT. That meteor happened to land in Northern Arizona. The Meteor Crater Visitor Center is located at the rim with an amazing view of the massive crater. Learn about Meteor Crater, experience the Discovery Center, see artifacts and exhibits on space, catch the Collision! 4D Experience Room, or snag a snack at the Blasted Bistro. Meteor Crater is a fun experience for all ages.

Sunset Crater (115 miles)

Black ash and volcanic rock are just two amazing things to see when visiting this otherworldly site. Sunset Crater Volcano National Monument is home to a dormant volcano whose last eruption was just a thousand years ago. Just a short drive from lively Flagstaff, this destination offers hiking trails, a visitor center and amazing views.

Arizona ADVENTURES

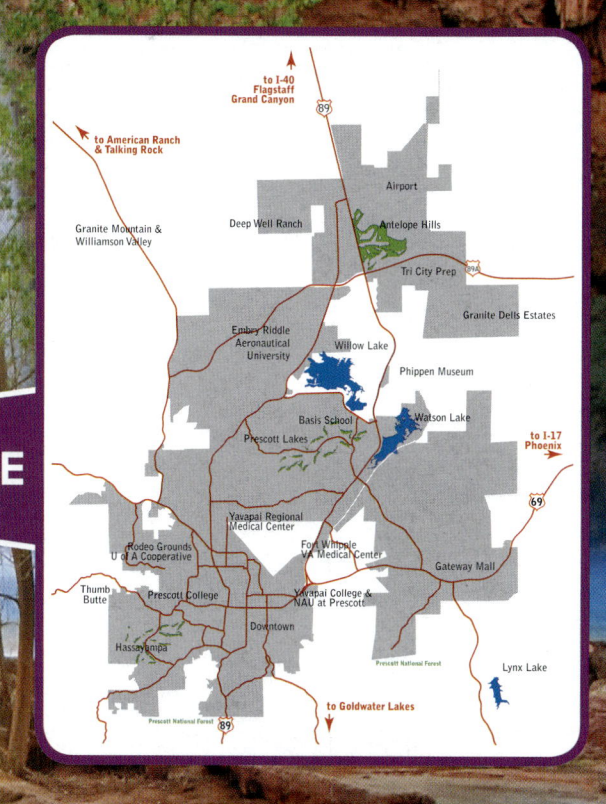

YOU ARE HERE

PRESCOTT IS THE PERFECT SPOT TO LAUNCH THESE DAY TRIPS:

- **Carefree/Cave Creek** *(90 miles)* Trail Rides, Antiques, Massacre Cave
- **Camp Verde - Cottonwood** *(43 miles)* Verde Canyon Railroad, Wineries
- **Flagstaff** *(96 miles)* - Snow Bowl, Lowell Observatory, Meteor Crater
- **Grand Canyon** *(123 miles)* - Hiking, White Water Rafting
- **Jerome** *(35 miles)* - Art Galleries, Gold King Mine and Ghost Town
- **Kingman** *(149 miles)* - Grand Canyon West, Skywalk, Zipline
- **Lake Havasu City** *(191 miles)* - Casinos, London Bridge, Boating
- **Navajo Nation** *(228 miles)* - Antelope Canyon, Canyon de Chelly
- **Payson** *(99 miles)* - Tonto National Forest, Mogollon Rim, Rim Country Museum and Zane Grey Cabin
- **Sedona** *(67 miles)* - Galleries, Slide Rock State Park, Oak Creek Canyon
- **Scottsdale** *(109 miles)* - Shopping, Dining, OdySea Aquarium
- **Wickenburg** *(59 miles)* - Western Museums, Vulture Mine and Ghost Town
- **Williams** *(69 miles)* - Grand Canyon Railroad, Grand Canyon Deer Farm, Bearizona

Photo: Blushing Cactus Photography

Lantern Festival
in·tro·spect
intrō'spekt

verb: examine one's own thoughts or feelings
~ Merriam-Webster

Locals Insider Tips for *Beautiful Gardens*

Mountain Gardening for Newcomers

by Lisa Watters-Lain, Arizona's garden gal

High-altitude gardening is different from gardening at lower elevations. Combine our altitude with Arizona's dry climate, bright air and ever-present mountain winds, and you pretty much can forget what you learned from gardening in other parts of the country. The high country of Arizona is unique, from its water to the soil, or lack thereof. If you've moved from the deserts or low country of Southern California, you really, really need to read on to learn how to be a successful gardener in these conditions.

Our local USDA garden zone is 6b with a definite influence from zones 7 and 8. This defines our area as mild, but we experience a distinct winter with nightly freezing temperatures. The secret when buying plants is to look for those that grow in zones 7 and lower. Stay away from growing desert plants meant for zones 10 and 11.

Low-winter temperatures provide the chill necessary to grow all the deciduous fruits and perennials that thrive in colder climates. The list includes apples, peaches, cherries, grapes and berries. This climate also is conducive to blooming deciduous shrubs such as lilacs, forsythias, hardy camellias, rose of Sharons, butterfly bushes and Russian sages.

Our cool season is so mild we can garden and design landscapes 12 months of the year. Broccoli, spinach, cabbages, a variety of lettuces and Brussels sprouts are available at local garden centers and can be planted in early summer for harvests at Thanksgiving and Christmas. Few places in the country allow this type of two-season harvests. Visit Watters Garden Center for my free Vegetable Planting Calendar for Prescott gardens.

A mild, cool season also is a boon for gardeners who grow for color. A splash of flowers blooming through the snow is an oasis of cheer during our winters. Our best winter-blooming flowers include pansies, snapdragons, violas, dusty millers, Johnny-jump-ups and ornamental kales.

All are available at garden centers and should be planted before the cold weather makes its debut so they are entirely rooted. I fully expect my garden to provide brilliant color for each of our family's holiday parties and on through the rest of the winter.

Never underestimate the Arizona sun, wind and dry air at this elevation. They are major influences in determining which plants do well in our landscapes and which ones don't.

Informed selectivity is essential when choosing plants for an Arizona mountain landscape. This region does best with plants that have thick, leathery leaves because they allow plants to retain extra moisture and to be less prone to tearing during the area's fierce windstorms. This is when it pays to talk to a gardening expert with experience dealing with local landscapes; it can save you a whole lot of time, energy and expense in creating your landscape.

Mountain soils change from home to home, even on the same street. In many landscapes, the soil in the front yard is different from that in the backyard. You need to learn how plants react in each new garden location.

Local soils typically are either sandy or heavy clay with very little organic material; soil preparation for planting is of extreme importance. It demands the addition of organic mulch to your soil to either hold in the moisture for granite soils or to keep clay soils from compacting. Our soil is alkaline, so don't add either lime or wood ashes as they increase its already high pH. Instead, local gardens benefit from additives that lower the soil's pH.

Lisa Watters-Lain can be found throughout the week at Watters Garden Center, 1815 W. Iron Springs Road in Prescott, or contacted through her website at WattersGardenCenter.com or FB.com/WattersGardenCenter.

9 Best-Smelling Spring Flowers for Mountain Landscapes

by Lisa Watters-Lain, Arizona's garden gal

Due to the genetic manipulation that has gone into their creation, many modern flowers no longer are fragrant. The plants have been bred to be full and bushy, disease resistant or perpetually blooming, and these virtues often come at the sacrifice of scent. Heirloom flowers are usually the best bet for a scented garden. If you'd like to include some fragrance in your garden, here are tips for getting the most from your scented flowers. Plant them where you'll be able to enjoy their fragrances most frequently: alongside paths, patios, near windows that can be opened and in containers by doorways. Plants smell their best early in the morning and at dusk. Plant in large clumps for the most substantial impact. The scent of flowers will dissipate if they are planted in wide open, windy areas. Spread fragrant plants throughout the yard so different scents don't compete with each other. Some plants are most fragrant in the evening. Plant them near your dining/entertaining areas. Plants with fragrant leaves are even more potent when the leaves are crushed underfoot. Look for fragrant ground covers and lawn alternatives that can withstand foot traffic.

Here are the top-scented local plants known for their unique scents. They are listed by general seasons but may bloom earlier or later in individual gardens.

No. 1 Carnation (*Dianthus*)
Summer Blooming Perennial
The spicy scent of carnations is one of the most familiar flower fragrances. Make sure you purchase a variety that says explicitly it is fragrant because many have been bred for larger flowers and longer blooms but have little to no scent left.

No. 2 Daphne (*Daphne cneorum*)
Spring Blooming Perennial
Daphne is a beautiful knee-high shrub with glossy green leaves and flowers with a true perfume quality scent that is a mix of sweet florals and earthy undertones. It is easily grown in shady mountain gardens and retains its green leaves right through winter.

No. 3 Fragrant Columbine (*Aquilegia*)
Spring Blooming Perennial
Aquilegia fragrans is slightly different from the more common garden columbines, although they are almost as easy to grow. They have creamy

Gardenia

white flowers that give off a lovely honeysuckle-like scent.

No. 4 Gardenia (*Gardenia jasminoides*)
Summer Blooming Perennial

Gardenias are one of the most fragrant flowers; some noses even find them too strong for close encounters. Several new mountain introductions can now be grown outdoors perennially, remaining evergreen through winter.

No. 5 Lavender (*Lavendula*)
Summer Blooming Perennial

Lavender has one of the most beloved scents of all flowers. When used in cooking its musky floral fragrance even will permeate the palate.

No. 6 Lilac (*Syringa vulgaris*)
Spring Blooming Perennial

The sweet, floral fragrance of lilacs announces spring. You can get a hint of it as the buds start to swell, but once the flowers open, lilacs can perfume the entire neighborhood. New dwarf varieties bloom for months of lilac enjoyment; like the new Bloomerang lilac that blooms multiple times each year.

No. 7 Lily of the Valley (*Convalariam*)
Spring Blooming Perennial

With their rich, sweet fragrance, lilies of the valley flowers are a favorite addition to commercial perfumes. Enjoy the scent throughout the shady parts of mountain landscape.

No. 8 Peony (*Paeonia*)
Spring Blooming Perennial

Peonies would be beautiful enough to grow just for their flowers, but the lush blooms also have a bright, clean scent very similar to roses. Very long lasting as cut flowers, the plant is a low-water user, distasteful to animals.

No. 9 Sweet Alyssum (*Lobularia*)
Spring through Fall Annual

This low-growing plant is so covered with flowers it looks like a white carpet on the ground or turns containers into giant snowballs. Its fragrance is a unique blend of a honey-like quality with a floral finish.

Greater Prescott LIVING at Its Best! 201

serene
/sə-ˈrēn/

adjective: clear and free of storms or unpleasant change

~ Merriam-Webster

Photo: Rod Hendrick
Goldwater Lake

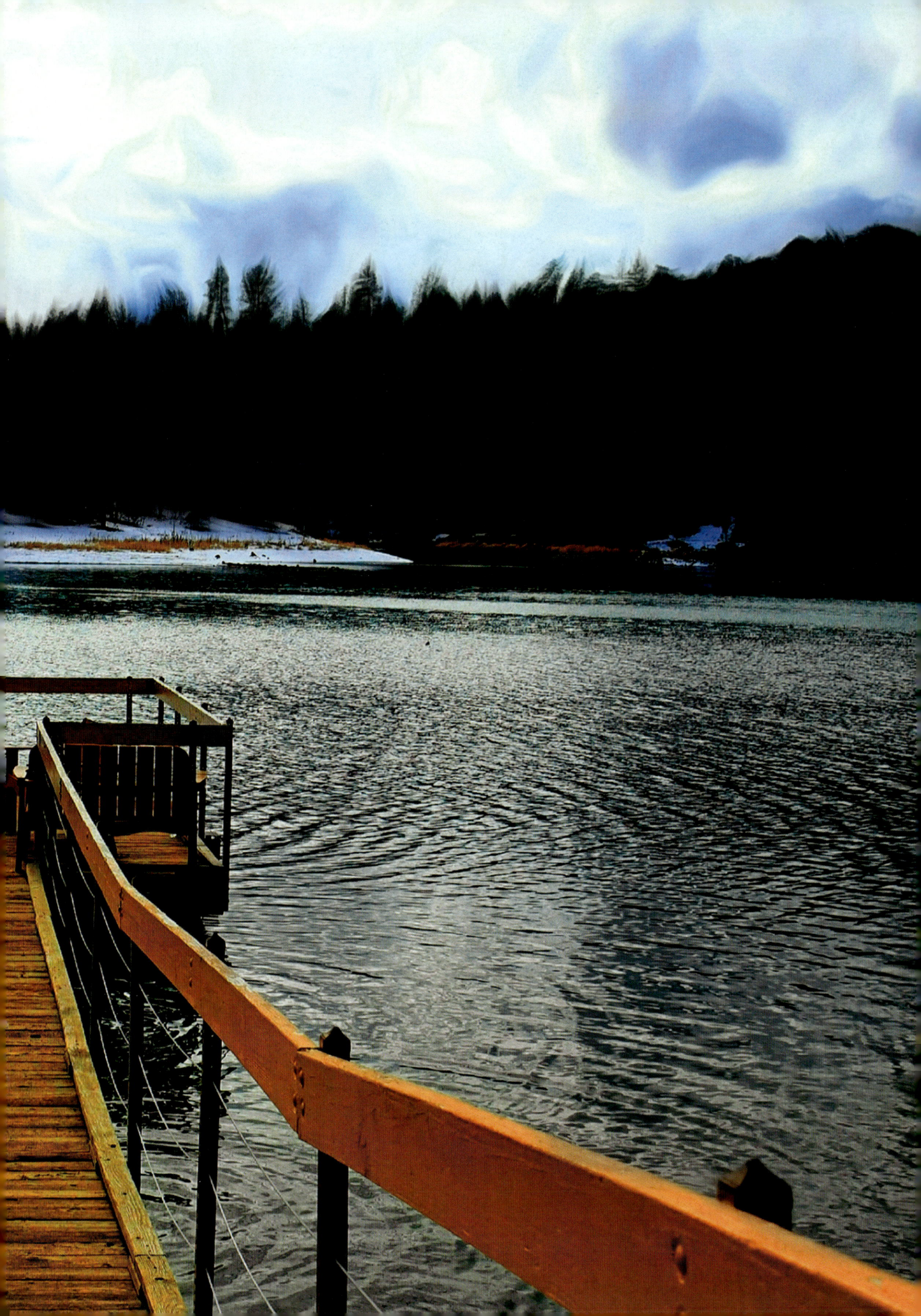

YRMC and the Community
Over 75 Years of

by Ken Boush, Director, Marketing and Communications, Yavapai Regional Medical Center

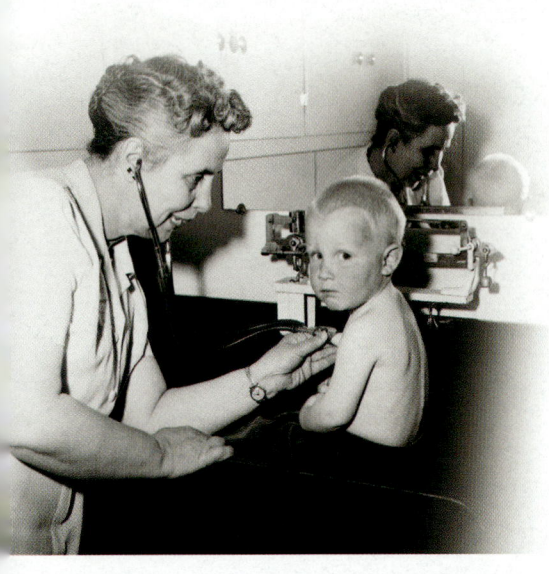

Dr. Florence Yount delivered the first baby born at Prescott Community Hospital, now Yavapai Regional Medical Center, on March 1, 1943.

Prescott Community Hospital – now Yavapai Regional Medical Center – was converted from a grade school.

On March 1, 1943, Prescott Community Hospital – now Yavapai Regional Medical Center (YRMC) – opened its doors to care for patients. By 9 p.m. that day, Florence Yount, M.D., had delivered the first baby born at the new hospital.

"This marked the official launch of an important relationship between YRMC and the community," said John Amos, President and CEO of YRMC. "From the beginning, the people of this community understood the significance of creating a health-care delivery system to meet their unique needs. They believed firmly that lots of good would result from neighbors caring for neighbors."

A History of Community Support

That belief was clear as community members pitched in to ensure Prescott Community Hospital – converted from Jefferson Elementary School on Marina Street – was equipped and ready to care for patients.

Many longtime Prescott residents and community leaders were involved in efforts to establish the hospital as a nonprofit provider, available to all people in the community. A group of community members wrote the cornerstone document – "Prescott Community Hospital Association Inc., a Non-Profit Corporation in the State of Arizona" – that designated the hospital as a community-based, not-for-profit provider. They also selected the previously closed Jefferson Elementary School – which was purchased for $1,000 – as the location of the hospital.

These same people, and many others in the community, were involved in ensuring the hospital was equipped and ready to provide care.

Dr. Yount traveled the region looking for beds, stoves, tables – any kind of hospital equipment she could buy. Her efforts helped convert the school cafeteria into an operating room. Physicians' spouses went door-to-door for donations. All of the businesses stepped up so the community could open a hospital in the abandoned school building.

A Milestone Vote

Fast forward several decades and the community was again at a crossroads that concerned health care.

In 1960, the community voted to establish the Central Yavapai Hospital District. This was followed in 1962 by a vote to build a new hospital to replace Prescott Community Hospital.

There was lots of excitement in the community surrounding the vote. Many believed it was the first time – at least in Arizona – that a nonprofit, local association took over a government hospital. The agreement involved the hospital providing a clinic that would replace the county hospital. Then, with a Hill-Burton Grant from the federal government, a wing was built to the south that would become a dedicated hospital.

An article in the Prescott Evening Courier characterized the vote as part of a larger effort that would allow the community to "attract new industry and other economic assets, including college and tourism, so that local residents will benefit from more job opportunities and a higher standard of living."

In 1964, the new hospital relocated to its current location on Willow Creek Road and changed its name to Yavapai Community Hospital. The hospital underwent another name change in

Yavapai Regional Medical Center East in Prescott Valley

Community - Based Health Care

Yavapai Regional Medical Center's Hybrid Operating Room – considered to be one of America's finest

1984, becoming Yavapai Regional Medical Center. This change reflected the scope of its advanced medical services and growing service area.

YRMC Heads East to Prescott Valley

The rapid growth of Prescott Valley helped spur another important milestone for the community: the opening of YRMC East in 2006.

"People were waiting for YRMC to open. They wanted it here. They needed the medical services," said former Prescott Valley Mayor Harvey Skoog, who had long advocated for the hospital. "We had the opening of the hospital, and here I thought it would just be a hospital, but we have all these other services, like the BreastCare Center and Imaging Services. Today we have approximately 45,000 people, and this is just a phenomenal part of our growth."

YRMC's Journey: Moving Forward, Maintaining Original Values

For Robbie Nicol, MBA, CFRE, Executive Director of Community Outreach and Philanthropy at YRMC, our journey illustrates the community's commitment to locally operated health care as well as its support for advanced facilities and services.

"This is part of the DNA of our community," she said. "I think about how the community coalesced to equip the cafeteria-turned-operating-room at the first hospital on Marina Street. Then I think about the support YRMC received for its hybrid surgical suite at YRMC West. Both were possible because the people we serve believe in community-based health care and support state-of-the-art services."

Today, YRMC accomplishes this through a vast network of health-care services throughout the community. In addition to YRMC West and YRMC East, the community has access to excellent health care through a total of 26 primary and specialty YRMC PhysicianCare Clinics in Prescott, Prescott Valley, Chino Valley and Bagdad.

"YRMC also cares for people with chronic and specialized needs," Nicol said. "The BreastCare Center at YRMC and the James Family Heart Center at YRMC are examples of lifesaving, specialty services."

Telling the Story of Health Care in Our Community

During YRMC's 75th anniversary celebration in 2018, many Prescott and Prescott Valley residents shared their stories of life in the community. Their video interviews, stories and images were gathered as part of the YRMC Memory Catcher project. Visit YRMC HealthConnect (yrmchealthconnect.org/memory-catcher) to explore YRMC's history as told by the community.

Memory Catcher visitors will meet folks who have grown up in the community or are new to the area with wonderful, interesting and amusing stories to share. These anecdotes create a tapestry that tell the story of YRMC and its more than 75-year relationship with the community.

John Amos, President and CEO of Yavapai Regional Medical Center, tours the new Cardiac Catheterization Laboratory at YRMC West during its construction, which took place in 2018 and 2019.

The frog in the well knows nothing of the mighty ocean.
- Japanese Proverb

Photo: Blushing Cactus Photography
Watson Lake

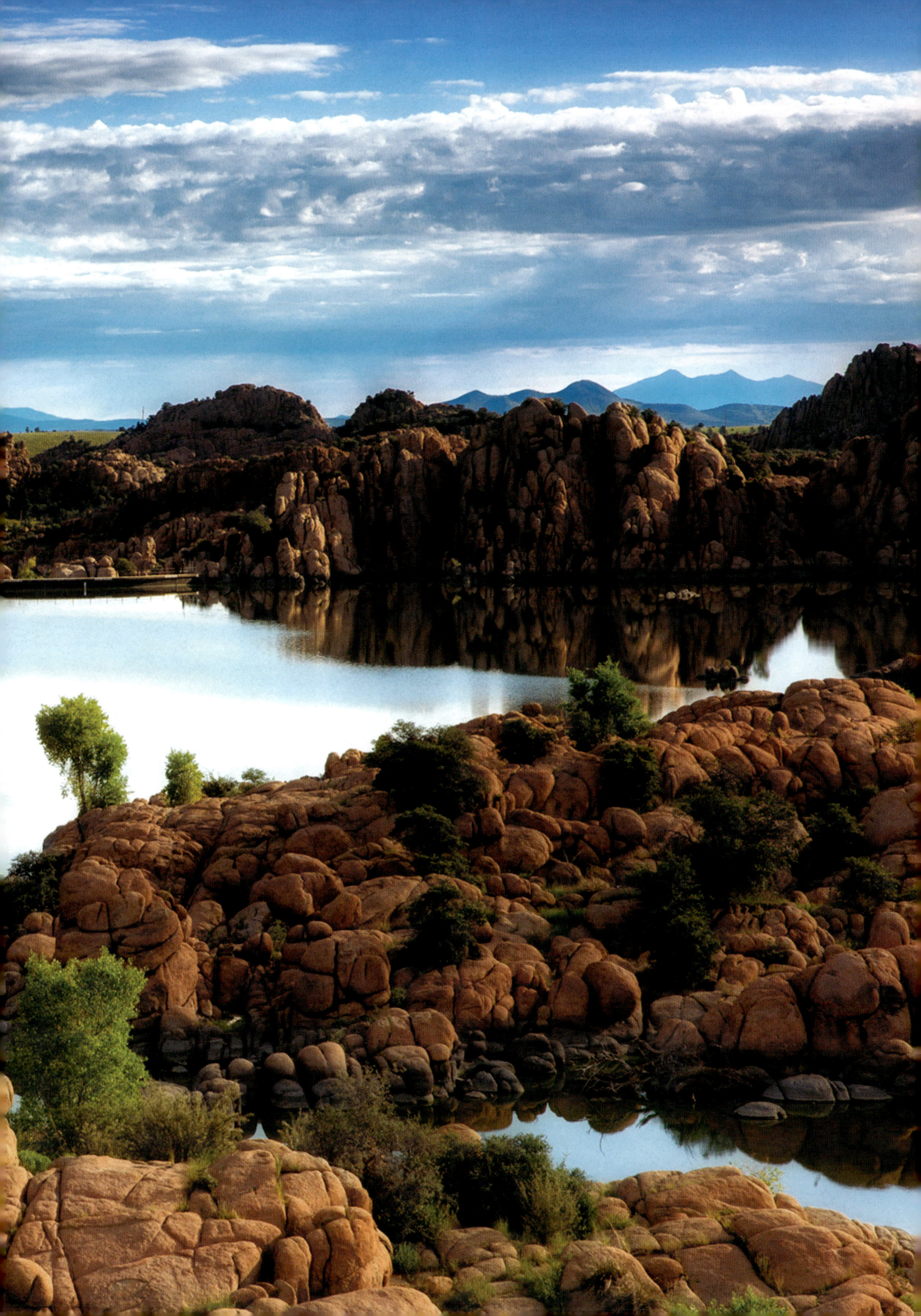

World's Largest Gingerbread Village

Photo: Lynne LaMaster – eNews AZ

Photos: Bea Lueck

Photo: Lynne LaMaster – eNews AZ

208 ANNUAL SHOWCASE EDITION 2020

go.

Wahiba Sands, Oman, 2019

rox travel
roxtravel.com
800-690-7660

Special Section: Restaurants

Greater Prescott

PRESCOTT

American

AUGIE'S
1721 AZ-69
928-777-0330
www.augiesprescott.com
American food with unique flare, bar, chefs table

BIGA
623 Miller Valley Rd.
928-227-2543
www.bigaprescott.com
American cuisine and Farm-to-Fork Family Suppers

BISTRO ST. MICHAEL
205 W. Gurley St.
928-778-2500
www.bistrostmikes.com
Signature cuisine where locals eat, full bar

DRY GULCH
1630 Adams Ave.
928-778-9693
www.drygulchsteakhouse.com
Western style steak house, bar

GURLEY STREET GRILL
230 W. Gurley St.
928-445-3388
www.gurleystgrill.com
Light fare, cold beer, burgers and wraps

PRESCOTT JUNCTION
1121 E. Sheldon St.
928-778-4029
www.prescottjunction.com
Comfort food and all-you-can-eat breakfast bar

BiGA

THE OFFICE
128 N. Cortez St.
928-445-1211
www.theofficerestaurant.com
Sports bar, southwestern dishes, burgers

THE PALACE RESTAURANT & SALOON
120 S. Montezuma St.
928-541-1996
www.whiskeyrowpalace.com
Historic old West bar and restaurant

WAFFLE IRON CAFE
420 E. Sheldon St.
928-445-9944
Waffles, pancakes flavorful breakfast, brunch

WAFFLES-N-MORE
1365 Iron Springs Rd. Ste 1
928-778-3039
Local favorite, breakfast, brunch, family style

Asian

CHI'S CUISINE
114 N. Cortez St.
928-778-5390
Common, authentic Thai and Chinese food, crab puffs

Bakery

WILDFLOWER BREAD
3201 State Hwy 69
928-717-1700
www.wildflowerbread.com
Soups, salads, sandwiches, pasta

Bar

BIRDCAGE SALOON
160 S. Montezuma St.
928-778-9921
Funky, old-timey watering hole & live music

JERSEY LILLY SALON
116 W. Montezuma St.
928-541-7854
www.jerseylillysaloon.com
The only balcony overlooking the Courthouse Square!

JJ'S SALOON
444 W. Goodwin St.
928-445-9867
Dive Bar, Karaoke, Pub

Murphy's

LYZZARD'S LOUNGE
120 N. Cortez St.
928-778-2244
Lyzzards Specialty Elixirs and Draft Beers!

PUDGE & ASTI'S SPORTS BAR & GRILL
721 6th St.
928-778-2893
Full bar, 24 beers on tap, limited lunch & dinner.

THE FINAL SCORE SPORTS BAR & GRILL
1011 Commerce Dr., Suite A
928-778-2211
Sports Bar & Grill

THE WINDSOCK LOUNGE
1365 W. Iron Springs Rd
928-776-7309
www.thewindsocklounge.net
Bar, live entertainment, shuffleboard and pool tables

THE POINT BAR AND LOUNGE
114 N. Montezuma St
928-237-9027
www.thepointbarandlounge.com
A prohibition-era style speakeasy, live music

BBQ

LUCY DEE'S BBQ
669 E. Sheldon St.
928-237-5765
www.lucydeesbbq.com
Meats are smoked daily on premise, fresh sides

MARK'S BEER GARDEN
1590 Swenson St.
928-515-1044
www.marksbeergarden.com
Beer, wine and food, BBQ, live music, karaoke

UNCLE BUD'S PLACE
1781 E. HWY 69
928-227-0092
www.unclebudsplace.com
Cajun, BBQ, family recipes, Homestyle take-out

Brewery

PRESCOTT BREWING COMPANY
130 W. Gurley St
928-771-2795
www.prescottbrewingcompany.com
Traditional pub food, fresh, handcrafted beer.

COPPERTOP ALEHOUSE
220 S. Montezuma St.
928-351-7712
www.coppertopalehouse.com
Traditional European alehouse, German-style grub

GRANITE MOUNTAIN BREWING
123 N. Cortez St.
928-778-5535
www.granitemountainbrewing.com
Small-batch brews, mead, cider, Arizona wine

LAZY G BREWHOUSE
220 W. Leroux St.
928-445-2994
www.lazygbrewhouse.com
Craft beer, American cuisine and dog-friendly

Burgers, Ice Cream, Gelato

MARINO'S MOB BURGER & ICE CREAM
113 S. Cortez St.
928-515-1690
Historic Burger, Breakfast, Ice Cream and Gelato Shop

210 ANNUAL SHOWCASE EDITION 2020

Special Section: Restaurants

Dining Directory

CAFE

DINNER BELL CAFE
321 W. Gurley St.
928-445-9888
Delicious food and nice atmosphere

PARK PLAZA LIQUOR AND DELI
402 W. Goodwin St.
928-541-9894
www.parkplazaliquor.com
Wood-fired pizza & wings, liquor/beer/wine/cigars

ZEKE'S EATIN' PLACE
1781 E. Route 69, Ste. 35
928-776-4602
www.zekeseatinplace.com
Western country-style food with huge portions

CHINESE

BEIJING GARDEN
1042 Willow Creek Rd., #105
928-778-5276
Traditional Mandarin Chinese food

CANTON DRAGON
377 N. Montezuma St.
928-771-8118
Cantonese style food. generous portions

COFFEE

THE ESPRESSO BARN
1301 E. Gurley St., Ste. B
928-288-2052
www.theespressobarn.com
Bakery and collectibles, comfy coffee shop

THE PORCH
226 N. Montezuma St.
928-227-2790
Coffee shop, scones, crepes, bagels and quiche

THIRD SHOT COFFEE
3106 Gateway Mall
928-227-3465
www.thirdshotcoffee.com
Coffee house, bakery, breakfast and lunch

WILD IRIS COFFEEHOUSE
124 S. Granite St, Ste. E
928-778-5155
www.wildiriscoffee.com
Coffee, bakery, pastries, sandwiches

DISTILLERY

THUMB BUTTE DISTILLERY
400 N. Washington Ave.
928-443-8498
www.thumbbuttedistillery.com
Distillery for whiskey, gin and vodka

FINE DINING

MURPHY'S
201 N. Cortez St.
928-445-4044
www.murphysprescott.com
Prime rib, seafood, burgers, sandwiches

THE FINN
3150 Touchmark Blvd.
928-708-3131
www.thefinnprescott.com
Fine dining, fresh, local food, signature cocktails

Hawk & Hound
Photo - Jordyn Vixie

THE PEACOCK DINING ROOM
122 E. Gurley St.
928-778-9434
www.hassayampainn.com/dining
American cuisine, lounge, full bar, entertainment

FUSION, AMERICAN, VEGETARIAN FRIENDLY

ATMESFIR
232 S. Montezuma St.
928-445-1929
www.atmesfir.com
The best local ingredients at the peak of their season

GASTROPUB

BARLEY HOUND
234 S. Cortez St.
928-237-4506
www.thebarleyhound.com
Gastropub, beer, craft cocktails, fun atmosphere

GREEN CAFÉ

RAVEN CAFE
142 N. Cortez St.
928-717-0009
www.ravencafe.com
Burgers, small bites, sandwiches

HEALTH FOOD, VEGETARIAN, VEGAN

FARM PROVISIONS
148 N. Montezuma St.
928-776-3001
www.farmprovisionsaz.com
True farm to table experience, seasonal menus

MS. NATURALS
318 W. Gurley
928-515-1584
www.msnaturalsprescott.com
Smoothies, sandwiches, bagels, salads. vegan

THE LOCAL
520 W. Sheldon St.
928-237-4724
www.localprescott.com
Unique and creative food, made from scratch

INDIAN

TAJ MAHAL RESTAURANT & BAR
124 N. Montezuma St.
928-445-5752
www.aztajmahal.com
Indian Cuisine, bar, live entertainment.

ITALIAN

CARMELLA'S
120 N. Montezuma St.
928-277-4948
www.carmellasprescott.com
Authentic Mediterreanean Italian dishes, bar

LIMONCELLO
218 W. Goodwin St.
480-399-9978
www.limopizzeria.com
Homemade Italian food, salads, pasta & pizzeria.

PAPA'S ITALIAN RESTURAUNT
129 N. Cortez St.
928-776-4880
www.papasitalianrestaurant.com
Pasta, pizza, full Bar

ROSA'S PIZZERIA
330 W. Gurley St.
928-445-7400
www.rosaspizzeria.com
Authentic Sicilian and Southern Italian recipes

JAPANESE

SUSHI MAN
1355 W. Iron Springs Rd
928-227-2151
www.sushimanprescott.wixsite.com
Authentic Japanese Cuisine

MEXICAN

ARTUROS MEXICAN RESTAURANT
503 Miller Valley Rd.
928-445-5787
www.arturosaz.com
Mexican food, prepared daily, fresh ingredients

Bistro St. Michael

CASA ALVAREZ
321 W. Gurley St.
928-445-9888
Homemade Mexican-style food from Jalisco, Mexico

Special Section: Restaurants

FARM Provisions

CASA SANCHEZ
1459 W. Gurley St.
928-771-9505
Homemade Mexican-style food from Jalisco, Mexico

LINDO MEXICO
1260 Gail Gardner Way, Suite 101
928-227-0924
www.lindomexico.netwaiter.com
Mexican Food, full bar

MAYA'S RESTURANT
512 S. Montezuma St.
928-776-8346
www.mayarestaurant.com
Authentic Mexican food, BYOB

SPICY STREATS
1201 Iron Springs Rd, Ste. 13
928-277-8210
www.spicystreats.com
Authentic Mexican street food

TACO DON'S
624 Miller Valley Rd.
928-778-6246
Mexican food, drive thru, inside seating.

Night Club

MATT'S SALOON
112 S. Montezuma St
928-776-2974
www.mattssaloon.com
Drink specials, off-track betting, live music

Pizza

BILL'S PIZZA
107 S. Cortez St.
928-443-0800
www.billspizzaprescott.com
Pizza, salads, local micro brews and wines

TWO MAMA'S PIZZA
221 N. Cortez St.
928-443-9455
www.twomamaspizza.com
Specialty pizza, sandwiches, salads, desserts

Pub

PRESCOTT PUBLIC HOUSE
218 W. Gurley St.
928-277-8062
www.azprescottpublichouse.com
Local craft beer, small bites & BBQ.

Southwest Inspired Tapas & Cuisine

EL GATO AZUL
316 W. Goodwin St.
928-445-1070
www.elgatoazulprescott.com
Over 50 Tapas, pasta, seafood, live music

Southwest, American

LONE SPUR CAFE
106 W. Gurley St.
928-445-8202
www.lonespurcafe.com
Cowboy food, cowboy service and cowboy charm

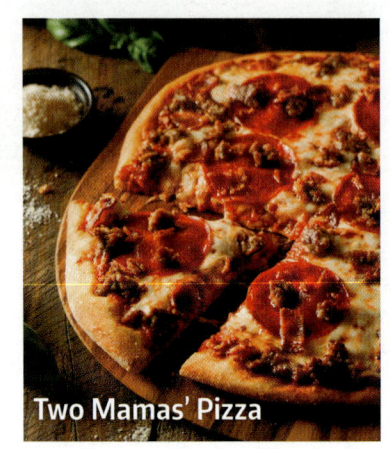

Two Mamas' Pizza

Southwest, Cajun & Mexican Cuisine

IRON SPRINGS CAFE
1501 W. Iron Springs Rd.
928-443-8848
www.ironspringscafe.com
Cajun and Southwest cuisines

Steakhouse

JOHN'S CHOPHOUSE
217 W. Gurley St.
928-458-7393
Steak, wild game, seafood, vegetarian, vegan dishes

TEXAS ROADHOUSE
3310 Gateway Blvd.
928-778-7427
www.texasroadhouse.com
Hand-Cut Steaks, ribs, made-from-scratch sides

Tasting Room

BACK ALLEY WINE BAR
156 S. Montezuma St. (Back Alley)
480-570-5131
Arizona wine flights, craft beer and cider, live music

FLYING LEAP VINEYARDS TASTING ROOM
124 S. Granite St.
520-954-2935
www.flyingleapvineyards.com
Tasting room, full-service, direct distributor

SUPERSTITION MEADERY
120 W. Gurley St.
928-458-4256
www.superstitionmeadery.com
More than 10 varieties of Mead, Tapas and dessert

Thai

TARA THAI
115 S. Cortez St.
928-772-3249
www.tarathaiprescott.com
Thai food, open lunch and dinner.

THAI HOUSE CAFE
230 N. Cortez St.
928-777-0041
Authentic Thai food, excellent curry

PRESCOTT VALLEY

American

BACKBURNER FAMILY RESTAURANT
8400 E. Long Mesa Dr.
928-772-9298
www.backburneraz.com
Omelettes, biscuits/gravy, burgers, sandwich

GABBY'S GRILL
2982 N. Park Ave. Suite B
928-775-6656
www.gabbysgrill.com
Upscale bar & grill, sandwiches, steaks, chicken

Spicy Streats

GABBY'S KITCHEN PV
8164 E. Spouse Dr.
928-277-1787
Family style restaurant, breakfast and brunch

JAMIE'S WAFFLE EXPRESS
3050 N. Windsong Dr.
928-772-3131
Mexican and American classics

Brewery

LONESOME VALLEY BREWING
3040 N Windsong Dr, Ste. 101
928-515-3541
www.lonesomevalleybrewing.com
Homemade pub food, craft brewery

Special Section: Restaurants

CAFE

SALLY B'S CAFE
7680 E. State Route 69
928-772-2053
Serves breakfast, lunch and dinner

ITALIAN

GABRIELLA'S RISTORANTE
8930 E. Valley Rd.
928-227-0358
Select your own' pasta & sauce, specialties

MEXICAN

LINDO MEXICO RESTAURANT
5684 E. State Hwy 69
928-227-1512
Mexican food, featured molcajetes

PLAZA BONITA
8280 Spouse Dr.
928-775-7014
www.myplazabonita.com
Traditional Sonoran style Mexican food, full bar

TASTING ROOM

RAFTER ELEVEN
2985 Centre Ct, Ste. B
928-227-2050
www.raftereleven.com
Wine, coffee, olive oils and spices

THAI

THAI CAFE
3050 N. Windsong Dr.
928-237-5293
www.thaicafearizona.com
Thai food with lots of choices

TOI'S THAI KITCHEN
7545 E. Addis Ave.
928-237-9099
www.toisthaikitchen.com
Fresh ingredients, Thai fare

DEWEY - HUMBOLT

BBQ

LUCKY'S BBQ & BURGERS
171 S. State Route 69
928-632-0077
Known for BBQ, brisket tacos.

Barley Hound Photo - Jordyn Vixie

CAFE

BLUE HILLS CAFE
12262 E. Bradhsaw Mountain Rd
928-772-7893
www.bluehillscafeaz.com
American Cuisine · Breakfast & Brunch

MAMMAS KITCHEN
2735 S. Hwy 69
928-632-5411
Kitchen Cafe, breadfast, lunch

RANDALL'S RESTAURANT
1030 Prescott Country Club Blvd
928-772-8812
American, breakfast, Italian

ITALIAN

JACKIE BOYZ LITTLE ITALY
12910 E. Main St
928-632-1010
www.jackieboyzlittleitaly.com
Authentic Italian Cuisine

MEXICAN

PUERTO VALLARTA
11901 E. State Route 69
928-772-4460
Mexican food, meeting room

PIZZA

GUIDO'S PIZZA
150 S. State Route 69
928-632-5950
Pizza, Italian food.

STEAKHOUSE

LEFT T'S STEAKHOUSE
150 S. State Route 69
928-632-1388
www.steaksaz.com
Steaks, Burgers, BBQ

CHINO VALLEY

AMERICAN

GABBY'S KITCHEN CV
2235 S. State Route 89, Ste. B2
928-636-6003
Family style restaurant, breakfast and brunch

BBQ

BIG DADDY E'S BBQ
380 Butterfield Rd.
928-515-2344
www.bdebbq.com
"Best BBQ in AZ" Smoke house BBQ, open for lunch and dinner.

BREWERY

BARNSTAR BREWERY
4050 N. Tonto Rd.
928-442-2337
www.barnstarbrew.com
Tastings, open Saturday and Sunday 12-5

BURGER

BONN-FIRE CHILLIN & GRILLIN RESTAURANT
1667 S. State Route 89
928-636-7410
www.bonn-fire.com
Homestyle recipes, made from scratch, open for lunch and dinner, Happy Hour 3-6 PM

LUCY'S BAR & GRILL
3020 AZ-89
928-636-7314
1/2 lb. burgers, thick fries, big salads

CAFE

SKILLETS CAFE
990 Arizona-89
928-237-5235
Breakfast & brunch, omelettes and more

EVENT/WEDDING

THE WINDMILL HOUSE
1460 W. Road 4 N
928-636-1700
www.windmillhouseaz.com
Premier wedding venue and event venue

ITALIAN

AROMA PIZZA
854 S. State Route 89
928-636-3770
East Coast style pizza and Italian food.

PASGHETTIS PASTA JOINT
1150 N. State Route 89
928-636-2921
www.pasghettispastajoint.weebly.com
Pasta, stromboli, salads, steaks, burgers

MEXICAN

ARTUROS MEXICAN RESTAURANT
900 S. State Route 89
928-636-0221
www.arturosaz.com
Serves lunch & dinner, Mexican food, catering.

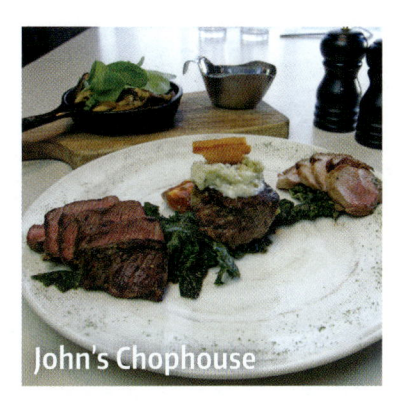

John's Chophouse

CASA GRANDE MEXICAN RESTAURANT
443 Butterfield Rd.
928-636-7275
Tex-Mex restaurant

EL CHARRO NORTE
2789 N. Arizona Trl.
928-460-5869
www.elcharronorte.com
Mexican Cuisine, steaks, specialty drinks

WINE BAR/TASTING

GRANITE CREEK VINEYARD
2515 N. Rd. 1 E
928-636-2003
www.granitecreekvineyards.com
Award-winning local Arizona wines

Special Section: Restaurants

MURPHY'S
An ESTABLISHMENT of GOOD TASTE
PRIME RIB · FRESH SEAFOOD · BAKERY

201 N. Cortez Street
928.445.4044
MurphysPrescott.com

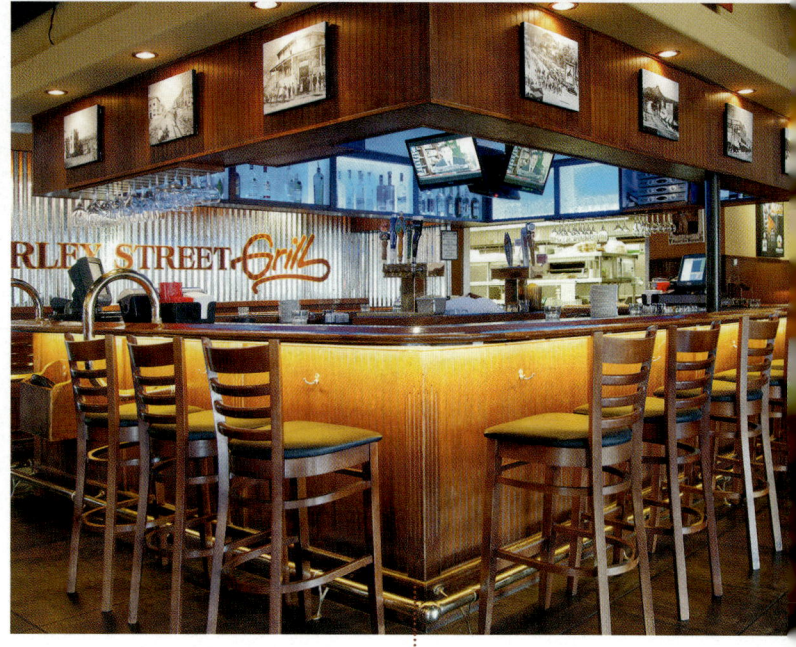

230 W. Gurley Street
928.445.3388
GurleyStGrill.com

GURLEY ST. Grill
DOWNTOWN PRESCOTT

The Office Cantina
Prescott, Arizona

128 N. Cortez Street
928.445.1211
TheOfficeRestaurant.com

Murphy's Restaurant

Enjoy sophisticated lunches, delectable dinners & relaxing Sunday champagne brunches in an elegant, historic setting.

- LUNCH
- DINNER
- SUNDAY BRUNCH
- PRIVATE ROOMS

With impeccable food, gracious service and the ambiance of yesteryear, life's moments are more memorable at Murphy's.

Gurley St. Grill

Prescott's favorite neighborhood restaurant and bar!
Dine on creative and delicious comfort food, enjoy a cold beer at the bar, or celebrate that special family gathering.

- BREAKFAST
- LUNCH
- DINNER
- PRIVATE ROOMS

Whatever you're craving, come on into the Grill. We'll cook it up fresh for you!

The Office Cantina

Where salsa and sports collide! Enjoy contemporary Southwestern dishes and home made margaritas while you watch your favorite sports team on one of 25 televisions.

- LUNCH
- DINNER
- PRIVATE ROOM

You can say you're staying late at the office! We won't tell!

Photo: Christopher Marchetti - The Palace Restaurant & Saloon

John's CHOPHOUSE
A CREATIVE DINING EXPERIENCE

Monday - Thursday 3 PM to 9 PM   Friday & Saturday 3 PM to 10 PM   Closed Sundays
217 W. Gurley Street, Prescott, AZ | 928.458.7393

BiGA.
fresh. modern. local.

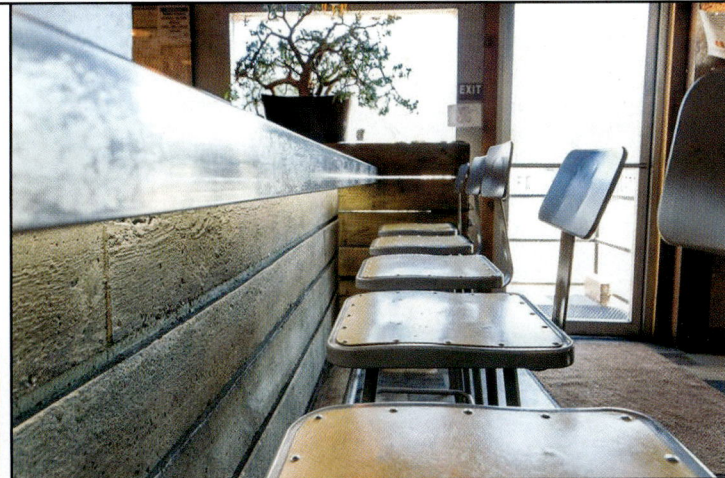

MONDAY-SATURDAY 11 AM TO 9 PM
623 MILLER VALLEY RD, PRESCOTT, AZ | 928.227.2543

Special Section: Restaurants

Two Mamas' Gourmet Pizzeria
The One That (Almost) Got Away
by Erica and Keith, Co-owners, Two Mamas' Gourmet Pizzeria

One 2013 summer evening while relaxing with my wife Erica in our home northwest of Chicago, the first of many phone calls came from Erica's sister in Prescott, Arizona. She wanted us to buy Two Mamas' Gourmet Pizzeria. Our first response was "No way." The calls continued every two to three months, and the next thing I know, it's January 2015, and we're driving a car full of our last personal belongings 1,800 miles to Prescott and Two Mamas Gourmet Pizzeria. We never looked back.

Two Mamas' is located one and a half blocks north of the Yavapai County Courthouse Plaza at 221 N. Cortez St. We feature over 25 specialty pizzas, but you can always build your own with more than 60 options of toppings and four different types of crust in four sizes each.

We make our own dough fresh daily (sometimes twice, if needed) along with our homemade sauces and dressings. We sell the sauces and dressings by the pint and quart because customers enjoy them so much. All produce, meats and cheeses are prepped each morning. Nothing is pre-packaged or pre-made to ensure that fresh-made taste.

We also have wings, calzones, pasta and subs all made fresh to order. We now carry four sizes of gluten-free pizza crust, two types of gluten-free pasta and even gluten-removed beer. We take special caution when preparing these dishes, but don't claim to be a gluten-free kitchen. We also recently added vegan cheese, vegan veggie patties and Beyond Meats crumbles as options for our pizzas.

Our pasta dishes are also "build your own." You choose the pasta type and sauce, then add meatballs, sausage, chicken, shrimp or primavera. We've expanded our pasta line from spaghetti, penne and rotini by adding ravioli, tortellini, baked ziti and chicken parmesan.

We have seven different salads in three sizes with your choice of eight dressings. You can also add chicken, shrimp, bacon or another veggie.

Our sub sandwiches are all toasted on French bread and come with chips and a pickle spear. There are 12 to choose from.

Chicken wings come in boneless, traditional bone-in and jumbo bone-in. You can have them tossed in your choice of seven sauces and choice of homemade ranch or chunky bleu cheese for dipping.

Build your own calzone with a choice of three sizes; always made with fresh ricotta cheese and our own red sauce.

Fun dine in: We have draft and bottled beer, wine by the glass or bottle and a full line of spirits for cocktails.

If there's any room left, we offer five desserts including cannolis with our own house-made filling!

We accept reservations, but they are not required. You can dine in, carry out or have our delicious food delivered.

So, whether a Prescott resident or someone just visiting, we hope you give us a try. You won't be disappointed.

See you soon.
twomamaspizza.com

> We offer five desserts including cannolis with our own house-made filling!

Signature Dishes

Specialty Pizzas
Hawaiian
Supremo
Margherita
Black and Bleu

Submarine Sandwiches
Italian Sausage
Philly Steak
Meatball
Chicken Parmesan

Pasta
Baked Ziti
Ravioli
Tortellini

221 N Cortez St
Prescott, Arizona
86301
(928) 443-9455
twomamaspizza.com

Two Mamas' Gourmet Pizzeria

Delivery, Dine in, Carry Out and Catering.

ORDER ON LINE @ TWOMAMASPIZZA.COM, DOWNLOAD THE MOBILEBYTES APP TO JOIN OUR REWARDS CLUB AND FOR APP ORDERING.

Two Mamas' Gourmet Pizzeria
221 N Cortez St
(928) 443-9455

Photos by: Gerry Groeber

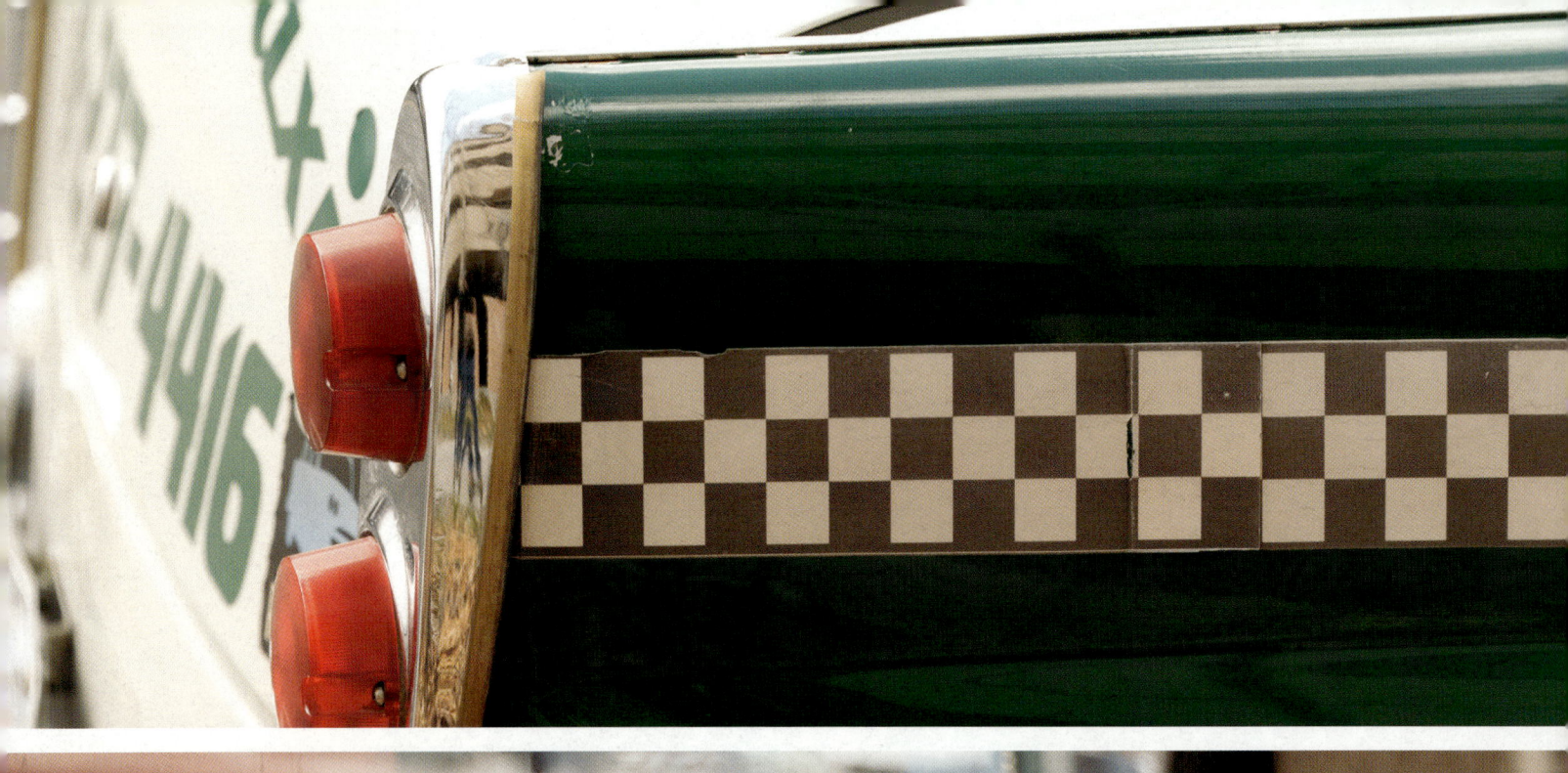

Photo by: Rod Hendrick

"What day is it?" asked Pooh.
"It's today," replied Piglet.
"My favorite day," said Pooh.
- A. A. Milne

Photo: Jess Berry

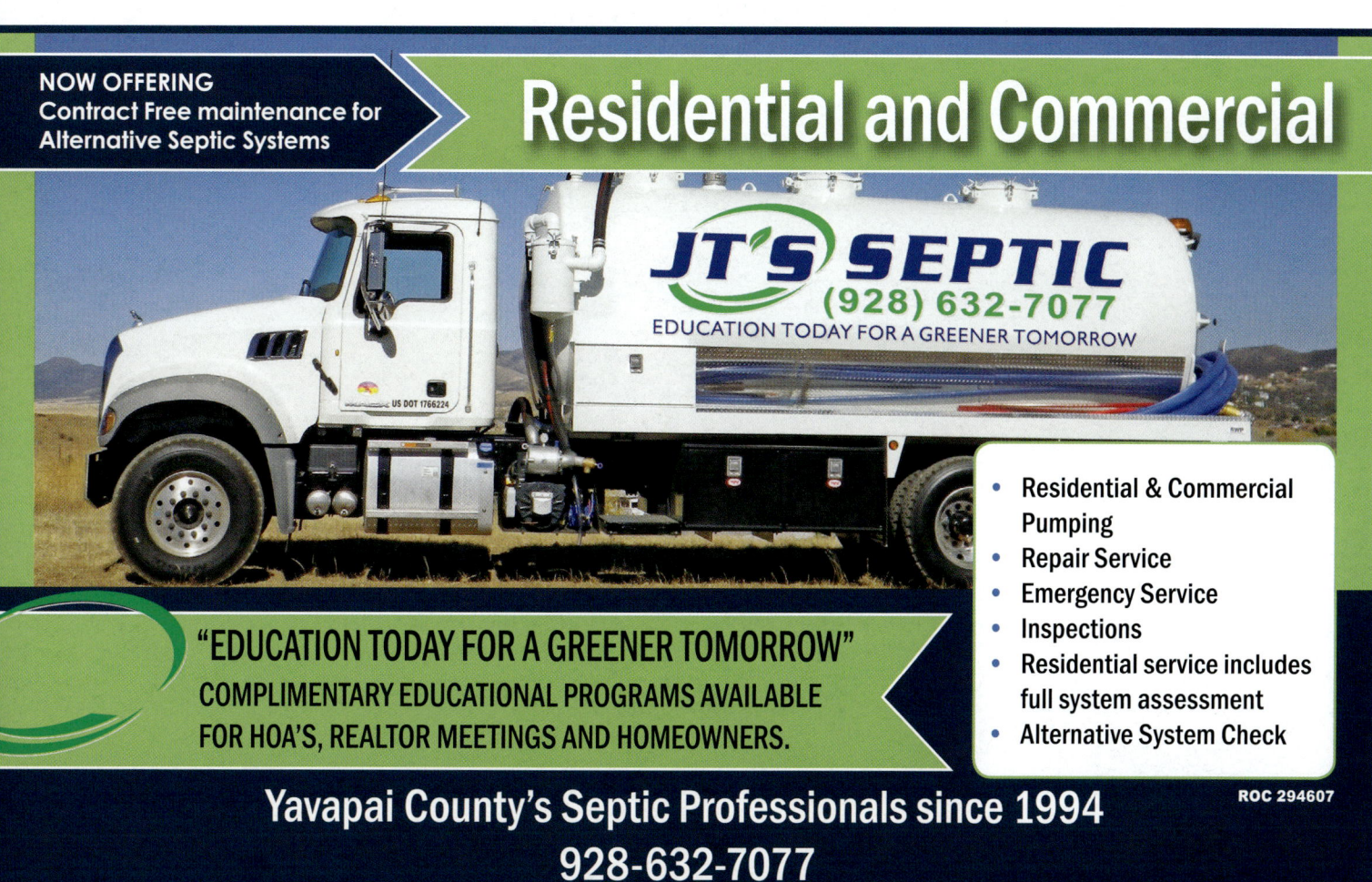

Photo: Rod Hendrick
"Snow at Watson Lake"

NOW OFFERING Contract Free maintenance for Alternative Septic Systems

Residential and Commercial

JT'S SEPTIC
(928) 632-7077
EDUCATION TODAY FOR A GREENER TOMORROW

"EDUCATION TODAY FOR A GREENER TOMORROW"
COMPLIMENTARY EDUCATIONAL PROGRAMS AVAILABLE FOR HOA'S, REALTOR MEETINGS AND HOMEOWNERS.

- Residential & Commercial Pumping
- Repair Service
- Emergency Service
- Inspections
- Residential service includes full system assessment
- Alternative System Check

ROC 294607

Yavapai County's Septic Professionals since 1994
928-632-7077
www.Jtseptic.com | Email: jt@jtseptic.com | Join us on f ACEBOOK

soar
/sôr/

verb: fly or rise high in the air.
~ Merriam-Webster

Photo: Michael Wilson

PEPE'S PAINTING INC.

- RESIDENTIAL REPAINTING
- COMMERCIAL PAINTING
- POWER WASHING
- DECK REFINISHING
- EPOXY / DECORATIVE CONCRETE COATINGS
- HIGH END CUSTOM REPAINTS
- STAIN REFINISHING
- ROOF COATINGS
- COLOR CONSULTATION
- NO OBLIGATION FREE ESTIMATES 7 DAYS A WEEK

Pepe's Painting, Inc.
RESIDENTIAL & COMMERCIAL

OFFICE: 928.445.7330
PAINHORSEPAINT@YAHOO.COM
PRESCOTT, AZ
ROC. 201565 K-34

Photo: Ruth Draeger

birth
/bərTH/

noun: the beginning or coming into existence of something.

~ Merriam-Webster

Photo: Wanderlux Photography & Portraits Out West - Willow Lake

maj·es·ty
/ˈmajəstē/

noun: impressive stateliness, dignity, or beauty

~ Merriam-Webster

Photo: Blushing Cactus Photography
Elks Theatre

New to the Quad Cities? Welcome!!

We are your 1-STOP cleaning SPECIALISTS

- LOCALLY Owned & Operated
- Deep and Regular House Cleaning
- Professional Window Cleaning
- Carpet, Tile & Grout Cleaning
- Power Washing
- We're BONDED & INSURED

Prescott Maid to Order LLC

Call Us Today! **928.899.8518**
"Simply the BEST Cleaning Service"

THANK YOU for keeping us #1 since 2005!
www.PrescottMaidtoOrder.com

HunterDouglas

VIGNETTE® MODERN ROMAN SHADES

season of style SAVINGS EVENT

Don't wait to get your home holiday ready with beautiful Hunter Douglas shades.

REBATES STARTING AT
$100*
ON QUALIFYING PURCHASES
SEPT. 14–DEC. 9, 2019

Prescott Window Coverings

Prescott Window Coverings Llc
1480 W Iron Springs Rd Prescott, AZ
M-F: 8:30 am - 4:30 pm
Sat: By Appointment Only
Sun: Closed
(928) 778-4799
www.prescottwindowcoverings.com

*Manufacturer's mail-in rebate offer valid for qualifying purchases made 9/14/19–12/9/19 from participating dealers in the U.S. only. Rebate will be issued in the form of a prepaid reward card and mailed within 4 weeks of rebate claim approval. Funds do not expire. Subject to applicable law, a $2.00 monthly fee will be assessed against card balance 6 months after card issuance and each month thereafter. See complete terms distributed with reward card. Additional limitations may apply. Ask participating dealer for details and rebate form. ©2019 Hunter Douglas. All rights reserved. All trademarks used herein are the property of Hunter Douglas or their respective owners. 19Q4MAGVIC2

art
/ärt/

noun; the conscious use of skill and creative imagination especially in the production of aesthetic objects
- Merriam-Webster

Photo: Kuki Hargrave - Hargrave Fine Art; "Mid-day Melt"

Looking to buy or sell? I sell houses all year round. Call me.

Debbie Dunbar

Prescott Native, Detail Oriented, Certified Military Residential Specialist.

Cell: 928.899.1867
2971 Willow Creek Rd
Prescott, AZ 86301
Debbie.dunbar@russlyon.com

Power Driven Performance

Russ Lyon | Sotheby's INTERNATIONAL REALTY

Each office is independently owned and operated.

Expert Hands, Natural Results

Dr. Paul K. Holden, MD
Facial Plastic Surgery

15757 N. 78th St, Suite A • Scottsdale, AZ 85260
480-787-5815 • www.ScottsdalePS.com

Scottsdale PLASTIC SURGEONS

Curiosity is the tip of the intelligence iceberg.
~ WB Dedman

Photo: Laura Zenari - Kayaking on Willow Lake

Accounting, Income Tax Preparation, Payroll, QuickBooks Services

Why Choose Us?

We are an excellent choice because we have:

- A Reputation for Excellence
- Experience and Trusted Business Consultants & Advisors
- Our Personal Attention That Produces Quality Results
- Reasonable & Transparent Fees

Premiere Tax & Accounting Services PLLC
928-460-5908
1235 Willow Creek Road, #A
Prescott, AZ 86301

Brenda Hershkowitz
President

PRESCOTT FLOORING BROKERS

Commercial / Residential   ROC192753 K08

Huge selection of Carpet, Hardwood, Ceramic, Rigid Core Water Proof Hybrid LVT, Custom Area Rugs, & more to choose from in our 3,100 Sq Ft showroom

Prescott's Premier Flooring Store Since 1973
M-F 8-4 Sat 9-12 | 401 W. Goodwin Street in Downtown Prescott, AZ 86303
www.PrescottFlooringBrokers.com | 928-445-2544

friend
/ˈfrend/
noun: a favored companion
~ Merriam-Webster

Photo:
Blushing Cactus
Photography
World's Oldest Rodeo

Women's Clothing and Accessories!

Purple Clover Boutique
130 West Gurley St # 205, Prescott | 928-499-5195
Located in Bashford Courts

ELKS THEATRE
PERFORMING ARTS CENTER

Whether you are in The Historic Elks Theatre or upstairs in the intimate setting of The Crystal Hall, The Elks Theatre and Performing Arts Center is *THE* place in the Quad City with GREAT live music, movies, comedy shows and more!

117 E. Gurley St. • info@etpac.org • PrescottElksTheater.com

kiln
/ˈkiln/

noun: an oven, furnace, or heated enclosure used for processing a substance by burning, firing, or drying

~ Merriam-Webster

Photos: Martha Court
Charcoal Kiln

Cactus in kiln wall

A VALLEY of VITALITY
WELLNESS STUDIO

The Daily Courier 2019 READERS' CHOICE AWARDS — 1st PLACE BEST MASSAGE — A Valley of Vitality Wellness Studio

We are your Destination for Rejuvenation

At A Valley of Vitality Wellness Studio, massage is not just a luxury but a path to a happier, healthier life. We are commited to providing the best treatment and creating a safe space for our clients to relax and regain their natural vitality.

- Vitality Wellnesss Memberships
- Theraputic Essential Oils
- Full Spectrum CBD
- Premium Add ons Available
- Stress Free Environment
- Purchase Self Care Items

2074 Willow Creek Rd. Prescott, az - 928.442.6026 - avalleyofvitality.com

PRESCOTT OUTPATIENT SURGICAL CENTER
Passionate   Outstanding   Specialized   Care

MISSION STATEMENT:
We believe in compassionate medicine, where our focus is on each individual patient.

Our experienced surgeons have dedicated themselves to caring for patients within Yavapai County for the past 30 years.

Our team of professionals are among the **highest-trained** and **most experienced** anywhere in Arizona.

REQUEST POSC AT YOUR PHYSICIAN'S OFFICE!

815 AINSWORTH DR., PRESCOTT AZ 86301 • 928.778.9770 • WWW.POSC-AZ.COM

We accept most insurance. Cash pricing and financing options available.

in·spi·ra·tion
/ˌinspəˈrāSH(ə)n/

noun: the drawing in of breath

~ Merriam-Webster

Photo: Michael Wilson - Granite Basin Lake
"Out of the Blue"

Photo: Martha Court – "Lynx Lake Watercolor"

Commercial Sales ~ Leasing ~ Property Management ~ Asset Disposition ~ Residential

Professional Property Management Matters.
Choose the right Management Company

Do you need the 5 essential aspects of a professional Property & Asset Manager?

- Identify areas of improvement or growth.
- Retain quality tenants.
- Attract desirable new tenants.
- Negotiate favorable leases.
- Control overhead and costs.

Our Property & Asset Management services include; , Leasing, Marketing, Accounting, Risk Management, Energy Cost Savings, and Maintenance Services. Contact us today to discuss how we can assist you.

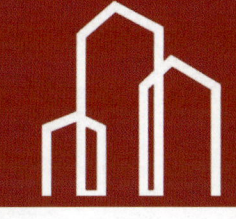

SUMNER
COMMERCIAL REAL ESTATE, INC.
sales • leasing • property management
www.sumnercre.com   @sumnercre

Angie Sumner
Broker
928-775-4227
angie@sumnercre.com

Greater Prescott LIVING at Its Best! 239

Photographers

PHOTOGRAPHERS NOT PICTURED:
- Kevin Attebery
- Ryan Closson
- Kialana Duenas
- Elaine Earle
- Catherine Fillebrown
- Michelle Haynes
- Chris Hosking
- Bill Kettler
- Lynne LaMaster, eNews AZ
- Jean Lopez
- Bea Lueck
- Teresa Mahan

Charles Ables
Charles Ables is a local photographer in and around Prescott Valley having resided here for almost 30 years. His goal is to always look for the challenging, unusual, different and every once in a while, a sprinkle of local contemporary photographs to shoot with either digital or film cameras.
chuckables.pixels.com

Ruth Draeger
Ruth loves the outdoors. She wants to share her experiences with others and feels the best way is through photography. It's strictly a hobby for now, perhaps after retirement it will become more.

Jess Berry
Jess' passion for stormy weather, gorgeous landscapes, adventures, and photography all came about early on in life and it seemed fitting to combine them. Her photography has been featured by newspapers, magazines and the National Weather Service in Flagstaff. Follow along with Jess' adventures at *jessberryphotography.com* and on Instagram @avidsleeperjess

Gerry Groeber
Gerry, an award-winning photographer, specializes in the American Southwest. Currently a contributing photographer for Arizona Highways magazine, his work has graced the pages of prominent photography magazines including Outdoor Photographer and Shutterbug Magazine.
gerrygroeber.com/
facebook.com/onelightimage
Instagram @gerry.groeber

Blushing Cactus Photography: Tracy Fultz & Jeremiah Scheffer
We are Blushing Cactus Photography, a husband and wife team based in Prescott, Arizona who document the human connection - everything from musicians to entrepreneurs, events to intimate family portraits, and best of all, couples on their wedding day.
www.blushingcactus.com

Kuki Hargrave
Kuki grew up around the corner from Disneyland and works near downtown Prescott. She's been an artist, photographer and designer most of her life, with award-winning works in collections worldwide, including those of rock stars, celebrities and a U.S. president.

Martha Court
Martha moved to Prescott after being drawn to the natural beauty of the area. She's always enjoyed taking photographs, but her involvement in what was a hobby has soared to new levels here, expanded by the spectacular landscapes.

Rod Hendrick
Rod is retired after 40 years working as a drywall finisher and has been an artist his whole life. He and his wife Lisa live in the Prescott area, and he enjoys hiking, kayaking and always has his camera ready.
facebook.com/HendrickArts

- » Miller Photo
- » Tony Munshi
- » Alexandra Rhody
- » Helen Schmeck
- » Dave Suggs
- » Kelly Tolbert
- » Treerose Photography
- » Jordan Vixie, Barley Hound
- » Jordan Vixie, Hawk & Hound

Thank you!

Christopher Marchetti
An expert in lensmanship, Christopher is noted for his commercial and corporate photography. Based in Prescott's Old Masonic Temple for over 25 years, he travels extensively. His work can be seen in publications including Southwest Arts Magazine and Arizona Highways.
www.marchettiphoto.com

Rob Strain: Wanderlux Photography & Portraits Out West
Rob focuses on fine art landscape photography and western outdoor portraiture. He guides other photographers on adventures to both iconic and secret locations. With his photographer wife, Barbara, they constantly explore new locations in and around town. Dr. Rob also practices the art of dentistry in Prescott as a first career. Their photography website is at wanderluxphotography.com

Nancy Maurer
Nancy has lived in Prescott for 14 years and serves on the board of directors for the Highlands Center for Natural History. She specializes in nature and landscape photography endeavoring to capture the wonder, beauty, and awe we may find in nature and everyday life.
www.nancymaurer.com

Daryl Weisser
Daryl is a photographer based in Prescott Valley, and his wide range of subjects includes blues musicians and horse show exhibitors. He enjoys being around these talented people, and his work is featured in blues and horse-related publications. Some samples of Daryl's photos are posted at DarylWeisserPhotos.com

Jody L. Miller
Jody was born in Brooklyn, but it was always her father's idea to raise the family in the country. She met her first horse while living in Illinois and it was love at first sight. She hopes viewers can sense feelings of strength and freedom well up within them as they see her work.
JodyLMiller.com

Michael Wilson
Michael grew up in Prescott, leaving only to earn a degree from ASU. His "geeky" side drew him to technical aspects of photography; its creativity made it his passion. His goal is to evoke how he felt at each location.
www.michael-wilson.com

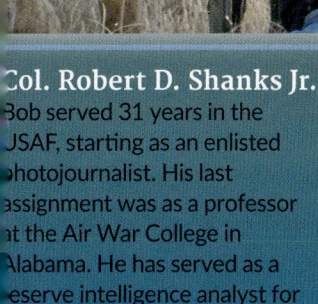

Col. Robert D. Shanks Jr.
Bob served 31 years in the USAF, starting as an enlisted photojournalist. His last assignment was as a professor at the Air War College in Alabama. He has served as a reserve intelligence analyst for federal law enforcement.

Laura Zenari
Born and raised in Chicago, Laura realized she would not stay, as she loved the outdoors and nature. One night, her aunt in Arizona suggested the Prescott area. She now thinks of it as her little "heaven on earth."

We are everybody's home-town dealer!

Findlay Prescott TOYOTA

findlaytoyotaprescott.com
3200 Willow Creek Rd, Prescott, AZ 86305

The local dealership that supports your community!

Findlay Prescott GMC

findlaybuickgmc.com
1006 Commerce Dr, Prescott, AZ 86305

Findlay
PRESCOTT

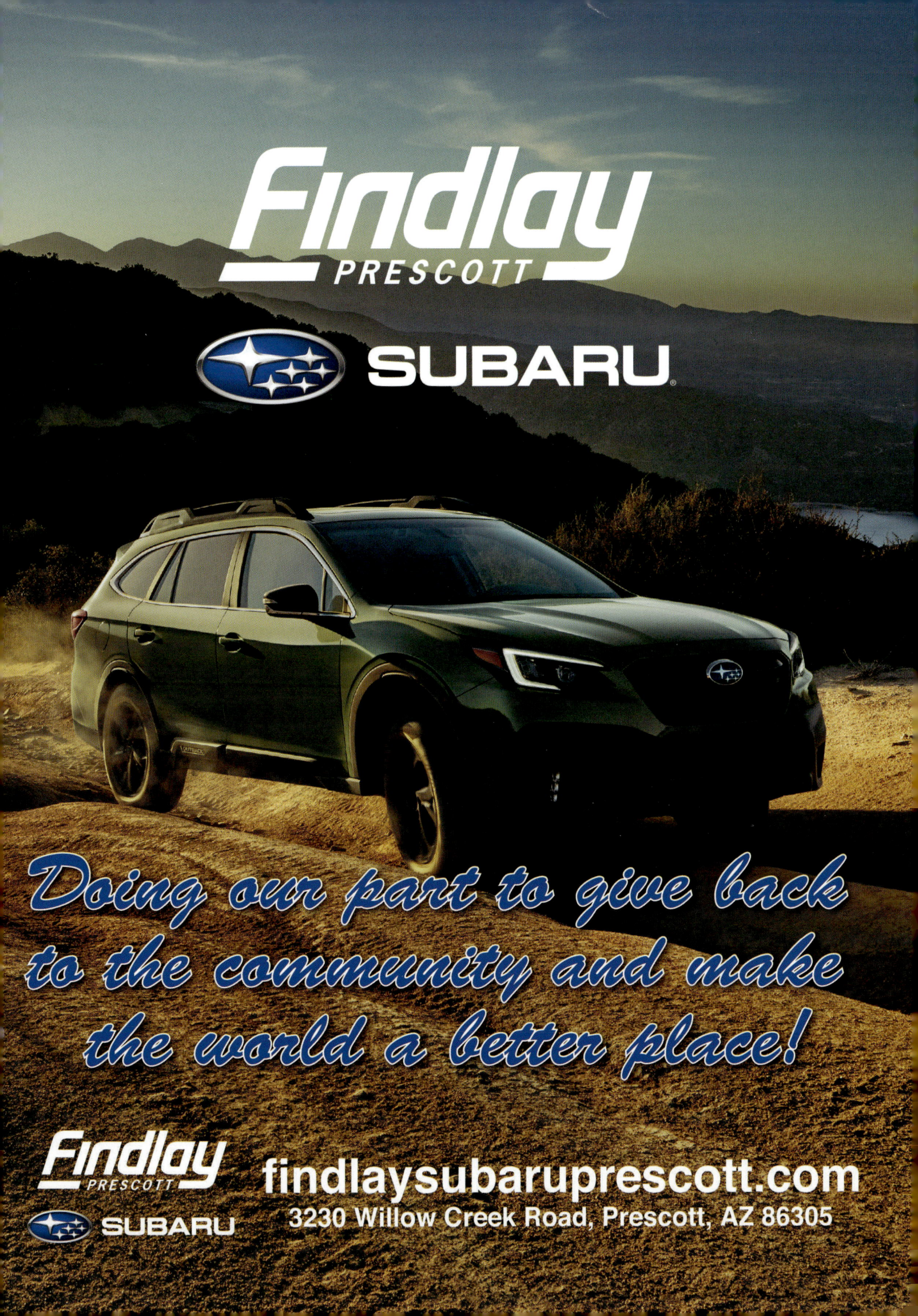

SUBARU

Doing our part to give back to the community and make the world a better place!

Findlay PRESCOTT
SUBARU

findlaysubaruprescott.com
3230 Willow Creek Road, Prescott, AZ 86305

A Big THANK YOU to Greater Prescott for being so AWESOME to capture in this book! We hope that you enjoyed reading it as much as we enjoyed putting it together.

– Until next edition… ROX Media Group

Photo: Blushing Cactus Photography - Granite Mountain